D0408469

THE OBAMA QUESTION

THE OBAMA QUESTION

A Progressive Perspective

Gary Dorrien

ROWMAN & LITTLEFIELD PUBLISHERS, INC.
Lanham • Boulder • New York • Toronto • Plymouth, UK

Published by Rowman & Littlefield Publishers, Inc.
A wholly owned subsidary of The Rowman & Littlefield Publishing Group, Inc.
4501 Forbes Boulevard, Suite 200, Lanham, Maryland 20706
www.rowmanlittlefield.com

Estover Road, Plymouth PL6 7PY, United Kingdom

British Library Cataloguing in Publication Information Available

Library of Congress Cataloging-in-Publication Data
Dorrien, Gary J.
 The Obama question : a progressive perspective / Gary Dorrien.
  p. cm.
 Includes bibliographical references and index.
 ISBN 978-1-4422-1537-5 (cloth : alk. paper) — ISBN 978-1-4422-1539-9 (electronic)
 1. Obama, Barack—Political and social views. 2. Progressivism (United States politics—History—21st century. 3. United States—Politics and government—2009- 4. United States—Economic policy—2009- 5. United States--Social policy—1993- I. Title.
 E908.3.D67 2012
 973.932092—dc23

                                                                2011051197

∞™ The paper used in this publication meets the minimum requirements of American National Standard for Information Sciences—Permanence of Paper for Printed Library Materials, ANSI/NISO Z39.48-1992.

Printed in the United States of America

For Eris, whose greater beauty is inward.

Contents

Acknowledgments

GRATEFUL ACKNOWLEDGMENT IS MADE to *Cross Currents* for the right to adapt previously published material from Gary Dorrien, "Beyond State and Market" (Summer 1995); *Religion & Ethics Newsweekly*, a PBS production of Thirteen/WNET New York, for material from Dorrien, "Yes We Can . . . Change the Subject?" (August 26, 2008), "Visible Man Rising" (September 2, 2008), and "Back to the Subject" (September 9, 2008); *The Christian Century*, for material from Dorrien, "Hope or Hype?" (May 20, 2007), Dorrien, "Health Care Fix: The Role of a Public Option" (July 14, 2009), and Dorrien, "The Common Good" (April 19, 2011); Columbia University Press, for material from Dorrien, *Economy, Difference, Empire: Social Ethics for Social Justice* (2010); and Wiley-Blackwell, for material from Dorrien, *Social Ethics in the Making* (2009).

1

Shortcut to Redemption

O N NOVEMBER 4, 2008, I GOT IN LINE at Riverside Church in New York City to vote for Barack Obama. The mood was unusually spirited for a polling place—mostly buoyant, with lots of expectant smiles, mixed with an undertow of anxiety. John McCain could not have gotten many votes at Riverside. Suddenly my friend Elisabeth Sifton came out of a polling booth and approached me. Elisabeth, a former editor at Viking, is the daughter of Reinhold Niebuhr. She was raised on hard-edged, pragmatic, liberal Christian realism, and she had worried for a while that Obama shot into prominence too quickly for him to be electable. By election day, however, Elisabeth was long past "Can he win?" anxieties. She had no doubt that Obama would win and that his election would be a watershed moment in U.S. history. Hugging me, Elisabeth exclaimed, "Gary, this is better than we deserve!"

Yes, exactly. The same nation that enslaved African Americans until 1865 and imposed a vicious century-long regime of segregation and everyday abuse upon them was about to elect an African American to its presidency. The same nation that elected twelve slavemasters to its presidency was about to elect a president whose wife was a descendant of American slaves. The same nation that never would have elected a veteran of the civil rights movement to national office was about to fulfill some of the movement's most idealistic hymnody. The same nation that prattled about its exceptionalism and superiority was on the verge of a democratic breakthrough that could not have happened in any European nation. The same nation that made "USA" synonymous with imperial smashing in Iraq and torturing prisoners at Guantanamo was bidding to dramatically change its international image.

We seemed to be taking a shortcut to some kind of national redemption, electing an inspiring, eloquent, dignified, reflective type who embodied America's racial and multicultural complexity even as he played it down. But it *was* a shortcut, which is problematic in politics, even when a shortcut takes us someplace that we need to go.

Politics is always about power and only sometimes about social justice. It has a relation to redemption—the healing of life and the world (Hebrew *tikkun*)—only through its connection to social justice. The Obama movement of 2008, though long on redemptive aspects for a political campaign, wrought nothing like redemption for centuries of slavery and discrimination in the United States, and it did not change the fact that African Americans are subjected to unemployment, imprisonment, and bad schools at higher rates than other groups. Even as ordinary politics, the Obama campaign was a shortcut. Otherwise Obama would not have been compelled to play down the memories, ideals, and struggles that tied his campaign to the civil rights movement. And otherwise it would not have mattered so much that Obama's many political talents include his Oprah-scale capacity for making white Americans feel good about themselves and their nation.

Obama was only the third African American to serve in the U.S. Senate since Reconstruction, and he had been there for only three years when he ran for president. He skyrocketed to national prominence, and then the presidency, on the strength of his once-in-a-generation talent, intelligence, self-confidence, and Oprah-likeness. In the Senate he pleaded with supporters to give him time to accomplish something before they talked up a run for the White House; Michelle Obama was adamant on this theme.

All was to no avail. The vast crowds of mostly white liberals and moderates who packed into Obama's speaking engagements could not wait for him to run on his record. Since Obama had planned all along to run for president as soon as possible anyway, he had only to change his mind about when it was timely to do so. One kind of shortcut, a very early run for the White House, led to another.

Electing Barack Hussein Obama to the presidency fulfilled much of America's idealistic rhetoric about itself. Unlike any president before him, Obama was already a historic figure on his first day in office, and he bore the hope of being a transformative one. Favorable views of the United States soared by 30 to 40 points in most nations after he was inaugurated, a phenomenon lacking any precedent.

But Obama is a figure of protean irony and complexity. He wrote a lengthy autobiography in his early thirties, yet he is short and guarded on what makes him tick. He is audacious about himself and his career, with enormous ambitions for his presidency, yet he governs with deep caution, even timidity, even as he pushes for huge, risky, historic things. He is disciplined to the point of having disciplined even his feelings. He is almost eerily self-possessed, more comfortable in his skin than any major political figure since Ronald Reagan, who, like Obama, was often described as an actor portraying a politician. Reagan was more complicated than he seemed; Obama, by contrast, is obviously complicated, much more than the average American president, which unnerves many Americans. Yet Obama's blend of extroverted charm, informality, centered ease, reasonableness, and personal guardedness epitomizes the style of sociability prized by American professional and business culture. Obama developed his affable cool in a place, Indonesia, where being affably cool helped him get along, negotiating his outsider status. Had he grown up in the continental United States, he might not have developed the distinctly complex social personality that lifted him to the White House.

Obama had barely been elected president when he had to start governing, and he was in full governing mode before he was inaugurated, pushing a huge stimulus bill that he wanted to sign on his first day in office. A month after he was inaugurated he signed seven landmark bills at once—the largest tax cut for the middle class since the Reagan administration, the biggest infrastructure bill since the Eisenhower administration, the biggest education bill since the Johnson administration, the biggest antipoverty and job training bill since the Johnson administration, the biggest clean energy bill ever, and huge investments in housing and scientific research.

But he wrapped these items together as one bill to ensure that everything passed, and he settled for a smaller stimulus than was needed without fighting about it publicly—a sign of things to come. Had Obama pushed these initiatives separately, he would have received more credit for achievements that ranked with the New Deal and the Great Society. To him it was more important to prevent layoffs immediately and to revive the economy as quickly as possible. Obama is not one to emote with prophetic passion about the poor and vulnerable, yet he pushed through the best antipoverty bill in forty years, which he played down, because drawing attention to it might have jeopardized it. Then he pulled off a colossal antipoverty reform of historic proportions by attaining health coverage for 34 million uninsured people, all the while insisting that the best antipoverty program is a world-class education.

Obama defied his entire senior staff by rolling the dice on national health insurance, an issue with forbidding politics and a record of eight presidential failures—seven, if one discounts Gerald Ford's very brief attempt. Obama eliminated the worst abuses of the insurance companies and accomplished more reform for preretired people than any president before him. But he alienated his liberal base by approaching health care reform in a timid, temporizing, opportunistic fashion. He backed away from demanding universal coverage. He bought off as many special interests as possible. He failed to fight for a public option, which infuriated his liberal base.

By the end of Obama's first year in office, progressives were angry that he eased off on employment spending, abandoned the public option, and escalated the war in Afghanistan, while conservatives and many independents were appalled that he stepped on the Keynesian gas, rescued General Motors and Chrysler, and asked Americans to extend health coverage to the poor and vulnerable. A year later, after the Democrats were routed in the midterm elections, progressives were furious that Obama extended the Bush tax cuts for the wealthy, albeit in a hostage situation. The following year Obama disastrously capitulated to Republican extortion on the debt ceiling, agreeing to spending cuts that slash social programs and federal agencies in exchange for averting a federal default. By the time that Obama allowed Republican extremists to take his administration and the country hostage, he had enormous problems with his liberal base and special problems with much of the country, all on top of inheriting the worst economic crisis since the 1930s, the two longest wars in American history, and a cyclone of national debt caused by the economic crisis, the wars, and the Bush tax cuts.

It did not take long to see what Obama's special problems are. More than one-fourth of the American population, when polled on such questions, claim to believe that Obama was not born in the United States, is not a legitimate president, is a Muslim, is a Socialist, and either definitely or probably sympathizes with the goals of Islamic fundamentalists who want to impose Sharia law throughout the world. In some polling, up to a third of Americans have tagged Obama as sympathetic with Islamic radicalism, and over half have tagged him as a Socialist. More than two years into Obama's presidency, television celebrity and putative presidential contender Donald Trump was able to stoke a weeks-long national media frenzy by charging that Obama is not a legitimate president. Over half of registered Republicans agreed; another 20 percent reported that they weren't sure. In a country where such stunningly preposterous beliefs are professed on this scale, Obama pays a steep price for representing the USA better than it deserves.

Obama's election set off a howling alarm of anxiety and fear for Americans who could not see him as an American leader. Before he was elected, there was already a best-selling literature portraying him as a corrupt, alien, mendacious, anti-American Socialist and elitist who covered up his ties to radicals and plotted to destroy America. Accusations of this sort heated up numerous campaign rallies in the closing weeks of the 2008 election. After Obama was elected, the conspiracy blogs and books got even more unhinged. Within weeks of Obama's inauguration, "I want my country back" became a staple of Republican rallies. The placard version featured an image of America's first black president, just in case anyone needed an interpretation. Fox television star Glenn Beck, fueling this reaction, declared that Obama "has exposed himself as a guy over and over and over again who has a deep-seated hatred for white people or the white culture." Beck allowed that Obama had quite a few white people in his administration. However, "I'm saying he has a problem. This guy is, I believe, a racist." It did not help, for Beck's audience, that Obama told his personal story as an illustration of American exceptionalism. In fact, it was offensive that he did so.[1]

Normal political trading stopped with the coming of Obama, notwithstanding his pleas for civility and political cooperation, and notwithstanding that the country was in the throes of an economic crisis when he was inaugurated. Conservative radio star Rush Limbaugh declared, "I shamelessly say, no, I want him to fail." Republican leaders were equally resolute, spurning any pretense of working with the new administration to solve the nation's problems. Senate minority leader Mitch McConnell was adamant from the beginning that Republican cooperation with Obama would not be tolerated. Twenty-one months after Obama was elected, McConnell was still saying it, now for public consumption: "The single most important thing we want to achieve is for President Obama to be a one-term president." Pressed on whether he meant to say it quite so directly, McConnell was emphatic. His party's top priority was to take down Obama.[2]

The stimulus bill was the first test of that resolution. Obama's textbook attempt to revive the economy in the face of a free-falling economic crash garnered almost no Republican support in the Senate and no Republican support whatsoever in the House of Representatives. Instead he set off a huge conservative reaction against saving capitalism from itself.

Barely a month after Obama was inaugurated, Rick Santelli, a self-described "Ayn Rander" and second-string business correspondent for CNBC, launched an ostensibly spontaneous rant that sparked the Tea Party reaction. Speaking from the CME trading floor in Chicago, telecast live by CNBC, Santelli exclaimed: "This is America! How many of you people want to pay for your neighbor's mortgage that has an extra bathroom and can't pay their bills?" Obama's Homeowner Affordability and Stability Plan had nothing to do with preventing a depression, Santelli insisted. It was a straightforward giveaway to society's losers, rewarding the kind of people who just wanted to drink the water at the expense of those who carried the water. Santelli admonished, "If you read our Founding Fathers, people like Benjamin Franklin and Jefferson—what we're doing now in this country is making them roll over in their graves." He had a parting shot, seemingly an afterthought: "We're thinking of having a Chicago tea party in July." Within hours there was a website called ChicagoTeaParty.com, registered by a producer for a popular Chicago right-wing radio host, and the Tea Party reaction was born.[3]

In parts of the country the Tea Party movement is simply the Christian Right under a different guise. In other places it nudged aside or blended with the Christian Right, quickly becoming the new engine of the Republican Party. It rings the alarm about something terribly real—a soaring national debt that has increased by over $500 billion each year since 2003 and now equals the size of the American economy. Getting control of the debt problem is imperative for the United States. But most of the current debt problem was created by the policies of George W. Bush. Cutting spending in a depressed economy is misguided, as Franklin Roosevelt proved in 1937. And the debt problem as a whole is a by-product of tax policies that have fueled massive structural inequality since the early 1980s. It cannot be solved with any moral decency without rectifying the legacy of Ronald Reagan, the gold standard president for the Republican Party.

Reagan led the Republican Party into temptation by persuading it that deficits don't matter because tax cuts pay for themselves, especially at the upper end. When Reagan took office in 1981, the national debt was $907 billion, approximately 26 percent of gross domestic product. Eight years later the debt stood at $2.7 trillion, representing 40 percent of GDP. In eight years Reagan tripled the country's accumulated debt by cutting the marginal tax rate from 70 percent to 28 percent and cutting the top rate on capital gains from 49 percent to 20 percent—social engineering on a staggering scale that fueled a huge inequality surge. George H. W. Bush, vowing to maintain Reagan's winning approach, let the national debt escalate to $3.9 trillion, which scared him enough to break his vow, raise the marginal rate to 35 percent, demoralize his party, and lose a second term.[4]

The only break in America's post-1980 record of escalating debt was the Clinton administration. The national debt crossed the $4 trillion mark during Clinton's first year in office, 1993. Clinton raised the marginal rate to 39.6 percent, which Republicans warned would destroy the economy. At the end of Clinton's presidency the national debt was $5,674,000,000 and heading downward, as Clinton rang up budget surpluses of $70 billion in 1998, $124 billion in 1999, and $237 billion in 2000. According to the Congressional Budget Office, had the United States stuck with Clinton's fiscal policy, the cumulative budget surplus would have reached $5.6 trillion by 2011, wiping out the national debt.[5]

All of that was quickly squandered by George W. Bush's tax cuts and ramped-up military expenditures, plus a prescription benefit lacking a pay-for. Bush's tax cuts blew a $2 trillion hole in the deficit. He was the first president in American history not to raise taxes to pay for an expensive war.

Official expenses for the two wars that Bush charged exceeded $1 trillion, with long-term costs that will triple that figure. He added a $1 trillion Medicare prescription drug benefit without paying for it either, a windfall for the pharmaceutical industry, creating the first entitlement in American history lacking a revenue source. Then the casino economy that Bush deregulated crashed. In eight years the Bush administration piled up new debt and new accrued obligations of $10.35 trillion, and it doubled the national debt from $5.7 trillion to $11.3 trillion, not counting the $5.4 trillion of debt inherited from the federal takeovers of Fannie Mae and Freddie Mac. Bush amassed more debt in eight years than America's previous forty-two presidents combined, breaking the record of the previous debt champion, Ronald Reagan, and the record keeps growing, as three-quarters of the debt amassed on Obama's watch is the outgrowth of Bush's unpaid tax cuts, unpaid wars, and unpaid drug benefit, and much of the rest is cleanup for the financial crash.[6]

Obama inherited a deflating economy teetering on an outright depression, a skyrocketing debt, the structural legacy of thirty years of politically engineered inequality, and two wars. When he took office in January 2009 the U.S. economy was losing 741,000 jobs per month, and the Congressional Budget Office projected a $1.2 trillion deficit for 2009. The economy had lost $13 trillion of net worth over the past eighteen months and 2.6 million jobs over the past twelve months. The government had pledged $9 trillion in loans, investments, and guarantees to fill the chasm. And the economy was shrinking by nearly 6 percent annually. Had these losses continued, the United States would have been in a depression by September. Instead, by January 2010 the job loss figure had been cut to 20,000 and the economy was growing at nearly 6 percent annually.[7]

In a rational world, huge political benefits would accrue to a leader who staves off a depression and stabilizes the system. However, people are not that rational, and neither are markets or politics. Nobody gets reelected to national office by saying, "Things are really bad, but they could have been much worse. We plugged some gaping holes with a stimulus that was just enough to end a recession." In this case, the Republican Party made a dramatic comeback by protesting that Obama's $787 billion of Keynesian stimulus was outrageously radical, socialist, un-American, and unsustainable.

That was absurd; the Obama stimulus was modest for a deflating economy dominated by dysfunctional banks holding $2 trillion of toxic assets. When Obama took office the big players were sitting on their bailouts, because they had faked themselves out from knowing what their assets were worth, and because the Bush administration let them sit on their bailouts. Nobody trusted each other's balance sheets or their own. The case for a big stimulus bill was overwhelming. There was no monetary solution because the Federal Reserve had already cut interest rates to zero and credit was frozen. As it was, the Fed did what it could to prevent a depression by backstopping the financial system with $13 trillion in guarantees.

Yet Republican leaders, fixating on the politics, were suddenly reborn as deficit hawks and opponents of fiscal priming. It did not matter, somehow, that Republican policies were the main driver of the debt spiral; or that in February 2008 Republican leaders had approved Bush's $150 billion stimulus plan to head off an economic disaster; or that five months later they handed Treasury Secretary Henry M. Paulson Jr. a blank check to save the mortgage companies Fannie Mae and Freddie Mac from crashing—the Housing and Economic Recovery Act of 2008; or that in October 2008 they showered Wall Street banks with $700 billion. By the time that Republicans found themselves lavishing taxpayer billions on too-big-to-fail banks, most of them had a sick feeling, and with the turn of an election and the rise of the Tea Party, they were reborn as opponents of feeding the recovery, after the disaster had occurred.

The Republican Party denied the necessity of stimulating the economy and conveniently ignored the absurdity of branding itself as the party of fiscal rectitude after quadrupling the debt under Reagan and Bush and doubling it again under Bush. Textbook economics were thrown away. In a struggling economy, the government spends to spur growth; then it cuts after the economy takes off. Republican leaders dispensed with history and economic knowledge, fixating on one thing—cutting spending without raising new revenue. They took pride in ignoring what is known about fiscal policy. They had no proposal whatsoever for preventing the financial industry from gambling the economy to another crash. And they worked assiduously to prevent any financial reforms from being enacted.

Republican leaders, however, got one thing terribly right. To their credit and reward, they conveyed to Americans that the country was in crisis and that taxpayers had been ripped off by deal-making elites playing by a different set of rules. Republican officials seized the advantage that came with speaking to the rage of an enraged public. President Obama, meanwhile, meeting with the CEOs of the nation's thirteen largest financial institutions on March 27, 2009, tellingly cautioned them, "My administration is the only thing between you and the pitchforks."[8]

Obama took for granted that his first job was to stabilize a free-falling economic system. The first important decision that he made was to choose his Treasury secretary. Obama had an eminent candidate for the position—former Federal Research chair Paul Volcker, who was critical of the derivatives-driven casino economy that deregulation created, and who wanted the job. But after Obama was elected he narrowed his choice to two candidates closely tied to Wall Street—Timothy Geithner and Lawrence Summers. Geithner, as president of the Federal Reserve Bank of New York, had cut the bailout deals with the megabanks, and Summers, as Treasury secretary under Clinton, had helped tear down the wall between commercial and investment banking. Obama chose Geithner, a personality much like his own, for the Treasury, appeasing Summers with the National Economic Council. Both appointments symbolized that Wall Street had little or nothing to fear from the coming of Obama. Geithner, having played matchmaker for the megabank mergers, was naturally averse to breaking them up; Summers, having advocated the most disastrous deregulation bill since the Depression, was averse to apologizing for the wreckage; both assured Obama that Volcker's time had passed.

On the right, Obama's special problems are toxic and short on facts, and even the one real problem—the mounting debt—is invoked by Republicans mostly as cover for their obstructionism. Republican leaders care more about preserving the unfairness of the tax system than about debt reduction or anything else, and they have fought Obama with the most relentless obstructionism ever faced by an American president. On the left, on the other hand, bitter disappointment with real things is closer to the norm—and politically perilous for Obama.

To a considerable extent the Obama administration has replayed the debates of the Clinton years over how much a centrist Democratic administration that is liberal on some issues should be able to accomplish in a nation that self-identifies as 20 percent liberal or progressive, 30 percent conservative, and 40 percent moderate. (The remaining 10 percent "don't know.") Obama's ideological rudder is vaguely liberal-leaning in Clinton's fashion, and he has energized the same right-wing noise machine that constantly accused Clinton of fraud, thievery, murder, rape, drug running, and treachery. In some ways, the things that the Right has made up about Obama are not as bad as the things it made up about Clinton.

But hardly anyone thought that Bill Clinton was better than we deserved. Clinton was a skilled politician, long on charm and cunning, who did not suffer from having stirred messianic expectations, and the Right mostly stuck to criminality fantasies in making up things about him. Obama, more deeply than Clinton, has anguished many of the very people who believed most in him, and an ample portion of the Republican Party seriously believes that Obama is a seething, alien radical bent on destroying America.

The progressive critique of Obama begins with Geithner and Summers. It proceeds to most of his cabinet and top staff, which he stocked with Wall Street apologists, Republican defense officials, and retreads from the Democratic establishment. He sought and attained a smaller stimulus package than his own economic advisers thought was necessary to break the unemployment spiral. He took his eye off the jobs crisis a few months after taking office. He escalated the war in Afghanistan and expanded America's military empire.

He created an aggregator bank to bribe hedge funds and private investors to buy up the toxic debts of the big banks. His initial financial reform plan did nothing to curtail the use of bespoke derivatives. He watered down the reform bill as it moved through Congress, accepting carve-outs for corporate users of derivatives and opposing proposals to force banks to spin off their trading operations in derivatives. He spurned a crucial amendment to the financial reform bill that would have imposed sensible limits on the size of megabanks. He took a passive approach to health care reform legislation, letting a Democratic Congress write the bill, and refused to press for a public option. He contended that beneficiaries and health care providers have no right to sue state officials to challenge cuts in Medicaid payment rates. He supported free-trade deals that harmed American unions and failed to push a card-check union organizing bill through the Senate. He put off a decision on the Keystone Pipeline until 2013, wavering on a boondoggle for the burning of dirty fossil fuels that would spill acidic bitumen for thousands of miles. He rolled over on tax cuts for the rich, breaking a campaign promise. He gave Republican-lite speeches about debt reduction and capitulated to Republican extortion in averting a federal default.

Repeatedly he surrendered in the third quarter, or punted on third down, or whatever sports metaphor one prefers for this objection. Conciliation was not merely Obama's default mode, as progressives had worried in 2008. It was his chief operating mode, which led him to surrender, disastrously, in the third year of his administration, to the debt ceiling extortion of the Republican Party.

Although Obama rediscovered his populist voice after the debt ceiling debacle, he spent most of his term seeming to be averse to conflict, and thus demoralized his supporters. So much better was expected of him by progressives, like me. We wanted Obama to appoint some progressives to his cabinet, get out of Afghanistan, scale back the military empire, shrink the megabanks, create a public bank, push hard for a public option in health care, push through a second stimulus bill to save and create jobs, and end the Bush tax cuts. Or at least, allowing for political reality, I wanted Obama to take a stand on any two of these things, fighting on principle and risking legislative defeat for things that are important enough to fight about. Above all, when Republicans drove the nation to the edge of default over raising the debt ceiling, we wanted Obama to fight for Democratic principles and, if necessary, invoke the 14th Amendment to prevent Republicans from dictating the terms of ransom.

But temperamentally, and by political conviction, Obama is predisposed to the role of mediating reconciler who leads the country beyond its divisions. In December 2010, when Republicans coerced Obama into extending the Bush tax cuts, Obama did not demand to dispose of the debt ceiling threat in exchange. He assured that Republicans would be responsible when the debt ceiling came up. That was spectacularly not to be. The following August, when Republicans took the nation hostage over a debt ceiling vote, Obama did not invoke the 14th Amendment or even threaten to do so. One act of anguished capitulation led to another.

Every week on the lecture trail I meet progressives who are demoralized and/or infuriated by Obama's performance as president. In some venues more than half of them insist that they will not work for him again or even vote for him. They are finished with Obama. Many have signed petitions vowing to waste no more time, money, or effort on his behalf. The Occupy Wall Street movement is teeming with them.

Princeton philosopher Cornel West epitomizes the problem that Obama has with his progressive base. West worked hard for Obama in 2008, speaking at sixty-five campaign events, lending his celebrity and moral authority to Obama's candidacy. Privately he worried that Obama was "the Johnny Mathis of American politics," gliding to success in the smoothly tame manner of the crooner's early career. Moreover, it troubled West that Obama gave him little personal time or thanks for his efforts, even though many others who helped the campaign got plenty of time and thanks. West feared that Obama's success delegitimized any expression of outrage by African Americans in American society and that Obama shrewdly endeavored to achieve this outcome. But West stifled his inner doubts, plugging hard to win support for Obama wherever the campaign sent him.

When Obama appointed Geithner and Summers, West felt betrayed. He had similar feelings when Obama retained Bush's defense secretary, Robert Gates, and appointed a McCain Republican, retired Marine general James L. Jones, as national security adviser, and recycled veteran Middle East adviser Dennis Ross. West later recalled, "I said, 'Oh my God, I have really been misled at a very deep level. I have been thoroughly misled, all this populist language is just a façade." He had pictured Columbia University economist Joseph Stiglitz and Princeton University economist Paul Krugman running Obama's economic policy, or at least, progressive Keynesians of lesser stature with a track record of giving priority to the working poor and unemployed. Two years into Obama's presidency, West described him bitterly as "a black mascot of Wall Street oligarchs and a black puppet of corporate plutocrats. And now he has become head of the American killing machine and is proud of it."[9]

Rabbi Michael Lerner, a prominent progressive and editor of *Tikkun* magazine, went through a similar metamorphosis more gradually. Lerner hoped that Obama would commit his administration to something like *Tikkun*'s idea of a "caring society" that emphasizes cooperation with others to achieve environmental sustainability, nuclear disarmament, human rights, and the abolition of global poverty. For two years, Lerner and *Tikkun* protested that Obama lacked a consistent worldview or vision. It was hard to say what Obama thought he was doing, besides shoring up the establishment; *Tikkun* kept editorializing that it was not too late for Obama to proclaim a progressive story about where America has been and where it should go. Lerner wanted Obama to emphasize cooperating with others to achieve a global common good.

After Obama delivered his 2011 State of the Union address, however, Lerner stopped complaining that Obama had no vision, because he had clearly come up with one. It was a variation, Lerner protested, on the same worldview that Republicans have advocated for eighty years: "Economic nationalism backed by a competitive ethos domestically and a strong military internationally." To Lerner, Obama's aggressive talk about competing to "win the future" was a sad echo of the last Democratic administration, recycling the very slogans and pro-corporate agenda by which Clinton demoralized the Democratic Party in the 1990s. For Lerner, therefore, betrayal was exactly the point. He had met with Obama in 2006 and later advocated on his behalf; now he regrets having believed in Obama: "We accomplish little by dwelling for the next few years on how dishonestly Obama manipulated us."[10]

Cornel West and Michael Lerner are treasured friends to me. Both are generous-spirited types who balked at criticizing Obama so personally, and on most issues we have the same politics. But we disagree about the importance of not giving up on Obama. Here I make three brief points as a preface to what follows. (1) The United States and the world would be much better off had there been a Gore administration. (2) The progressive litany of criticism, though valid on most of the particulars, exaggerates the betrayal trope. (3) Obama, for all his temporizing and capitulation, is America's most progressive president since FDR, and electing a more compelling human being to the White House is probably impossible in this country.

Had there been a Gore administration, the United States would not have invaded Iraq. The United States would have responded to 9/11 by hunting down al-Qaeda and building new structures of collective security. President Gore would not have showered the rich with tax cuts they don't need, he would not have doubled the U.S. debt, and he would not have let the oil companies devise America's policies on energy and environmental issues. In the 2000 presidential campaign, Bush claimed that the government had too much money and that tax cuts pay for themselves anyway; Gore rightly countered that taking Bush's path would be disastrous for America. The left-liberals who sat out the 2000 election or that supported Ralph Nader had ample cause to be frustrated with Clinton's legacy and put off by Gore's candidacy. But the differences between the Gore administration that should have been and the Bush administration that occurred were enormous, vastly outstripping the reasons that progressives gave for spurning Gore.

As for betrayal, this charge registers surprise or double-dealing. But Obama has advocated the very policies and governed in the very manner of liberal-leaning moderation and accommodation that he espoused in the 2008 campaign. He did not have a single risky position in his campaign agenda. His opposition to the Iraq war played to his favor in the Democratic weeding-out process, and he had committed himself to it long before he became a national figure. On everything else he was no more progressive than his chief Democratic rivals, Hillary Clinton and John Edwards. On some things, he was clearly less so, and he evinced less fighting spirit than Clinton and Edwards. Progressives who campaigned for Obama had a saying on this topic, which they muttered off camera, which Henry Louis Gates eventually uttered for the record: "Well, you know, Obama's only radical belief is that he can be elected president." But too many progressives and others imagined they were electing Martin Luther King Jr., which set them up for a mighty disillusionment.

Obama did not promise to get out of Afghanistan; he promised to escalate there. He did not promise to scale back the military empire; he promised to expand the Army, emphasize emergency warfare and counterterrorism, and shift the military away from preparing for World War III. He never promised to break the banking oligarchy or to create a public bank. He did not claim that he would *fight* for social justice causes, and he did not act like someone who would; he claimed that he would advance the struggle for social justice by persuading Democrats and Republicans to work together. For a while he debated whether to advocate a gas tax, but he decided that was too risky. His campaign supported a public option in health care, but very quietly; for most of the campaign, health care reform was a secondary issue for Obama. He eventually folded on military trials at Guantanamo Bay, but for two years he tried to close the Gitmo prison and to prosecute suspected terrorists in civilian courts.

The two biggest examples of "betrayal" that one might cite are Obama's capitulation on the Bush tax cuts for the rich in December 2010 and his subsequent months-long capitulation on spending cuts tied to the debt ceiling drama. In the former case, Obama broke a major campaign promise; in the latter case, he wrongly signed off on assaults on Medicaid and Medicare. But in both cases he was ensnared in hostage situations in which Republicans took pride in their willingness to take the nation hostage.

Obama had been president for barely a year when he appointed the Bowles-Simpson commission in February 2010 to find savings in the federal budget. The following November, after Democrats were routed in the midterm elections, Obama strengthened his resolve to show that he was serious about

deficit reduction. Republican leaders told Obama they would not allow exten-
sions of unemployment compensation or the middle-class tax cuts if he did
not cave on tax cuts for the rich, and so he caved. Then Republican leaders
turned a mere formality—raising the debt ceiling—into a massive extortion
threatening default on the national debt.

There is no exaggeration in describing this strategy as a species of extortion.
McConnell and the *Wall Street Journal* editorial board put it as bluntly as any
progressive critic. On August 1, 2011, the day after Obama cut a deal with
McConnell and House Republican leader John Boehner to avert a default,
the *Journal* declared, with an eye on history, "The debt ceiling is a political
hostage the GOP could never afford to shoot, and this deal is about the best
Republicans could have hoped for given that the limit had to be raised." The
Journal was grateful that Republican officials seemed truly willing, even eager,
to shoot the hostage; otherwise they could not have extorted the maximum
deal from Obama. Nonetheless, the *Journal* assured, "Sooner or later the GOP
had to give up the hostage."[11]

Unfortunately for the hostage, Obama let the extortion play out to the last
day; then he capitulated as though he had no leverage. Franklin Roosevelt
would not have allowed that outcome; even Bill Clinton would have invoked
the 14th Amendment to protect the nation. Obama made brutal concessions
that cannot be cleaned up. In April 2011 he cut Medicaid to get a budget
deal, which is morally indefensible. In the debt ceiling bargaining, he offered
to raise the entry age for Medicare, which is the opposite of what America
needs to do in health care; he dragged Social Security into the bargaining,
even though Social Security is solvent; and he cut an atrocious deal ceding to
Republicans, on Boehner's estimate, 98 percent of what they wanted. Any serious defense of Obama has to acknowledge the damage that his capitulation
to Republican extremism has caused. I take for granted that Medicare must be
reformed. Medicare, from the beginning a bureaucratic contraption of political compromises based on fee for service medicine, needs to be reorganized
to work more efficiently. Ensuring the solvency of the entitlement programs is
imperative. But none of that justifies doing harm to the poor and vulnerable.
Any progressive case for Obama has to bank on his commitment to limit the
damage from his own concessions and redeem the transformational promise
of his presidency.

This promise is still in play because Obama is singularly gifted, and he has
historic accomplishments to his credit to build upon—achievements that
too many progressives and others fail to acknowledge. Obama abolished
the United States' use of torture and the CIA's secret prisons. He restored
the liberal internationalist approach to foreign policy and made a historic
outreach to the Muslim world. He stabilized an economy that was spiraling

into a deflationary abyss. He expanded the earned income tax credit and made historic investments in job training, education, infrastructure, clean energy, housing, and scientific research. He saved the automobile industry and the economies related to it by saving General Motors and Chrysler. He expanded the State Children's Health Insurance Program (SCHIP), the last remnant of the Clinton health care initiatives, which Bush had vetoed twice. Obama forced the health insurance companies to stop excluding people with preexisting conditions and to stop dropping people when they got sick. He made an enormous and historic gain toward universal health care. He signed a financial reform bill that established a new consumer protection agency and put most derivative trading on an open exchange under the regulatory umbrella. He has gradually withdrawn American troops from Iraq exactly as he promised. He helped to inspire, and adeptly responded to, a history-changing wave of democratic revolutions in the Arab world. He relieved the world of Osama bin Laden and helped to end the murderous regime of Muammar Qaddafi. He has tried to reinstate excise taxes on the oil and chemical industry to revive the Environmental Protection Agency's Superfund program, though without success. He ended the Pentagon's Don't Ask, Don't Tell mistreatment of gays and lesbians in the military. He terminated the Justice Department's legal challenges to the Defense of Marriage Act, which bars the federal government from recognizing same-sex marriages or extending to them the benefits granted to heterosexual unions. He blocked Republicans from eliminating federal funding for Planned Parenthood. He suspended deportation proceedings against illegal immigrants lacking a criminal record. He has supported family unity in immigration policy, interpreting "family" to include the partners of lesbian, gay, and bisexual people. And he has represented the United States with consummate dignity.

Obama is a pragmatic, liberal-leaning centrist who prizes collaboration and accommodation, and a big-thinking ambitious type who wants to leave the largest possible legacy while governing cautiously yet taking a few risks. He advocates, and exemplifies, the communitarian approach of pulling people together to advance the common good. I believe that Obama would have done better to spend his political capital on job creation for a clean energy economy. He got diverted from what should have been his highest, everyday, ongoing priority, and for two years he wrongly lifted debt reduction above pushing for an infrastructure bank, renovating public schools, and making other socially beneficial investments that scale up. But it was not an overcautious trimmer who spent his political capital covering 34 million people lacking health insurance, and Obama still holds an essentially progressive vision of the presidency that he wants to have. When Obama thinks about the kind of legacy that he wants to leave, he thinks of FDR and Reagan, figures who changed the trajectory of American society. If, however, Obama is to reverse thirty years of capitulating to the interests of corporations and the wealthy, he must be pushed.

The Republican Party has wholly committed itself to an extreme ideology that abdicates responsibility for governing and that clings to disproven fantasies about tax cuts paying for themselves. Having lurched so far from being a normal party, it almost doesn't matter anymore which particular Republicans emerge as party leaders. Grover Norquist, president of Americans for Tax Reform, is more important than any congressional Republican leader. In the 112th Congress, 235 House members and 41 senators have taken the Norquist pledge to oppose any increase in the marginal tax rate for individuals or businesses and any elimination of tax breaks not matched dollar for dollar by reducing tax rates. All but two signers in the House and two in the Senate are Republicans; in the entire Congress, there are only seven Republican representatives and seven Republican senators who have not taken the Norquist pledge. The Republican Party, once home to moderate types with a sense of balance, has opted wholly for "starve the beast" extremism, never mind that slashing government spending in a weak economy is a sure way to deepen the misery, and that bond raters tend to look down on nations lacking stable political procedures or any capacity to raise new tax revenue. When "starve the beast" is axiomatic for every Republican leader, the slight differences among the party's Wall Street, social conservative, and Tea Party factions hold little significance.

The further-Right-than-ever Republican Party would rather default on the federal debt than make the wealthy pay taxes at the Clinton rate or even eliminate tax breaks for oil and gas companies. It drove the nation to the edge of default to get its way and damaged the nation's bond rating in the process. It wants yet another whopping tax cut for the wealthy. It claims to have been right, somehow, in opposing Obama's rescue of the automobile industry. It wants to break America's social contract with the elderly and the poor, replacing Medicare with a voucher system, turning Medicaid into a block grant program, and abolishing the new health insurance bill. It wants a balanced budget amendment to the Constitution that caps federal spending at 18 percent of the total economy, a figure last reached in 1966, which would require draconian cuts in everything, including Social Security. It wants to abolish the capital gains tax and all taxes on interest, dividends, and inheritance, recycling the same slogans that created the Reagan and Bush deficits. It has enacted reprehensible anti-immigrant laws in Alabama and Arizona, with promises of more to come. It wants to abolish Planned Parenthood and *Roe v. Wade*, plus the recent gains in rights for gays and lesbians, all with pledge-group ultimatums of their own modeled on the Norquist pledge.

People who hate the government have no business running it. The Tea Party has pulled the Republican Party further to the right on economic policy, but the Tea Party alone—numbering sixty members among House Republicans—could not have pulled off the debt ceiling ransom of 2011. Tea Party hatred of government now animates most of the Republican Party, setting its agenda for whoever proposes to be the party's putative leader.

In the early going, when the Republican presidential field had nine contenders, all of them pledged to never, never, never support any measure that yielded any new tax revenue, even if Obama delivered a fantasy ratio of 10-to-1 spending cuts to new revenue. Mitt Romney, the Wall Street candidate, supports the ludicrous "cut, cap and balance pledge" to gut the federal government and distort the Constitution. To make himself eligible to win Republican primaries, he had to disavow his previous positions on gay rights, abortion rights, gun control, campaign finance reform, immigration, reduction of greenhouse gas emissions, and whether health insurance reform would be good for any states besides Massachusetts. In July 2011, Romney had nothing to say as his party drove the country to the edge of default; then he blasted congressional Republicans for accepting less than 100 percent of what they wanted, sniffing that he would not have eaten "Obama's dog food."[12]

Rick Perry is more aggressively and convincingly far-Right, viscerally championing the Tea Party's rage against government. Perry says that America made terrible mistakes by establishing the income tax (in 1913) and Social Security (in 1935). He is against everything that came from the 16th and 17th Amendments and the New Deal, claiming that the income tax, Social Security, Medicare, Medicaid, clean-air laws, bank regulation, and much more are violations of the constitutional order established by the American founders. Perry is devoted to the interests of his corporate benefactors, especially big oil; he is anti-science concerning evolution and global warming; he is devoted to states' rights and a regressive flat tax; and he thuggishly warned Ben Bernanke against committing treason by printing more money.[13]

Rick Santorum boasts that no one in the Republican field surpasses his animus against feminism, contraception, abortion, rights for gays and lesbians, and Islamic radicalism; Santorum also wants to cut the marginal tax rate to 28 percent and cut the capital gains rate in half.

Michele Bachmann adds that global warming is a hoax; gay sexuality of "part of Satan," gay marriage is a threat to American society, the New Deal was a disaster for American society, and defaulting on the nation's debt obligation is better than raising the debt ceiling.

Newt Gingrich, the long-reigning king of moral hypocrisy, egomania, and venomous tactics in American politics, pushes a ridiculous theory about Obama's anticolonial vengefulness. In Gingrich's telling, Perry has the correct analysis of America's problems, but Gingrich, his prodigious baggage notwithstanding, is the candidate best suited to carry it out.

Faced with an opposition that has careened so far into a bizarre world of antigovernment extremisms and other irrational obsessions, Obama is naturally tempted to play for the safe middle ground. But that would be less than we deserve.

Notes

1. Beck comments on *Fox & Friends*, Fox television network, July 28, 2009, youtube.com.

2. "Rush Limbaugh's Shocking Words for President Obama," Rush Limbaugh interview with Sean Hannity, Fox News, January 22, 2009, www.foxnews.com/story/0,2933,481484,00.html; Mitch McConnell, interview with Major Garrett, *National Journal* (October 25, 2010), reprinted in "Mitch McConnell: I Want to Be Senate Majority Leader in Order to Make Obama a One-Term President," Think Progress, October 25, 2010, http://thinkprogress.org; "McConnell: Hold Obama to One Term," UPI, November 4, 2010, www.upi.com/Top_News.

3. "CNBC's Rick Santelli's Chicago Tea Party," February 19, 2009, youtube.com.

4. "Historical Debt Outstanding: Annual 1950–1999; Annual 2000–2010," Treasury Direct, www.treasurydirect.gov/govt/reports.

5. "President Clinton Announces Another Record Budget Surplus," CNN Politics, September 27, 2000, http://articles.cnn.com; "Historical Debt Outstanding: Annual 2000–2010"; Tax Policy Center, Urban Institute, and Brookings Institution, "The Tax Policy Briefing Book," 2011, www.taxpolicycenter.org.

6. Alan Greenspan, *The Age of Turbulence: Adventures in a New World* (New York: Penguin, 2008), 186; Linda J. Bilmes and Joseph E. Stiglitz, "The $10 Trillion Hangover: Paying the Price for Eight Years of Bush," *Harper's* (January 2009), 31–35; "Historical Debt Outstanding: Annual 2000–2010"; "The Tax Policy Briefing Book"; Joseph E. Stiglitz and Linda J. Bilmes, *The Three Trillion Dollar War* (New York: Norton, 2008).

7. Laura A. Kelter, "Substantial Job Losses in 2008: Weakness Broadens and Deepens across Industries," *Monthly Labor Review* (March 2009), 20–26; U.S. Department of Labor, Bureau of Labor Statistics, "Employment Situation, February 2009," "Employment Situation, February 2010," www.bls.gov; Eamon Javers, "Inside Obama's Bank CEOs Meeting," *Politico* (April 3, 2009), www.politico.com/news; Rick Klein, "Obama to Bankers: I'm Standing 'between You and the Pitchforks,'" ABC News, The Note, blogs.abcnews.com/thenote/2009/04.

9. Chris Hedges, "The Obama Deception: Why Cornel West Went Ballistic," *truthdig* (May 16, 2011), www.truthdig.com.

10. Michael Lerner, "A Progressive Strategy for 2011–2012," *Tikkun* (Spring 2011), 6–7.

11. Editorial, "A Tea Party Triumph," *Wall Street Journal* (August 1, 2011).

12. See Mitt Romney, *No Apology: Believe in America* (New York: St. Martin's Griffin, 2010).

13. Rick Perry, *Fed Up! Our Fight to Save America from Washington* (New York: Little, Brown and Company, 2010).

2

Becoming Obama

B ARACK OBAMA SHOT INTO NATIONAL PROMINENCE so quickly that catching up never quite occurred. He hurtled into national prominence on July 27, 2004, with a sensational keynote speech at the Democratic Party convention in Boston. Six months later he joined the U.S. Senate as its only African American member. Four years after that he was inaugurated as America's 44th president.

Nothing in American presidential history compares to this meteoric ascent, yet for no American president has the backstory loomed so large or symbolized so much. Obama knows the power of his story and has relied upon it throughout his career. When he entered electoral politics in 1996 at the age of thirty-five, he had already published a 440-page autobiography, *Dreams from My Father*. In his career as a state senator he told his story repeatedly, playing lightheartedly on his name, although after September 11, 2001, he had to tread carefully in joking about his name. He had barely started his 2004 convention speech when he launched into a capsule version of his story. Four years later he began his convention speech accepting the Democratic nomination for president by retelling his story. He featured his story in a second book, *The Audacity of Hope*, and on the 2008 campaign trail, notably in the famous "race speech" of March 2008. Not telling his story was not an option for Obama, as everything about him was too exotic not to explain to American voters. The meaning of Obama is inextricably linked with his story.[1]

The capsule version features geographic and cultural leaps: Born in Honolulu, Hawaii, in 1961 to a Kansas-born mother, Stanley Ann Dunham, and a Kenyan father, Barack Hussein Obama, who met in a Russian class as students at the University of Hawaii. Left behind at the age of eleven months by his father, who studied economics at Harvard before returning to Kenya to work as a government economist. Moved to Jakarta, Indonesia, in 1967 after Obama's mother married an Indonesian foreign student, Lolo Soetoro. Returned to Hawaii in 1971 to live with his maternal grandparents, Stanley and Madelyn "Toot" Dunham, where Obama attended an elite school, Punahou, adapted to Aloha culture, was reunited with his mother for three years, studied enough to earn Bs, smoked the normal amount of dope, played a reserve role on the basketball team, and graduated in 1979. Started college at Occidental College near Pasadena, California, where Obama loafed to easygoing Bs and hung out with stoners and lefty political types. Transferred to Columbia University in 1981, where Obama buckled down, gave up reefer, studied, kept to himself, worried about world poverty, and earned a degree in international relations. Worked for a year at Business International, working up to a research position, which bored him; Obama got clear that corporate life was not for him.

The gold standard for Obama, by the end of his college years, was the long-past civil rights movement, on which his mother had waxed idealistically in his youth. He read books about it and tried to find a vestige of it in New York, unsuccessfully. He got as close to the movement as he could by opting for three years of church-based community organizing in Chicago, which gave him an opportunity to live in a black community for the first time in his life. Had Obama opted for Harvard Law School straight out of Columbia, the corporate world might have snared him. As it was, when he enrolled at Harvard Law School in 1988 he had the worldview and street experience of an antipoverty organizer.

At Harvard Obama flourished, comparing very favorably to his high-aspiring, ideologically polarized classmates, which confirmed his self-confidence. In the summer after his first year he returned to Chicago to work as an associate at the Sidley & Austin law firm, where Michelle Robinson was his mentor. In his senior year he was elected president of the *Harvard Law Review*, which won him a book offer. Obama was twenty-nine years old when he signed the contract for *Dreams from My Father*. Then he returned to Chicago, married Michelle Robinson, worked for a law firm specializing in civil rights and antitrust cases, and led a successful voter registration drive.

That was his story when he wrote *Dreams from My Father*, a book that was supposed to range over civil rights law, affirmative action, Afrocentric education, community organizing, grassroots democracy, and his story. But Obama struggled with the manuscript for three years, losing his contract with Simon & Schuster in 1993. Luckily, Simon & Schuster didn't make him repay the half of his $150,000 advance that he had already received and spent, as Obama and Michelle were buried in student loan debts. Obama's agent, Jane Dystel, promptly landed a contract with Times Books (Random House) for the book, but he still struggled with it. At some point Obama realized that his story was more interesting than his thoughts about civil rights litigation or Afrocentric pedagogy. How and when, exactly, he reshaped the book, and to what extent he attained help from book doctors, are matters of speculation and dispute.

In 2009 veteran journalist Christopher Andersen reported that Obama got important help from his neighborhood friend Bill Ayers, an education professor and former 1960s Weather Underground revolutionary. According to Andersen, Obama admired the artful style of Ayers's recent book, *To Teach*, which Obama sought to emulate, partly by getting Ayers to work with him. Andersen's account was seized upon by anti-Obama conspiracy theorists who already contended that the chief influences on Obama's thought and career were a former terrorist (Ayers), a Communist poet (Frank Marshall Davis), a pro-Palestinian radical (Rashid Khalidi), and a radical liberationist preacher (Jeremiah Wright). The conspiracy literature is wild and excitable on the topic of Obama's purported debts to anti-American radicals; Ayers heads the list of conspiracy obsessions. In the real world, Obama and Ayers worked together on various projects during Obama's Chicago years, mostly on education reform; Obama admired Ayers's writing, publishing a favorable review of Ayers's book *A Kind and Just Parent*; and Ayers apparently gave Obama editorial help. In the conspiracy world, Ayers wrote *Dreams from My Father*, and Obama's presidency is a conspiracy to impose small-c communism, anti-imperialist revenge, and other anti-American radicalisms on America.[2]

At some point Obama realized that the most compelling parts of his story had little to do with his education at elite schools. The book morphed into an artful, shape-shifting memoir about being biracial and growing up multicultural in a multiracial extended family. It had three sections, titled "Origins," "Chicago," and "Kenya." In each section Obama experienced a tearful epiphany at the end. In "Origins" he saw his father in a dream and resolved to search for him. In "Chicago" he wept at finding a faith and a spiritual community at Trinity United Church of Christ. In "Kenya" he wept at his father's grave, accepting his family and his past after learning that his father bore little resemblance to the heroic figure that Ann Dunham had portrayed to enhance Obama's self-esteem and aspiration.

Dreams from My Father contained composite figures and other literary devices, especially Homeric tropes about finding a father and a way home, plus a layered skepticism about the stories that people tell about themselves, their loved ones, and their groups. Obama declared at the outset, "I learned long ago to distrust my childhood and the stories that shaped it." Stanley Dunham told his grandson that he had moved from Texas to Seattle to escape Southern racism, but Obama, years later, gave more credence to his grandmother's explanation that a job opportunity was the deciding factor. Hawaii's celebrated Aloha culture was real, Obama acknowledged, especially its wide-ranging racial inclusivity. On the other hand, the conquest of Hawaii by white European settlers who displaced the native population left ugly scars, and Hawaii had a grim legacy of plagues, missionary imperialism, and economic exploitation. Obama realized that his memoir colored events and experiences in ways that favored him, and he may have realized that his mother got less than her due in a story that played up his search for a father and a home.

Ann Dunham married an African at a time when nearly two dozen states outlawed intermarriage. She moved to Indonesia in the aftermath of an anti-Communist bloodbath and immersed herself in the nation's culture. She earned a doctorate in a field almost exclusively dominated by men. She took up community organizing before Obama did, helping poor Indonesians, especially women, get access to credit. But Obama had reasons for short-changing his mother, and he stressed that it was no easy thing to grow up black—and thus nearly alone—in Hawaii. *Dreams from My Father* reverber-ated with the story of Obama's attempt to live up to a well-intentioned myth of paternal grandeur, his search for the missing father, and his struggle to construct an identity.

In his early youth Obama barely noticed that his mother and maternal grandparents were white Americans from Kansas, his absent father in the photographs was a black African, and he and his younger sister Maya Soetoro were differently biracial. Later he found all of it confusing and unsettling. In his telling he developed a skeptical armor while growing up in Indonesia, and at the age of twelve or thirteen he stopped advertising his mother's race, because he suspected that he did it to ingratiate himself with white people. Obama struggled with his racial identity at Punahou and Occidental, even as he struck acquaintances as being happy and well adjusted.

Stanley Ann Dunham was seventeen years old when she met Barack Hus-sein Obama in September 1960; he was twenty-four. She had almost enrolled at the University of Chicago, but her parents dragged her to Hawaii, where she lived with her parents and started going by her middle name. Ann had never had a romantic relationship. At college she fell hard for the brilliant, gregarious, worldly Obama. Some of their classmates found him charming, and some found him aggressively full of himself. Obama Sr. had a deep, loud, captivating voice. He gave newspaper interviews and spoke at schools. And he loved to tell the story of his father, Onyango Obama, who had converted from Roman Catholicism to Islam while traveling with the British colonial forces in India and Zanzibar, who was jailed by the British in 1949 for his involvement in the Kenyan independence movement, and who was a polygamist. Barack Obama Sr. apparently did not let on, at first, that he was a polygamist too.

Classes began in late September. By November Ann was pregnant. A discrete wedding was held in February 1961, although there are no official records of it. Soon afterward Ann realized that she was in over her head. It is unknown when, exactly, Ann learned that her husband was already married and a father, with a second child by his first wife, Kezia, on the way. It is known that he became imperious and demanding after he married Ann. On one occasion Obama Sr. hurled a plate of food that she had prepared for him against a wall and shouted at her. Ann told a friend that she knew where this story was going when the plate hit the wall. Obama was born in August 1961, by which time his parents' marriage was effectively over. Ann left Hawaii first, in the spring of 1962, enrolling at the University of Washington in Seattle, where she had friends from high school. The elder Obama graduated from Hawaii that spring and chose Harvard for graduate school, where he had no financial support beyond tuition remittance, passing up a fellowship at the New School for Social Research in New York. By choosing Harvard, he opted for closure on his second marriage; meanwhile Ann Dunham Obama returned to Hawaii so her parents could help her.[3]

Ann's second husband was a Javanese graduate student, Lolo Soetoro, who arrived at the University of Hawaii in 1962. The youngest of ten children in a family from Yogyakarta, Lolo belonged to the second wave of Indonesian students to study at Hawaii on East-West Center grants. By temperament he was kindly and cheerful, plus affectionate with Ann's toddler son; by temperament and Javanese culture he was calm, considerate, and not inclined to argue, traits that Ann found refreshing after her marriage to a volubly intense type. Lolo planned to return to Indonesia for a career as a university professor, which appealed to Ann. In 1964, shortly after Ann was divorced from Obama and Lolo earned a master's degree in geography, she and Lolo married. But Lolo did not get the career that he wanted.

Indonesia, a nation of 17,500 islands, got its independence in 1949 after centuries of domination by the Dutch. In 1963 its postcolonial titan and first president, Sukarno, suspended elections in the midst of an economic crisis featuring 700 percent inflation. The following year Sukarno proclaimed a "year of living dangerously," and in September 1965 six Indonesian army generals and a lieutenant were killed in what may have been a coup attempt planned by the Communist Party. Everything is disputed about what happened, except that the "coup" incident, after being put down, set off a bloodbath that killed somewhere between 200,000 and 1,000,000 people. Suharto, a major general in the Indonesian army, launched a massive purge of Communists and suspected sympathizers that led to Sukarno's overthrow. Much of the killing was carried out by civilian vigilantes and militias backed by the army, many of whom went door to door, wielding bayonets. Adrian Vickers, in *A History of Modern Indonesia,* observes: "The best way to prove you were not a Communist was to join in the killings." Suharto was appointed acting president in 1967 and president the following year. Lolo was called home in the midst of the overthrow, conscripted straight off the plane from Hawaii. He was sent to work as an army geologist in the jungles of New Guinea for a year, mapping the border of Irian Barat, a contested area that later became the nation's twenty-sixth province, Papua. When Ann joined Lolo in Jakarta in 1967, he was completing his tour in the army. She was twenty-four years old and knew very little about the nation's upheaval; her son was six years old.[4]

Lolo told them as little as possible, traumatized by the mass killings and turmoil. His cheerfulness vanished; in addition, he became a different kind of husband in his home context, clashing with Ann about her independence, forthright opinions, and disinterest in dressing up or wearing makeup. Ann had to learn from others about the massacres that had just ended in Indonesia, and she took no interest in being a doting wife. Lolo, falling into depression, nursed his demons with imported whiskey. He barely spoke to anyone; Obama recalled that it was as though Lolo had come to distrust words.

Ann prized truthful directness in nearly all things; by all accounts she was cheerful, disorganized, restless, idealistic, and easily moved to tears; and her parenting style included occasional resorts to guilt. She was fond of saying that guilt was an underrated emotion. Lolo told her that she had no idea what it was like to have no power and to be constantly at risk of losing everything. Indonesians had to scrape for survival, he explained. Avoiding conflict was far more important than candor, and guilt was a luxury that only foreigners could afford. Ann's heredity protected her even if she disclaimed it. She could always fly home to America if things got messy.

Lolo was good to Obama, however, teaching him how to negotiate the street life of Jakarta—a place of adventure that young Obama greatly enjoyed. The family's first home in Indonesia was a tiny bungalow on a dirt road outside Jakarta, where cockatoos, chickens, baby crocodiles, and a pet monkey roamed the backyard. After Lolo took a government relations job with an American oil company, he became more Americanized, consorting with American oil businessmen, to Ann's dismay. She had not moved to Indonesia to associate with obnoxious Americans who believed in American supremacy, white supremacy, and/or Texas supremacy. It grieved her that Lolo settled for such mediocrity, lamenting that "power" had taken him just as he was about to do something interesting with his life. Ann begged off from making social appearances that might help his career in oil company culture. Instead she immersed herself in Indonesia's prodigious cultural complexity, in some ways becoming more Indonesian than her husband, which laid the groundwork for her subsequent doctoral work in anthropology. And she and Lolo gradually drifted apart.

For two years Ann worked at the U.S. Embassy in Jakarta, supervising an English language program for Indonesian business executives and government officials. She loathed the job, shuddering at the chasm between the elite that she served and the rest of the country. Obama later explained that the businessmen made passes at her, and she didn't much care for the U.S. State Department careerists either. After two years she made a breakthrough, founding a business communications division for a management training school, where she became a popular teacher. In both positions, every weekday at 4:00 a.m., Ann awoke Obama for three hours of English lessons before she headed off to work. He protested constantly, to no avail; Ann Dunham Soetoro was devoted to her son and determined not to deprive him of a productive life in his native country. Obama later recalled that even as his mother plunged into Indonesian culture, she was mindful that the life chances of an Indonesian did not remotely compare to those of an American: "She knew which side of the divide she wanted her child to be on."[5]

From an early age, however, according to Obama, he tuned her out when she waxed philosophical about how to live a good life. Later, in his telling, he made a similar judgment about his mother's grasp of racial realities. In Indonesia, Ann told her son that if he wanted to grow into a human being, he needed to develop some values, especially honesty, fairness, directness, and independent judgment. The core virtues were virtuous and enabling wherever one lived.

Obama doubted that his mother knew what she was talking about. Ann believed that people shape their own destiny and that the key to having a good life is to apply one's intelligence to problems. This belief was something like a religious faith to her, although she never called it that. Obama put it sharply in *Dreams from My Father*: "My mother's confidence in needlepoint virtues depended on a faith I didn't possess, a faith that she would refuse to describe as religious; that in fact, her experience told her was sacrilegious: a faith that rational people could shape their own destiny."[6]

Obama learned a different lesson from the streets and from observing his stepfather: that fatalism is a necessity for poor people struggling to survive. One cannot survive poverty and powerlessness without adopting, to some degree, a fatalistic attitude about the situation into which one has been thrown. From an early age, in Obama's telling, he sensed the chasm between his mother's faith in homespun Kansas virtues and the reality of the Indonesian street, where people struggled to survive Third World poverty and corruption. Ann's romantic idealism and somewhat reckless naïveté, in Obama's reckoning, made her allergic to some of life's prosaic realities, notwithstanding her openness to cultural difference: "She was a lonely witness for secular humanism, a soldier for New Deal, Peace Corps, position-paper liberalism."[7]

The only impressive argument that she had for her faith was the distant authority of Obama's father, who exemplified the truism that one could overcome any obstacle by working hard and intelligently. Ann told Obama that his father had "grown up poor, in a poor country, in a poor continent." He became a person of distinction by working hard, being unequivocally honest, and applying his acute intelligence. Obama's father, she explained, adhered to principles that demanded a distinct form of toughness. He developed a strong moral character that saw him through all manner of hardships, becoming powerful through achievement, developing powers of mind and will that set him apart from others.

This part of his mother's spiel got to Obama, who imagined life as a challenge to live up to his father's noble example. Obama loved and admired his mother. He realized that much of his success owed much to her intellectual curiosity and resilience and her devotion to him. He got his desire to help hurting and excluded people from his mother, and her later work as a type of community organizer gave him a model for it. After Ann died, a few months after *Dreams from My Father* was published, Obama got better at saying so. In the preface to the book's 2004 edition, he recalled poignantly: "I think sometimes that had I known she would not survive her illness, I might have written a different book—less a meditation on the absent parent, more a celebration of the one who was the single constant in my life. In my daughters I see her every day, her joy, her capacity for wonder." Obama professed that his mother was "the kindest, most generous spirit I have ever known, and that what is best in me I owe to her." The following year he dedicated his book *The Audacity of Hope* to the women who raised him, his grandmother Tutu (the Hawaiian term of affection for grandmothers), who was his "rock of stability throughout my life," and his mother, "whose loving spirit sustains me still." By the time that he ran for president, the latter tribute flowed readily out of him.[8]

But *Dreams from My Father* said very little about Ann Dunham; it skewered her idealism, and Obama spent much of his adolescence feeling abandoned by her. In his telling, his longing for a home traced directly to his mother's reckless wanderlust and disorganization. In the White House he told an interviewer that Ann's life was chaotic in every way and that his life could have turned out very differently without the saving support of his grandparents. In *Dreams from My Father* he stressed that his mother's simplistic bromides about living a good life went hand in hand with an equally naïve idealism about race. Ann's rendering of black American culture was a lot like her romanticized account of Obama's father. Thus, she was no help with Obama's struggle to achieve a racial identity, except for the picture that she provided of Obama's father, which turned out to be fictional.[9]

Ann Dunham, in her son's telling, had a Black History Month version of history, emphasizing black heroes: "She would come home with books on the civil rights movement, the recordings of Mahalia Jackson, the speeches of Dr. King. When she told me stories of schoolchildren in the South who were forced to read books handed down from wealthier white schools but who went on to become doctors and lawyers and scientists, I felt chastened by my reluctance to wake up and study in the mornings." Obama wearied especially of the hero trope, which his mother applied to all black people: "Every black man was Thurgood Marshall or Sidney Poitier; every black woman Fannie Lou Hamer or Lena Horne. To be black was to be the beneficiary of a great inheritance, a special destiny, glorious burdens that only we were strong enough to bear. Burdens we were to carry with style."[10]

Obama realized that he could have done much worse in the birth lottery. Moreover, his mother loved him so fiercely that she never criticized his father, even though the elder Obama had mistreated and abandoned her. Nurturing her son's ego, Ann built up a myth about Obama Sr. that sustained Obama's self-image and sense of purpose well into his twenties.

As a grown man, making a pilgrimage to his father's grave in Kenya, Obama got a chastening taste of how his life might have gone otherwise. Meeting his father's embittered third wife, Ruth Nidesand, and her son Mark, Obama cringed as Ruth rattled off a stream of insults about her purportedly crazy, mean, drunken former husband. Obama couldn't wait to get away from her. Instead, Ruth subjected him to her family picture album, which cut Obama deeply. He realized that he had spent his youth wishing to be reunited with his father, which would have been disastrous. After only a few minutes he had to look away from the pictures; he couldn't bear projecting himself into them.

He was one of the lucky ones, despite having a mother who could not help him with his racial identity and who was not there when he struggled with it. Obama spent four years in Jakarta, where he withstood taunts about his dark skin and curly hair by learning to be calm and self-controlled. In manners, Obama was shaped by his Indonesian experience, developing the habits of self-control, politeness, and cool reasonableness that his Javanese classmates respected. Then he was put on a flight to Hawaii after completing the fourth grade.

Stanley Dunham, an insurance salesman with a volatile, restless, garrulous personality and a history of conflict with his daughter, doted over Obama. Toot Dunham, a more stable but less warm personality, became the family's chief provider while working her way up to a bank vice presidency. Though Stanley had little education, his boss had graduated from Hawaii's finest private school, Punahou. On the strength of that connection and the school's eagerness to diversify its image (it had four black students at the time), Stanley got Obama into Punahou, an upscale paradise with a seventy-five-acre campus where students dressed as if headed for the beach or a party. For a year Obama adjusted to Hawaii, before Ann and Maya rejoined him; Ann returned for three years of graduate study in anthropology. She tried to be helpful to Obama as he negotiated adolescence, but she had struggles of her own getting through graduate school as a single mother of two children, and her sentimental view of race was hard to bear, although she later protested that Obama exaggerated her naïveté.

The Black Power movement confused and unsettled Ann Dunham. She had trouble assimilating black rage; she idealized the 1950s phase of the civil rights movement; she told Obama that she didn't *feel* white, which embarrassed him; and her head was filled with sentimental images from her favorite movie, *Black Orpheus,* which deeply embarrassed Obama when he realized it in his twenties. Ann returned to Indonesia to do fieldwork for her dissertation during Obama's high school years. Later she worked for the Ford Foundation and the World Bank in Indonesia. One summer, arriving at the airport in Jakarta to pick up Obama, Ann panicked at not finding her short, stocky, chubby-cheeked son. Finally a tall, thin, deep-voiced young man approached her, towering over her. Ann was stunned at not having recognized her son—a clue to her slight role in his memoir.

Obama later recalled that Ann combined deep personal convictions and a strong sense of herself with "a certain recklessness." Restless and headstrong, and proud to identify herself as a citizen of the world, she never stopped searching for something: "She wasn't comfortable seeing her life confined to a certain box." Elsewhere he recalled: "The idea of being a citizen of the world somehow didn't feel right for me. I wanted to be rooted in an American city and an American context and then venture forth. There was a weightlessness to that life, in the sense of at some level always being an outsider." Obama's sister Maya Soetoro-Ng, who lived with her mother in Indonesia, Pakistan, Thailand, India, and other places for years at a time, put the same thing differently: "We were all a little *untethered.*" Maya internalized more of Ann's wanderlust; later she reflected: "Probably some of our mother's decisions may have looked selfish in comparison." Certainly that helped to explain Obama's fixation with a father that he did not know. *Dreams from My Father* was appropriately titled, even though Obama's singular object of reference and imagination was a man he had met only once after his infancy, for a month.[11]

In 1971, a few months after Obama returned to Hawaii, Toot told him that they would have a special guest for Christmas—his father. Ann came to Honolulu for the occasion, leaving Lolo and Maya in Indonesia. Obama was apprehensive, but Ann told him not to worry. She had maintained a correspondence with her former husband during her years in Indonesia; the elder Obama knew all about his son; and he had five sons and a daughter in Kenya.

Obama employed a skeptical dangling verb in recalling her assurance: "'You two will become great friends,' she decided." Ann tried to compensate for years of not yielding much real information about the elder Obama by pouring out facts about Kenya and the Luo tribe, which Obama supplemented with a public library book on East Africa. Obama, ten years old, shuddered at the thought of living among a tribe, raising cattle, living in a mud hut, eating something called millet, and wearing a leather thong. He also feared being exposed at school, since he had told classmates that his father was an African prince, the son of a tribal chief. Years later Obama learned that his father had, in fact, come to Hawaii to bring him, Ann, and Maya to live with him in Kenya.[12]

The visit was strained and unnerving for Obama. Pilgrimages were made to his father's former residence and to the hospital where Obama was born. The elder Obama chastised Ann and her parents for spoiling Obama and for not pushing him hard enough to study. An appearance at Obama's school went better than he expected, as his father spoke impressively about Kenya's post-colonial struggle for freedom and said nothing about mud huts: "He told us of Kenya's struggle to be free, how the British had wanted to stay and unjustly rule the people, just as they had in America; how many had been enslaved only because of the color of their skin; just as they had in America; but that Kenyans, like all of us in the room, longed to be free and develop themselves through hard work and sacrifice." This sentence later caused excitement in the Right blogosphere as a clue to how Obama got to be such a seething, vengeful anticolonialist. In Obama's telling, however, the classroom episode was mostly a relief to him, not a revelation, and overall he decided that he preferred the distant image of his father as a figure of grandeur to the disapproving, elusive figure that he briefly met in the flesh: "If my father hadn't exactly disappointed me, he remained something unknown, something volatile and vaguely threatening."[13]

That was all that he had to work with upon entering adolescence, a ten-year-old's brief impression of a stranger. In high school Obama stopped writing letters to his father and took whatever instruction he could find about black culture from equally lonely black friends, black soldiers stationed on the island, and trips to a run-down bohemian section of Waikiki called "the Jungle." For one year he had an older friend, immortalized as "Ray" in *Dreams from My Father*, who talked a high-octane stream of black consciousness. "Ray" was Keith Kakugawa, the son of an Army transfer. He was later imprisoned for seven years on drug and auto-theft charges, and during the 2008 presidential campaign he set off a brief media flurry by asking the Obama campaign for money. Kakugawa, being homeless, explained that he routinely asked everybody for money and had no desire to injure Obama. According to Kakugawa, Obama exaggerated his racial angst in *Dreams from My Father*, underplayed his distress at feeling abandoned, and exaggerated Kakugawa's preoccupation with race. According to Obama, Ray helpfully introduced him to black sectors of Hawaii, and most of the time, Obama gently deflated Ray's bravado and racial stereotyping.[14]

In Obama's telling, Ray attributed his lack of a social life to the racism of white and Asian girls, and he attributed his and Obama's lack of playing time on the basketball team to the racism of their coaches. Obama needled his friend that not everything that happened to him was a racial incident (exactly what Kakugawa later claimed that he said to Obama). On the other hand, Obama savored Ray's company and eventually judged that Ray correctly diagnosed Obama's basketball problem. Obama had a black game modeled on Julius Erving and some local Army players, favoring behind-the-back passes and other playground flourishes. Punahou's varsity coach, Chris McLachlin, had an old-school white game modeled on Bobby Knight fundamentals featuring bounce passes, designed plays, and aggressive defense. On the playground, Obama could beat some of the players who played ahead of him. In the gym he steamed on the bench, eventually judging that his status had everything to do with racial prejudice. In one incident, which Obama did not retell, he punched a classmate in the face for calling him a "coon." In another incident, after a Punahou coach dismissed the opposing team as "a bunch of niggers," Obama hotly replied, "There are white folks, and then there are ignorant motherfuckers like you."[15]

One blinks with delight and surprise at this wonderfully unlike-Obama eruption. Even in a memoir of troubled, drifting, aimless adolescence, it stands out, although Obama finally made the varsity team in his senior year and played a few good games, on a team that cruised to a state championship. Basketball provided Obama's first and only focus of self-discipline in his teen years, plus a crucial source of friendship. His classmates, however, reading his memoir years later, were surprised that he described years of inner turmoil. He struck them as happy and pretty cool, an ornament of Aloha culture, always ready to party. Some had never thought of him as being black. In Obama's telling, he spent a good deal of his later adolescence pondering his racial identity, slipping back and forth between black and white worlds. He had white friends who loved him, treating him like they treated each other, yet he also half-agreed with Ray, or at least could not deny, that the world belonged to their white classmates.[16]

Ray, in the Obama version, was enraged at the white world, despite liking Obama's grandparents, the very people that Obama tried to distance himself from by hanging out with Ray. Obama told Ray that perhaps they should "give the bad-assed nigger pose a rest," saving it for when they needed it.

They were living, after all, "in goddamned Hawaii," not a housing project in Harlem. Ray, offended at the suggestion of posing, told Obama to speak for himself. That was a trump card, Obama recalled, because Ray understood something about him: "I had no idea who my own self was."[17]

Hawaii's most elite prep school was not a good place for him to make that discovery. Obama lived with his white grandparents, he had almost no black classmates, he ingratiated himself with "Miss Snooty Bitch" and other white teachers, and he moved in and out of agreeing with Ray, who assured him: "It's their world, all right? They own it, and we in it." No matter what Obama did, Ray contended, he had no real freedom of choice. Since white people owned the world and made the rules, it was always up to them to decide how much tolerance, opportunity, or respect to extend to any particular black person or to blacks as a whole. All that Obama could do was to accept his powerlessness or lash out at his white captors near and far. The former option meant withdrawing in defeat into a coil of rage. The latter option, Obama noted, carried a ready-made set of labels, all of them ostracizing: "Paranoid. Militant. Violent. Nigger."[18]

This section later provided quotable material for the Right blogosphere's hysteria about Obama's supposed Black Power radicalism. Moreover, his account of his inner struggle was undoubtedly colored by Frantz Fanon's classic account of black postcolonial consciousness, which Obama read in college. Fanon, a black Algerian psychiatrist, argued that blacks in postcolonial Algeria were fated to wear white masks over their faces, because white people wrote the rules and owned the world. Wearing the mask was a necessity, even if it violated one's dignity and even if one believed that self-determination should still be a possibility. In Obama's telling, Ray's Fanon-like challenge drove him to his room, brooding in isolation, where Obama read James Baldwin, W. E. B. Du Bois, Ralph Ellison, Langston Hughes, and Richard Wright, searching for an escape from a bad either/or. But every page of the African American canon conveyed to him that there was no escape: "I kept finding the same anguish, the same doubt; a self-contempt that neither irony nor intellect seemed able to deflect." In every case, the redeeming power of art brought no release or redemption. All the great black American writers, despite their learning and talent, ended up as "exhausted, bitter men, the devil at their heels."[19]

The only exception to this grim picture, as far as Obama could tell, was Malcolm X, who reinvented himself repeatedly, with fierce self-discipline and willpower, demanding to be respected. Malcolm refused to be cowed or defeated. Obama set aside Malcolm's black Muslim doctrine about the origin of white evil, which struck him as dispensable religious baggage that the later Malcolm relinquished. What mattered was that Malcolm radiated dignity, offering a model of vibrant, unyielding courage. Malcolm claimed his power unequivocally. Even if Obama, living in Aloha paradise and confused about his identity, was not ready for much self-discipline, he at least admired Malcolm's self-creating self-discipline. Kakugawa later confirmed that Obama went through a phase when he bored Kakugawa and their friends with constant chatter about Malcolm's greatness. Malcolm was a model, at least in theory. On the other hand, Obama gasped at Malcolm's insistence that he despised every ounce of white blood that coursed through his veins. Obama tried to imagine leaving his mother and grandparents "at some uncharted border."[20]

He moved past imagining it after learning that his beloved grandmother Toot harbored a special fear of black men that she encountered at the bus station. Here the Right blogosphere's second-favorite conspiracy figure, Frank Marshall Davis, enters the story, though in some versions, Davis is number one. Davis was an accomplished black poet and former Communist who moved to Hawaii in 1948 at the suggestion of his friend Paul Robeson. He lived in the bohemian section of Waikiki; he wrote highbrow articles about white supremacy, jazz, and sexual repression, dabbling as a nude photographer; and in 1956 he refused to answer questions by one of the McCarthy-era Senate committees investigating Communist influence in the United States. In parts of the anti-Obama blogosphere it is taken for granted that Davis was Obama's father, having impregnated Ann Dunham shortly after she arrived in Hawaii. In this telling, Davis and the Dunhams covered their embarrassment by drafting Barack Obama Sr. to play the beard, standing in briefly as the father and husband. Thus the entire African Obama business is a family fiction that would have died with Toot Dunham had Obama not aimed quite so high. Even for sectors of the conspiracy literature that don't leap this wildly, Davis is an intoxicating figure for purportedly indoctrinating young Obama in Communism and other radicalisms.[21]

Stanley Dunham occasionally took his grandson to Davis's home to hang out. He and Davis were friends, and Stanley realized that Obama should have an adult black male in his life. Not even the conspiracy bloggers charge that Stanley had any radical political motives, although, if one runs with the Davis-as-father theory, Stanley's friendship with Davis is hard to figure. Obama described his relationship with Davis with no suggestion of emotional freight or political indoctrination. He found Davis to be interesting, open, thoughtful, and accessible. In Obama's telling, while Dunham and Davis drank whiskey out of a jelly jar, Davis dispensed sage advice to Obama, who came to rely on it, sometimes visiting Davis on his own.

Obama, deeply troubled by a spat he had witnessed between his grandparents over Toot's bus station anxieties, paid a visit to Davis. He told Davis that Toot was afraid to take the bus on account of racial fear and that Stanley was ashamed of her fear. Davis told Obama that his grandparents were good people, but Stanley would never understand him (Davis) the way that Davis understood Stanley, and Toot had good reason to be scared of black men. Davis explained that Stanley had no trouble visiting him in his house, drinking his whiskey, and falling asleep in his chair, but it never worked the other way around. The friendship between them was not reciprocal, despite being a real friendship. Moreover, Toot understood that black people had ample cause to hate white people; thus, she was afraid of black males of a certain age or physical capacity. Nothing could be done about this, Davis advised; Obama was overdue to get used to it. Obama later recalled that as he walked away from Davis's home, he felt the earth shaking under his feet, threatening to crack open, as he realized for the first time "that I was utterly alone." The border was terribly real no matter how he felt about his white bloodline.[22]

After Obama entered the presidential race, this passage became a staple of the anti-Obama literature. Supposedly it showed that Obama was a proto-Communist, he hated white people, and he had no gratitude for a grandmother who rode the bus to work to support Obama and his self-righteous grandfather. In high school and at Occidental, Obama took pot and reefer breaks from thinking about such things; later he recalled: "Junkie. Pothead. That's where I was headed." At Occidental he hung out with alienated types whom he later spoofed as "the Marxist professors and structural feminists and punk-rock performance poets," although his classmates later remembered him as a "crossover guy," someone who moved easily between racial and ethnic communities, and the conspiracy theorists missed the tongue-in-cheek. Two of Obama's closest friends there, Mohammed Hasan Chandoo and Wahid Hamid, were Pakistanis; another, Vinai Thummalapally, was Indian; and Obama gave as much time to Salvadoran solidarity activism as to the Black Students Association (BSA). Louis Hook, a BSA leader, remembered Obama as someone who took part in the BSA without quite belonging to it. Unlike many black students at Occidental, Hook recalled, Obama did not need the reinforcement of African American culture; he had not grown up in it anyway. In Hook's perception, Obama was comfortable with African American culture and he was equally comfortable without it.[23]

But when Obama recounted this phase of his life, he did not portray himself as a multicultural type who identified with "multi-racial, not black." On the contrary, he insisted that even at Occidental, a college with 75 black students out of 1,600, and two black faculty, he was embarrassed by multiracial "individualists" and suburbanized blacks who did not self-identify as black.

"Joyce," a composite figure, represented both of the latter types. Joyce saw no reason why she should belong to the Black Students Association, since black was only one of her racial heritages. She told Obama that their white classmates treated her as a person; they were not the ones who told her that she had to choose her race. It was the black students who made everything racial, telling her that she had to choose. She was multiracial, not black; more importantly, she was *an individual* whose individual humanity transcended any racial marker.

Obama didn't buy it. The multicultural types like Joyce talked a good game about transcending binary oppositions and the like, but they had a pronounced tendency to avoid black people. Sometimes this was a conscious choice, Obama judged, and sometimes it wasn't. But in either case, the avoidance showed the gravitational pull of the dominant culture. Integration was about assimilating minorities into the dominant culture, not the other way around. Only white culture was racially neutral; only in white culture could one be nonracial. In white culture, one could be an individual, a right that whites of various ideologies claimed insistently, and which some extended to select individuals of other races. Obama recalled, "And we, the half-breeds and the college-degreed, take a survey of the situation and think to ourselves, 'Why should we get lumped in with the losers if we don't have to?'"[24]

Obama put it sarcastically to seal the point that he had never taken that option, despite understanding it terribly well, being tempted by it, and often accused of it. In his telling, he talked himself into becoming black before it really happened. Obama saw through the Joyce-types before he moved to Chicago and self-identified with the black community, and long before he married Michelle. After he became a national figure, it was not difficult for journalists to find classmates from Obama's past who remembered him as being much less black. Yes, Obama had dropped the boyish name "Barry" at Occidental, growing into his given name. Yes, he loved to tell the story of his father, who lifted himself from goat herder to government official. And yes, he occasionally made it to a Black Students Association meeting. But Obama, in their telling, was not the conflicted soul that he described. Everyone remembered him as an engaging and impressive character who was especially attractive to women. A few had felt that the early-college Obama was too smooth and sophisticated, already calculating his run for the White House. If he had really been so troubled as he claimed, why had they not seen it?

Obama's answer, which is plausible, is that he kept the hardest things pretty much to himself and cruised though life until he arrived at Columbia, where he acquired a new seriousness of purpose. He studied hard, adopted monkish habits, and started keeping a journal, which became a goldmine for his memoirs. Repressing his sense of humor, he bored acquaintances with moralistic lectures about world poverty. Reporters who tried to track down students that knew Obama at Columbia came up empty; nobody remembered him, which launched one of the conspiracy theories—that he made up the part about studying at Columbia. Ann Dunham, visiting Obama at Columbia, worried that he had taken a dour self-righteous turn; he replied that she was kidding herself about combating poverty. The World Bank and the other big development organizations made everything worse in the Third World.[25]

Obama tried to find a point of entrance into Harlem, but he didn't know how to go about it. If there was a community there to engage, he couldn't find it. New York City's colossal polarization along racial and class lines chastened him. From the in-between perch of a student, all that Obama could do was observe. The city was too much to assimilate, a mockery of his idealistic vision of making a difference. Obama realized that if he stayed in New York, he would eventually make a definite choice between its poor and not-poor sections, even if he didn't want to choose. It would happen when he started taking taxicabs at night instead of the subway, or when he began to pay for private school education for his children. Obama complained to friends that he didn't like being disillusioned so soon in life. They told him to get over it; New York was out of control. The city's monumental polarization was a natural phenomenon that could not be helped, like continental drift.

Self, Community, Faith

On November 24, 1982, Barack Obama Sr. got drunk at an old colonial bar in Nairobi, tried to drive home, and crashed into a gum tree, dying instantly. His American son was a first-semester senior at Columbia; the elder Obama had had previous drunken crashes; and thus he spent his last years walking on artificial legs. Obama wrote a letter of condolence to his father's family in Nairobi but did not attend the funeral.

After Obama graduated from Columbia he wrote scores of letters to civil rights organizations, black politicians, and community action groups, seeking a job, but received no replies. He took a job with Business International Corporation, a small firm that published newsletters on corporations operating overseas. In Obama's telling, he felt "like a spy behind enemy lines" at Business International, where he wore a suit and tie, with briefcase in hand, and had his own secretary, and where, in 1984, he was writing an article on interest-rate swaps when he received a fateful phone call from his half sister Auma, telling him that their brother David had been killed in a motorcycle accident.

There are problems with this story. David was not killed until 1987; Business International was not a high-powered outfit; its atmosphere was low-key and casual; and only the president had a secretary. Coworker Dan Armstrong, who liked Obama, later recalled that Business International was closer to a sweatshop than a high-end consultant firm and that nobody wore a suit or tie. Coworker Bill Millar, who didn't like Obama, recalled: "I found him arrogant and condescending. He just sort of rolled his eyes if you tried to explain something to him. I'll never forget it."[26]

Obama's line about "enemy lines" is a clue to the latter impression and to the exaggerated aspects of his account. Millar had a Wall Street background and a degree in finance, while Obama felt guilty about being a token black professional in corporate America. He apparently projected his guilt and derision at work, a feeling that colored his account of the place where he worked. In Obama's telling, the company's black secretaries treated him like their son, and a black security guard gruffly told him not to waste his time and moneymaking potential by becoming a community organizer. Obama was feeling guilty about climbing the corporate ladder when Auma called him out of the blue.

Probably he accidentally folded together conversations that occurred years apart. In Obama's telling, he had never before spoken to Auma, who was Kezia's second child. Obama was struck by Auma's soft voice and colonial accent, and she told him that David had been killed. Afterward, the conversation haunted him. Who were these strangers in a faraway land that still reached out to him? Who was he, who did not cry at the death of a brother? Recalling the incident years later, Obama wasn't sure if the call from Auma pushed him across a line, or if he would have taken up community organizing anyway. Perhaps he did receive his first call from Auma at this time, and perhaps it influenced his decision to become a community organizer, but a call about the death of his brother could only have occurred years later.

Obama had little idea of what organizers do when he set out to become one. At the New York Public Library on Forty-Second Street, reading an issue of *Community Jobs*, he came across an advertisement for a position with the Calamut Community Religious Conference, a coalition of Chicago South Side churches led by Jerry Kellman, an organizer in the Saul Alinsky tradition. Kellman needed a black organizer for a mostly black area containing numerous white clergy, a smattering of black churches, and academics from the University of Chicago.

Kellman taught his workers that people living in the poor black communities of South Side and West Side Chicago had little sense of community and that getting them to articulate their self-interests was very difficult because they refused to get their hopes up for things that would never happen. Life had taught them to keep disappointment to a minimum by not expecting very much. Community organizing, according to Kellman, was about building up communities and getting people to heighten their sense of possibility by working for things they needed—a local grocery store, a repaved street, a child care center, or the arrest of a drug dealer. In Chicago, aldermen and state representatives did not make the decisions that mattered; the key decisions were made by ward committee functionaries usually doubling as insurance agents, lawyers, funeral parlor directors, or the like. To get something done in Chicago, one had to operate at the ward level, helping disenfranchised people to identify and defend their interests.

Interviewing Obama, Kellman kept asking why he didn't go to graduate school or attach himself to a politician like Chicago's first black mayor, Harold Washington. Was he angry about something? Wasn't he too well adjusted to be an organizer? Repeatedly Obama replied that he was inspired by the civil rights movement and that he wanted to work at a grassroots level. Finally he added that he was also a writer looking for an identity, a community, and something to write about. To an Alinsky-style organizer, that was a much better answer. Obama was an outsider, having moved from one culture to another, largely without his parents. Kellman reasoned that an outsider either tried to join the mainstream or identified with other outsiders. He liked that Obama identified with outsiders.[27]

Except for his year of corporate existence and a brief public service job, Obama had been in school his entire life. He had never strongly identified with a neighborhood and had never lived in a place where race mattered so much. Moving to Hyde Park, he immersed himself in the South Side's neighborhoods, working mostly with middle-aged black female community activists, white clergy, and, less successfully, black ministers. Obama collected many mentors on his ascent to national prominence; Kellman was the first one.

Community organizing begins with interviews, canvassing people about their needs. The key is to find an issue that people care about, one that might catalyze them into action. One builds up power by mobilizing actions. Obama later recalled, "Issues, action, power, self-interest. I liked these concepts. They bespoke a certain hardheadedness, a worldly lack of sentiment; politics, not religion." But to build real power, community activists had to have an institutional base, an ongoing enterprise with a building and a network of social relationships. The unions were too weak and remote to play that role in Chicago; the only viable candidate was the church. So Obama operated out of churches for which the binary of "politics, not religion" did not apply. Or at least, it was part of his job to persuade them not to view community action in these terms. The church people for whom Obama worked had a community of faith and he did not. But they paid his salary to organize community actions. The tensions built into this arrangement worked on Obama from the beginning as he built up the Developing Communities Project, a coalition of religious communities. In the meantime he got a life-changing visit from Auma.[28]

Auma was a graduate student in linguistics at the University of Heidelberg. She was grateful for her education but ambivalent about Germany, explaining to Obama that although Germans tried not to be prejudiced against black Africans, beneath the surface they still regarded blacks as goblins, as in German fairy tales. Sometimes, feeling lonely in Germany, Auma reflected on what it must have been like for "the Old Man" to study in Hawaii and Cambridge, so far from home. Obama resonated with this name, "the Old Man," a blend of familiarity and elusive distance. He and Auma told each other their stories.

Obama revealed that in New York he had been in love with a white woman for almost a year. The relationship ended when he realized that if he stayed with his girlfriend, he would end up living in her world of wealth and family heritage. Her family was long-established; their country house was filled with pictures of dignitaries that the grandfather had known; to stay with his love interest, Obama would have to be the outsider who entered the establishment through romance. One evening he took her to a new play by a black playwright, where the dialogue was angry and funny, and the mostly black audience roared with delight. Obama's girlfriend unraveled, crying that she didn't understand why black people were angry all the time. She couldn't see how biting anger could be funny; she realized that she could never be black; she could only be herself.[29]

No one who knew Obama during his New York period, including his mother and sister, had any idea of this woman's existence. Three years later, during Obama's last year in Chicago, he had another romantic relationship with a white woman—an anthropology student at the University of Chicago—that cut him at breakup time, although this time the breakup was caused by his move to Harvard. The former story of romantic heartbreak, in Obama's telling, helped Auma and him get to the story of the father they shared.

Obama knew that his father had still been married to his first wife, Kezia, when he departed for the University of Hawaii in September 1959; that Obama Sr.'s first child was named Roy; that Kezia had been pregnant with Auma when Obama Sr. moved to Hawaii; and that Obama Sr. eventually had seven children, counting Obama. Kezia did not object to her husband taking a second wife, since Luo custom permitted plural marriages. When Obama was in college, Ann told him that his paternal grandfather Hussein wrote an infuriated letter to Stanley Dunham, protesting that he disapproved of the new marriage and that he did not want the Obama bloodline to be sullied by a white woman. Despite all that, Ann recounted, the marriage might have worked out, had Obama's father taken his doctorate at the New School, where he could have supported the three of them financially. But he went to Harvard, where he had no financial support besides tuition remittance, because Harvard was the best: "Barack was such a stubborn bastard, he had to go to Harvard. 'How can I refuse the best education?' he told me. That's all he could think about, proving that he was the best."[30]

Obama's father, upon returning to Kenya with the wealthy American teacher he had met in Cambridge, Ruth Nidesand, lived in Nairobi. Together they journeyed to a country village, Alego, to collect Roy and Auma, who were six and four years old at the time, living with their mother. Auma told Obama that she had never been near a white person; now this Ruth person was introduced as her new mother. The adjustment was harder for Roy, being older and having stronger memories of his mother. At first, Auma recounted, Obama Sr. did very well, working for Shell Oil Company. He was connected to top government people with whom he had gone to school, he had a big house, his American wife heightened his stature, and he openly maintained marital relations with Kezia, although he always traveled to Alego by himself. After he returned to Kenya he fathered two children with Ruth and two with Kezia.

Up to 1966, Auma told Obama, life was pretty comfortable in the Old Man's house. Ruth was a good mother and Obama Sr. was flourishing. But then things came apart. Ruth's attention shifted to her sons, Mark and David, after they were born. Obama Sr., probably aspiring to political office, took a job in the government of President Jomo Kenyatta just before the divisions between the Kikuyu and Luo tribes became toxic. Factional fighting intensified, Luos protested that Kikuyus got the best jobs, and Obama Sr. spoke up publicly, warning that the Kikuyus were exploiting their privileges and that tribalism was destroying the country. Obama Sr. seethed at taking orders from Kikuyu appointees lacking his academic credentials, and he believed that some government officials wanted to kill him for testifying in the trial against the accused killer of nationalist leader Tom Mboya. Besides being stubborn and proud, Obama Sr. had a tendency to be abrasive. Kenyatta told him to shut up, but the Old Man refused, which got him banished from government service. Auma apparently did not mention the ideological conflict between her father and Kenyatta over nationalizing the economy, which Kenyatta refused to do. In any case, she told Obama that after the Old Man's downfall no government ministry would touch him; he couldn't even leave Kenya, as the government revoked his passport. Finally a friend gave him a lowly job in the Water Department, a steep fall from the career that Obama Sr. had expected.[31]

According to Auma, the Old Man grew mean and bitter, drinking constantly. Ruth resented the change, raging back at him. Finally Ruth packed up her two children and left, shortly after Obama Sr., driving while drunk, had a serious car accident that killed the other driver. For almost a year the Old Man was hospitalized while Roy and Auma, aged fifteen and thirteen, fended for themselves at home; meanwhile he lost his job at the Water Department. When Obama Sr. got out of the hospital he told Roy and Auma that he was going to Hawaii to recuperate, and that he planned to bring Ann and Barack home with him. Auma recalled: "But you weren't with him when he returned, and Roy and I were left to deal with him by ourselves."[32]

Everything got worse after he returned. Obama Sr. had a bad temper and a load of shame at not being able to support his children. He fought furiously with Roy, until Roy stopped coming home, leaving Auma alone with her father. Sometimes he awoke Auma at night to rage that so many people had betrayed him, but only when he was drunk; when sober, he never admitted that anything was wrong. Auma told Obama that she never stopped being afraid of the Old Man and never really knew him. His drunken rages frightened her, he took no responsibility for the pain that he inflicted on his family and friends, and the rest of his life was equally chaotic: "His life was so scattered. People only knew scraps and pieces, even his children." It helped that Auma attended a boarding school during her high school years, supported by a scholarship: "I was glad not to have to live with him. I just left him to himself and never looked back."[33]

There was a slight upturn in the Old Man's last years, Auma noted. Kenyatta died in 1978, when Auma was a junior in high school, and Obama Sr. won a job with the Ministry of Finance. He started to make money again and acquired some influence. But he had already made a mess of his life, and he was bitter about it, believing that none of it was his fault. Auma recalled that her father insisted to the end that he had been a model father who had a right to tell her how to behave. She also told Obama that their father used to talk about Ann and Obama when he was down. He treasured Ann's letters, reading them to Auma repeatedly, and telling her that somebody out there truly loved him.

This stunning tale of waste and abuse shocked Obama: "I felt as if my world had been turned on its head; as if I had woken up to find a blue sun in the yellow sky, or heard animals speaking like men. All my life, I had carried a single image of my father, one that I had sometimes rebelled against but had never questioned, one that I had later tried to take as my own. The brilliant scholar, the generous friend, the upstanding leader—my father had been all those things." Somehow Obama had passed over the parts of this story that never fit his image of the great man. Throughout his youth Obama had watched flawed men like Stanley and Lolo cope with their failings and limitations. He could love them, but he did not emulate them. They were "white men and brown men whose fates didn't speak to my own." Obama wanted to be like Martin, Malcolm, Du Bois, and Nelson Mandela. He had projected his father onto these heroes, imagining Obama Sr. telling him: "You do not work hard enough, Barry. You must help in your people's struggle. Wake up, black man!"[34]

In one evening Auma had eviscerated Obama's imagined father. He recalled: "That image had suddenly vanished. Replaced by . . . what? A bitter drunk? An abusive husband? A defeated, lonely bureaucrat? To think that all my life I had been wrestling with nothing more than a ghost!" Obama wanted to laugh out loud, but not in front of Auma: "The king is overthrown, I thought. The emerald curtain is pulled aside. The rabble of my head is free to run riot; I can do what I damn well please." It was liberating, in a way, to realize that he could not do worse than his father. On the other hand, it was also unsettling. Who would warn him against all the dangers "that seem laid in a black man's soul?" The myth of his father had shielded him from despair, Obama reflected: "Now he was dead, truly. He could no longer tell me how to live."[35]

Obama had spent most of his life trying to live up to his father's expectations for him. Now he resolved to be a very different person than his father, making up for the Old Man's mistakes. His coworkers saw him change, doubling down on ethical determination. Barely an adult himself, Obama struggled with the gulf that separated him from urban youths defiantly asserting themselves into trouble. He tried to speak to them, while appreciating that many of them needed to shun him. He winced at the memory of having swaggered into high school classrooms either drunk or high, daring his teachers to say something. The world of his adolescent posing and spoofing had been far more forgiving than the one inhabited by these Chicago boys, he reflected: "These boys have no margin for error; if they carry guns, those guns will offer them no protection from that truth." Obama realized that he had been stupid and lucky, and that the youths he encountered would need to be luckier to make it.[36]

America dramatically escalated its so-called war on drugs during the period that Obama worked as a community organizer; thus he got a close-up view of its devastation. For a child of racial or class privilege, or a college student, a bit of drug use was usually no big deal. For a poor child of color, a bit of drug use became a ticket to a parallel social universe of imprisonment, branding as a criminal, and lifelong loss of one's civil rights not to be discriminated against. Imprisonment rates for African Americans skyrocketed by twenty-five times between 1983 and 2000, fueled by legislation providing federal funding to state and local law enforcement agencies for drug busts. In many states over 80 percent of the drug offenders sent to prison were, and are, African Americans—a species of social engineering driven by racial politics. Obama, increasingly frustrated by the limitations of community organizing, opted for law school, planning to specialize in civil rights law. Just before he moved to Harvard Law School, he settled the question of his religious identity by joining Trinity United Church of Christ.[37]

Obama's work as an organizer might have gone better had he joined a church sooner, but becoming a Christian was not a decision that he took lightly. His father was an atheist from a Muslim background. His maternal grandparents had dropped evangelical Protestantism in pretty much the same way that they dropped Kansas for Hawaii. Toot Dunham was a flinty empiricist who trusted only what she could see, and Stanley Dunham, the family dreamer, was too undisciplined and contrarian to get serious about anything, least of all ultimate reality. Ann Dunham had no fond memories of the Christians that she knew growing up in Kansas, Oklahoma, and Texas; she was caustic about fundamentalist beliefs; and she had no sense of having missed anything by shunning organized religion. She had a sense of awe at the mystery of life and an anthropologist's interest in comparative religion as a cultural phenomenon, but she took pride in her secularism.

In *The Audacity of Hope*, Obama stressed that having grown up with no religious faith, he was somewhat inoculated from wanting to be free from religion. In Chicago he felt his outsider status among the Christians with whom he sang and organized. He wanted to be a Christian before he became convinced that doing so with integrity would be possible for him. Could he join a religious community without suspending his critical reason? Could he claim a religious home without becoming religiously exclusive? Jeremiah Wright Jr., a brilliant preacher who turned Trinity United Church of Christ, Chicago, into a liberation theology megachurch, convinced Obama that he could convert to Christianity without sacrificing his intellectual or ethical integrity.[38]

Obama heard the gospel at Trinity Church and was claimed by it there. Wright's Afrocentric preaching featured the social justice message of the Hebrew prophets and Jesus, especially the theme that God is a liberating power taking the side of the oppressed in their struggle for freedom and dignity. In a sermon on "The Audacity of Hope," laced with jeremiads about white greed running a world in need, Wright preached about cruise ships throwing away more food in a day than Haitians in Port-au-Prince see in a year. But he also spoke of his grandmother singing, "There's a bright side somewhere . . . don't rest till you find it," and of God's abiding love. Obama, listening to this sermon, awaited the altar call that would mark his conversion to Christianity. He felt his three years in Chicago—all the people and stories in it—swirling together. Becoming a Christian connected him more profoundly to the people that he served and to the story of the Bible: "I imagined the stories of ordinary black people merging with the stories of David and Goliath, Moses and Pharaoh, the Christians in the lion's den, Ezekiel's field of dry bones. Those stories—of survival, and freedom, and hope—became our story, my story; the blood that had spilled was our blood, the tears our tears; until this black church, on this bright day, seemed once more a vessel carrying the story of a people into future generations and into a larger world."[39]

In Chicago, Obama found himself and something to write about, as he had hoped. He also found something more important, a larger world of faith in the preaching, singing, and practices of African American Christianity. His mother had been spiritually musical, he believed. She had a nature-mystical streak and an open delight in the profuse polymorphic strangeness of existence. Ann Dunham was happy to be a citizen of the world, drinking from many cultures and stitching together communities of friends wherever her sojourning spirit took her. She took pride in raising her children to be citizens of the world. Obama believed that had he not been attracted to the witness of the African American church, he probably would have followed his mother's example, straddling cultures and keeping a critical distance from belief systems. He said it explicitly in *The Audacity of Hope*, remarking that he probably would have opted for his mother's cosmopolitanism "had it not been for the particular attributes of the historically black church, attributes that helped me shed some of my skepticism and embrace the Christian faith."[40]

Obama treasured the black church's historic refusal to divorce personal salvation from social salvation, a refusal born of historic necessity. He embraced the black church's historic tendency to blur the line between sinners and the saved, a recognition that the sins of those who come to church are much like the sins of those who spurn the church. One comes to church precisely because one is of the world, not because one is separate from it: "In the day-to-day work of the men and women I met in church every day, in the ability to 'make a way out of no way' and maintain hope and dignity in the direst of circumstances, I could see the Word made manifest." On the day that he converted to Christianity at Trinity Church, he recalled, "I felt God's spirit beckoning me. I submitted myself to His will, and dedicated myself to discovering His truth."[41]

Then he went off to Harvard Law School to learn the currency of power. Obama flourished at law school for the same reasons that he later shot to the top of American politics: He was usually the smartest person in the room, and he was highly adept at winning people over. The fact that Obama got there after compiling an undistinguished college record enrages the anti-Obama bloggers and book writers. A leading figure in this genre, Jack Cashill, piles on by contending that Michelle Obama was even more unqualified to be at Harvard, although Cashill suspects that she felt some anxiety about it, unlike her future husband, who was too "self-deluding" to feel it. Cashill claims that Michelle Obama got through Harvard Law School because "the profs finessed her through." As for Barack Obama, he somehow excelled under renowned scholars Laurence Tribe, Mary Ann Glendon, Charles Ogletree, and Roberto Mangabeira Unger, to the point of making law review.[42]

By every account, acrimony prevailed at the law school during Obama's time there. Students were sharply divided along ideological lines; bitter fights over affirmative action, diversity, critical race theory, liberalism, feminism, and getting published in the *Harvard Law Review* were commonplace; law school professor Derrick Bell resigned dramatically from the faculty as a protest against the school's lack of faculty diversity. In this environment Obama aced his courses at the top of his class and honed his distinctively open-minded, consensus-seeking style of intellectual engagement.

Shortly after he took over as editor in chief of the *Harvard Law Review*, winning out over eighteen rival candidates, Obama mediated a controversy over affirmative action. On his watch the journal inaugurated a policy of affirmative action for the first round of its competitive process for choosing an editorial board. Making law review was a big deal, a springboard to professional success and prominence. Some racial minority students felt stigmatized by the new policy, protesting that it would diminish their achievements. At the same time, some female law students protested that they should have the same status as the minority students, benefiting from affirmative action. Writing in the *Harvard Law Record*, a student publication, Obama defended affirmative action for racial minorities, while explaining that women were not included because many women had made law review in recent years. Women, he reasoned, apparently did not need affirmative action to break down the gender barrier, although Obama was willing to put the question to a vote if the students wished. On the other hand, he urged minority students not to be defensive about receiving a boost from affirmative action. He observed that he had "undoubtedly benefited" from affirmative action during his academic career, but he had never felt stigmatized at the law school on that account. Obama's willingness to put it personally calmed the storm at Harvard. Later the same statement provided ammunition for people that could not accept him as an American president.[43]

The media splash announcing Obama's election as president of *Harvard Law Review*, besides leading to a contract for *Dreams from My Father*, contained a preview of it. There was a long feature article in the *Boston Globe* and a longer one in the *Los Angeles Times*. Both emphasized Obama's commitments to community organizing and social justice. Both described at length the education, achievements, and career arc of Barack Obama Sr. as an influence on his son, with quotes from the younger Obama. And both disposed of Ann Dunham in a sentence. The *Boston Globe* explained that Obama's mother was a white anthropologist from Kansas currently working as a development consultant in Indonesia; the *Los Angeles Times* was less expansive, noting that she was a white American anthropologist from Kansas. Ann Dunham, reading these articles, tried not to show that they wounded her. She told friends that she had been reduced to a sentence in the story of her son's life. *Dreams from My Father* evoked a similar reaction, but she refused to complain about it, telling friends that her son's identity "was something he had to work out."[44]

Obama worked for a law firm upon returning to Chicago, led a voter registration drive, married Michelle, got elected to the Illinois state senate representing South Side Chicago, and taught part time at the University of Chicago Law School. Ann Dunham felt a pang of regret that Michelle, despite having graduated from Princeton University and Harvard Law School, was somewhat provincial compared to Obama, although she otherwise liked Michelle. To Obama, Michelle's grounding in a working-class, conventional, churchgoing Methodist Chicago family was a strong point in her favor. At the University of Chicago, Obama taught civil rights law and thrived, but his heart was in politics. For six years, the best that he could do was the state senate, which exasperated Michelle. Obama had to bear Michelle's criticism that he was wasting his time driving back and forth to Springfield—accomplishing little, making too little money, and leaving her to raise their daughters, Sasha and Malia. He told Toot Dunham, "I love Michelle, but she's killing me with this constant criticism. She just seems so bitter, so angry all the time."[45]

Meanwhile, to succeed in his preferred vocation, he had to learn how to be charming at the level of retail politics. The early Obama sometimes came off as arrogant and withholding, plus overly restless and ambitious. He admitted to restless and ambitious, although he later claimed to have taken a break from both in 2002 and 2003. As for arrogance, he bristled at the charge, which discouraged his friends from pressing the point. Obama had to take a beating in 2000 before he did something about his air of superiority. Belatedly, taking instruction, he studied the extroverted charm of Bill Clinton and, much lower on the aptitude scale, that of Illinois governor Rod Blagojevich.

Obama's story was only moderately helpful to his state senate campaigns, and it did not work at all the first time that he aimed higher. In 2000 he challenged incumbent Bobby Rush, a former Black Panther, for his seat representing Illinois's First U.S. Congressional District. More than 70 percent of Rush's constituents were African American. From the beginning to the end of Obama's challenge, they told him that they did not like his presumptuous refusal to wait his turn. Neither did they appreciate his smooth-talking "turn the page" rhetoric, which smacked of "smarter than him," nor his habit of reciting his Columbia and Harvard resume, which smacked of "smarter than you," nor his frequent reminder that he could have made more money elsewhere, which smacked of self-congratulation. Repeatedly Obama was called dull, effete, arrogant, condescending, conceited, professorial, and, worst of all, not black enough. Rush chided that Obama's claim to the legacy of the civil rights movement was based on having read a few books about it. Even Michelle told him that he had "zero street cred" and no business running against Rush. The tally in Rush versus Obama was 61 percent to 30 percent. Obama took it hard, having little experience with defeat. Michelle Obama, sick of raising two children by herself, implored her husband to stop squandering his money-earning potential. To hold his family together, Obama had to promise that he would take only one more shot at reaching higher in the political realm.[46]

Very fortunately for him, a golden opportunity arose in 2004, a wide-open race for the U.S. Senate. It was not until Obama ran for the Senate that he and his political handlers discovered two things about him that set him apart from other politicians: He was electric on television, and he had an outsized knack for making white people feel good about themselves by winning their support. The end of his obscurity came quickly, after six years of seemingly dead-end toil in state politics. In the final three weeks of the Illinois Democratic primary, buoyed by television ads, Obama rose from 16 percent to 53 percent of the vote, and he was launched. John Kerry, recognizing Obama's star qualities, tapped him for a keynote at the Democratic National Convention. Obama, using a teleprompter for the first time, gave his spiel about blue-state people who worshipped an awesome God, red-state people who didn't like federal agents poking through their libraries, blue-state folks who coached Little League, and red-state folks who happened to be gay. America is not divided between blue and red states, he declared, nor is it divided among racial groups. America is one nation and people, the United States of America.

In the convention hall, Illinois politicos who knew Obama and had heard this song before judged that he did pretty well. Others at the convention gave him a rousing ovation. On television, Obama exploded off the screen. *Chicago Tribune* columnist Clarence Page wrote the following week, "A superstar is born. It is difficult for many of us to contain our enthusiasm for Barack Obama, yet we must try. We owe that to him. We should not reward his blockbuster performance last week at the Democratic National Convention by loading his shoulders with the fate of the nation. Not yet, anyway. That can wait, perhaps until, say, his 2012 Presidential campaign?"[47]

That prescient plea was spectacularly not to be.

Notes

1. See Barack Obama, *Dreams from My Father: A Story of Race and Inheritance* (1995; revised edition, New York: Three Rivers Press, 2004); David Remnick, *The Bridge: The Life and Rise of Barack Obama* (New York: Vintage Books, 2011); David Mendell, *Obama: From Promise to Power* (New York: Amistad, 2007); Janny Scott, *A Singular Woman: The Untold Story of Barack Obama's Mother* (New York: Riverhead Books, 2011).

2. Christopher Andersen, *Barack and Michelle: Portrait of an American Marriage* (New York: Morrow, 2009), 253–259; see Jerome R. Corsi, *The Obama Nation: Left-*

ist Politics and the Cult of Personality (New York: Threshold Editions, 2008); Aaron Klein, *The Manchurian President: Barack Obama's Ties to Communists, Socialists, and Other Anti-American Extremists* (Washington, DC: WND Books, 2010); Jack Cashill, *Deconstructing Obama: The Life, Loves, and Letters of the First Postmodern President* (New York: Threshold Editions, Simon & Schuster, 2011); William Ayers, *To Teach: The Journey of a Teacher* (New York: Teachers College Press, 1993); Ayers, *A Kind and Just Parent* (Boston: Beacon Press, 1997); Ayers, *Fugitive Days: A Memoir* (Boston: Beacon Press, 2001).

3. Scott, *A Singular Woman*, 84–94.

4. Adam Schwarz, *A Nation in Waiting: Indonesia in the 1990s* (San Francisco: Westview Press, 1994), 20–22; Adrian Vickers, *A History of Modern Indonesia* (Cambridge: Cambridge University Press, 2005), 158; Scott, *A Singular Woman*, 102–112, Vickers quote 108.

5. Obama, *Dreams from My Father*, quote 47.

6. Obama, *Dreams from My Father*, 50.

7. Obama, *Dreams from My Father*, 50.

8. Obama, *Dreams from My Father*, xii; Barack Obama, *The Audacity of Hope: Thoughts on Reclaiming the American Dream* (New York: Three Rivers Press, 2006), dedication page.

9. Scott, *A Singular Woman*, 353.

10. Obama, *Dreams from My Father*, 50–51.

11. Remnick, *The Bridge*, "a certain," "she wasn't," "we were," and "probably," 82; Richard Wolffe, *Renegade: The Making of a President* (New York: Three Rivers Press, 2010), "the idea," 29–30.

12. Obama, *Dreams from My Father*, 62–71, quote 64.

13. Obama, *Dreams from My Father*, 63.

14. Kristen Scharnberg and Kim Barker, "The Not-So-Simple Story of Barack Obama's Youth," *Chicago Tribune* (March 25, 2007); Maurice Possley, "An Old Friend's Troublesome Return," *Chicago Tribune* (March 25, 2007).

15. Obama, *Dreams from My Father*, quote 81; see Remnick, *The Bridge*, 90–92; Andersen, *Barack and Michelle*, 68.

16. See *Our Friend Barry: Classmates' Recollections of Barack Obama and Punahou School*, ed. Constance Ramos (Lulu, 2008), www.lulu.com; Scharnberg and Barker, "The Not-So-Simple Story."

17. Obama, *Dreams from My Father*, 82.

18. Obama, *Dreams from My Father*, 85.

19. Obama, *Dreams from My Father*, 86; see Frantz Fanon, *Black Skin, White Masks* (New York: Grove, 1967).

20. Obama, *Dreams from My Father*, quote 86.

21. See Frank Marshall Davis, *Livin' the Blues: Memoirs of a Black Journalist and Poet*, ed. John Edgar Tidwell (Madison: University of Wisconsin Press, 1992); Gerald Horne, "Rethinking the History and Future of the Communist Party" (March 28, 2007), www.politicalaffairs.net; Cliff Kincaid, "Obama's Communist Mentor," Accuracy in Media (February 18, 2008), www.aim.org; Cashill, *Deconstructing Obama*, 269–285. Cashill and his fellow bloggers at *WorldNetDaily* have pushed the father-

Davis story, though in *Deconstructing Obama*, Cashill gives priority to his theory that Obama published one of Davis's poems as his own—a poem purportedly suggesting that Obama knew that Davis was his father.

22. Obama, *Dreams from My Father*, 90–91.

23. Obama, *Dreams from My Father*, 100; Remnick, *The Bridge*, 101–102; James T. Kloppenberg, *Reading Obama: Dreams, Hope, and the American Political Tradition* (Princeton: Princeton University Press, 2011), 19.

24. Obama, *Dreams from My Father*, 100.

25. Janny Scott, "Obama's Account of New York Years Often Differs from What Others Say," *New York Times* (October 30, 2007).

26. Obama, *Dreams from My Father*, 136–138; Scott, "Obama's Account of New York Years"; Andersen, *Barack and Michelle*, quote 99.

27. See Remnick, *The Bridge*, 132–138; Obama, *Dreams from My Father*, 144–158; Andersen, *Barack and Michelle*, 103; Saul Alinsky, *John L. Lewis: An Unauthorized Biography* (New York: Putnam, 1949); Alinsky, *Rules for Radicals* (New York: Random House, 1971).

28. Obama, *Dreams from My Father*, quote 155.

29. Obama, *Dreams from My Father*, 210–212.

30. Obama, *Dreams from My Father*, 126.

31. Obama, *Dreams from My Father*, 214–215; see Barack H. Obama, "Problems Facing Our Socialism," *East Africa Journal* (July 1965), www.politico.com/static; Jomo Kenyatta, *Suffering without Bitterness* (Nairobi: East African Publishing, 1968).

32. Obama, *Dreams from My Father*, 216.

33. Obama, *Dreams from My Father*, 212, 217.

34. Obama, *Dreams from My Father*, 220.

35. Obama, *Dreams from My Father*, 220–221.

36. Obama, *Dreams from My Father*, 270.

37. See Michelle Alexander, *The New Jim Crow: Mass Incarceration in the Age of Colorblindness* (New York: New Press, 2010); Alexander, "Think Outside the Bars," *Yes* (Summer 2011), 18–22.

38. Obama, *The Audacity of Hope*, 202–206.

39. Obama, *Dreams from My Father*, 294.

40. Obama, *The Audacity of Hope*, 206.

41. Obama, *The Audacity of Hope*, 207–208.

42. Cashill, *Deconstructing Obama*, 172–173.

43. Kloppenberg, *Reading Obama*, 48–49.

44. Scott, *A Singular Woman*, 294–296; Andersen, *Barack and Michelle*, quote 262.

45. Remnick, *The Bridge*, 259–306; Scott, *A Singular Woman*, 296–297; Andersen, *Barack and Michelle*, quote 8.

46. See Mendell, *Obama: From Promise to Power*, 141–143; Remnick, *The Bridge*, 307–333; Ted Kleine, "Is Bobby Rush in Trouble?" *Chicago Reader* (March 17, 2000); Andersen, *Barack and Michelle*, 4–5.

47. Clarence Page, "Obama's Drama and Our Dreams," *Chicago Tribune* (August 1, 2004).

3

To the White House

W HEN OBAMA RAN FOR PRESIDENT IN 2008, the echoes of Robert Kennedy in 1968 were strong. No candidate had stirred such an intense reaction on the campaign trail since Kennedy, who might have won the White House had he not been assassinated. Like Obama, Kennedy ran against a controversial war and tapped the repressed hope and idealism of millions in a presidential campaign that he had not expected to wage.[1]

But Bobby Kennedy was already a totem of national memory and feeling when he ran for president. Most Americans remembered him as a former U.S. attorney general. Many regarded him as the successor to the tragically interrupted Kennedy presidency. Some hoped that he stood for something even better. Every American knew him as the brother of a martyred president.

In other respects, the Obama phenomenon was an echo of the political boon for Colin Powell that peaked in 1995. Powell might have won the presidency in 1996 had his wife Alma not declared that he would have to campaign as a divorcé; Alma Powell feared the part of white America that would not stand for a black president. Powell's memoir, *My American Journey*, sold nearly three million copies while he contemplated a run for the presidency. Many Americans got used to imagining a black president during the period that Powell decided whether to run.[2]

But Colin Powell, like Kennedy, had an ample public grooming before he seemed presidential. Americans did not need to read his memoir to learn that he had been President Reagan's national security adviser and served as chair of the Joint Chiefs of Staff during George H. W. Bush's presidency. By the end of George H. W. Bush's administration Powell was the most admired figure in the nation, a stature that became hard to remember after Powell disastrously helped George W. Bush make a bogus case for invading Iraq.

Obama rocketed into national politics with a swiftness and apparent ease that outstripped even these analogies. Two years into his brief career as a U.S. senator, he was candid on the matter of swiftness and only slightly defensive on the matter of ease. He wasn't just lucky, he insisted. He worked hard in 2004 to get elected to the Senate, and he had an appealing message. On the other hand, it was pointless to deny "my almost spooky good fortune."[3]

In 2004 he ran in a seven-way Democratic primary campaign that produced zero negative ads. In the final weeks of the primary campaign his chief opponent flamed out in a divorce scandal featuring allegations of verbal and physical abuse. A few weeks later the same thing happened to his Republican opponent, this time featuring stories about sex clubs in New Orleans, New York, and Paris. Then John Kerry handed Obama a convention keynote slot. Then the Illinois Republicans inexplicably selected Alan Keyes, an eccentric ideologue, to run against him. When Obama took office the following January, he was showered with hyperbolic media coverage treating him as the savior of politics while fellow politicians treated him as a political freak. A reporter asked Obama, on the day that he moved into his Senate office, to assess his place in history. Obama observed in reply that he had yet to cast a vote. For months afterward he played the story for laughs, which fed the demand for more of him.

Obama realized that his meteoric ascent was long on audacity and luck. For luck, one can only be grateful, plus ready to take advantage. Audacity is more slippery. Obama's audacity about himself and his career would be hard to exaggerate, a fact that sometimes registers as arrogance, even to close friends who otherwise praise him profusely. This partly explains his insistence that audacity is a central virtue in politics and a necessity for a politics of hope. In *The Audacity of Hope*, Obama offered many words on behalf of audacity and transformation; at the same time, his policy sections were cautious and moderate, and he played against his self-confident image by confessing that his years in the Illinois state senate nearly wiped out his self-confidence and political ambition.

For six years Obama labored in a Democratic minority in the Illinois state senate and accomplished little. In his seventh year the Democrats gained control and Obama pushed through over twenty bills, which felt better. But Obama was chastened at not feeling much better. The years of grinding, unrewarded labor had taken a toll on him, especially the commute between Chicago and Springfield. Obama was restless and dispirited, Michelle admonished him against continuing to waste his time, and being shellacked by Bobby Rush was humiliating. Then Osama bin Laden attacked the United

States, and Obama worried that his name might be hopelessly ruined for electoral politics. He later recalled:

> For the first time in my career, I began to experience the envy of seeing younger politicians succeed where I had failed, moving into higher offices, getting more things done. The pleasures of politics—the adrenaline of debate, the animal warmth of shaking hands and plunging into a crowd—began to pale against the meaner tasks of the job: the begging for money, the long drives home after the banquet had run two hours longer than scheduled, the bad food and stale air and clipped phone conversations with a wife who had stuck by me so far but was pretty fed up with raising our children alone and was beginning to question my priorities.

Even the policy making that drew him into politics began to feel small and inconsequential. Obama worried that major-league politics was out of reach for him; the dream was not going to happen.[4]

According to him, he accepted this state of affairs, which saved his career in politics. Obama says that after 9/11 he spent more time at home with his family, read some novels, exercised more regularly, and noticed that the earth rotated around the sun "without any particular exertions on my part." He caught his breath, accepting that life might not turn out as he had planned—performing on a national stage. Then the Illinois Senate race beckoned, and Obama, liberated from anxiety by low expectations, resolved to take one last fling at his dream. Audacity and a dose of humiliation worked together nicely for him. Careening around the state rather haphazardly, introducing himself to Democratic primary voters, Obama found his joy and energy returning.[5]

It struck him that most people have modest hopes and that a decent politics should be able to help people build a decent life. Here again, for Obama, audacity and modesty worked together. He appealed to the common sense of a broad, mostly goodwilled, largely nonideological middle sector that he found on the campaign trail. This sensible broad public cuts across the categories of race, region, religion, and class, he argued. Most Americans believe that anybody who is willing to work should be able to find a job that pays a living wage. They believe that every child should get a good education and that no one should be deprived of a college education merely for lacking financial resources. Most Americans think that no one should be threatened with bankruptcy merely on account of falling ill; they want to be safe from criminals and terrorists; they want to live in a clean environment; they want to be able to spend time with their families; and when they get old, they want to live with some dignity and respect.

This is a short list, and very modest, Obama stressed. Most Americans accept that how they do in life is mostly their responsibility, and that government cannot solve all their problems. But they also believe, rightly, that government should help in a few key areas to provide a measure of safety and fairness. Obama told his audiences that he stood for that much government and no more. Achieving a decent society was not out of reach, nor would it require any drastic change or heroic achievements in the political realm. It required only "a slight change in priorities." Campaigning on that theme, Obama rediscovered why he had gone into politics. Americans have a common fundamental decency, he argued. They only need a political culture that approximates their own basic decency.[6]

The Audacity of Hope was a product of Obama's 2004 U.S. Senate campaign and a catalyst of his 2008 presidential campaign. Usually one writes a campaign book to support a campaign that one has already decided to enter. *The Audacity of Hope* worked the other way around. Obama was already bored with the Senate when he started writing the book near the end of 2005. Being a rookie U.S. senator in a minority party was too much like his experience in the Illinois Senate; in some ways it was worse. In Illinois up to a hundred bills got passed per session; in the U.S. Senate the average was twenty. The pace was languid, the duties were grinding and routine, and committee hearings droned on mercilessly.

Feeding the media would have livened things up, but Obama entered the Senate vowing to keep his head down. He didn't want his colleagues or his Illinois supporters to tag him as a media hog. In the early going he turned down most out-of-state speaking invitations and the Sunday news programs, heading home on the weekends. He did not raise his national media profile until August 2005, when Hurricane Katrina slammed into Louisiana. Obama was in Ukraine, dealing with disarmament issues, when Katrina struck. Upon returning to the United States, he visited the Astrodome, where evacuees were sheltered. Obama realized that Katrina changed the national political picture. George W. Bush had won a second term only nine months earlier; now the Bush administration was reeling. Stepping into a national furor over Katrina, Obama declared on the Senate floor that the people of New Orleans were abandoned long before Bush took office. On the other hand, he told a gathering in Nebraska, Bush was well known for having declared that he opposed nation building. What Americans hadn't realized, until recently, was that Bush was talking about the United States.

Obama took heart that his office got few complaints from Illinois; his base wanted him to go national. He could feel the political clock speeding up. Something was happening; people swarmed to him wherever he went, urging him to run for president. Meanwhile, to his staff, Obama made no secret of being frustrated by the Senate. He greatly preferred writing his next book, which was about big issues, to voting on bills and attending committee hearings, where Senate windbags like Joe Biden blathered on and on. Obama's staffers judged that he even preferred fund-raising to committee work; he built up a campaign war chest called Hopefund while pouring himself into *The Audacity of Hope*.

In August 2006 Obama finished the manuscript and took a two-week trip to Kenya, Djibouti, Chad, and South Africa, which generated huge crowds and outsized media coverage. His favorable reception in Africa made a strong contrast to the global anti-Americanism set off by the Bush administration—a point that much of the media coverage featured, along with Obama's tender reunion with Sarah Onyango Obama (sometimes referred to as Sarah Ogwel), the third wife of Obama's paternal grandfather. Two weeks after Obama returned from a triumphal visit to Africa he attended Senator Tom Harkin's annual steak fry in Indianola, Iowa, where Harkin introduced him as a rock star surpassed only by Bono. Political operative and former Tom Daschle staffer Steve Hildebrand, stunned at the impassioned, clamorous reception that Obama got in Indianola, asked if this was a common reaction. Obama replied, "It's like this everywhere I go."[7]

Obama told the Iowa Democrats that Democrats have a different idea than Bush Republicans of what America is about. Republican partisans actually believe that the key to building a good society is to dismantle the government, he observed. Their fantasy is to break up the government piece by piece, handing tax cuts to the wealthy, privatizing Social Security, abolishing public schools, replacing police with private security guards, and turning public parks into privately owned playgrounds. Obama contended that this vision of an ownership society flagrantly favoring the rich lay behind nearly everything that Republicans do in Congress. Negatively, it is a vision resting on the denial that Americans owe any obligations to each other. Positively, in a weird sense of the term, it is the view that you're on your own in America.[8]

The Audacity of Hope, a book aimed at bigger game than the Iowa caucus, put it more gently, abounding with on-the-one-hand, on-the-other-hand formulations. Obama disclosed that he admired Franklin Roosevelt and John F. Kennedy above all twentieth-century presidents because they represented "transformative politics." Obama, however, advocated nothing comparable to the New Deal or even the Peace Corps. His policy sections were bland, cautious, and almost monotonously two-handed, establishing only that he aspired to the vague middle. The only risky position in his portfolio was his opposition to the Iraq war, which had been risky indeed when he committed himself to it on October 3, 2002, five months before the United States invaded Iraq. On that day, speaking to an anti-war crowd at Chicago's Federal Plaza, Obama declared that he did not oppose all wars; he opposed only dumb wars, like the one that Bush administration armchair warriors were cooking up for

Iraq: "That's what I'm opposed to. A dumb war. A rash war. A war based not on reason but on passion; not on principle but on politics."[9]

However, Obama was far from a national figure in 2002, and he admitted in *The Audacity of Hope* that afterward he had doubts about having stepped out so far. In the early going, buoyed by excited media coverage, Americans cheered as their country smashed into Iraq, and Obama worried that perhaps he overdid the "dumb" accusation. A bit later, his only proof that he could take a sizable political risk was a speech that he gave before he had much of a political career to put at risk.

Otherwise he held carefully to liberal-leaning middle ground. Obama supported universal health coverage but not a mandate for it. He was an advocate of breaking America's addiction to oil but declined to advocate a gas tax. He noted with seeming incredulity that America outspends the next thirty nations combined on defense, but a page later, he called for increased military spending. He admitted to being a liberal Democrat but lamented that too many liberal Democrats were stuck in "the old-time religion, defending every New Deal and Great Society program from Republican encroachment, achieving ratings of 100 percent from the liberal interest groups."[10]

For Obama, being African American was risk enough for a national political campaign. He was not radical about anything else; it was daring enough to think that he could be elected president if he handled the race issue with sufficient skill. Obama assured that he understood that some white Americans still harbor hostility toward blacks. But he refused to confer on such bigotry "a power it no longer possesses."[11]

This refusal was a key to the surging crowds that greeted Obama during the book tour period, when he generated intense excitement among vast audiences of white listeners and a more reserved response from African Americans. *Time* magazine writer Joe Klein asked Obama about his unusual appeal to white voters. Were white Americans desperate for validation from prominent blacks such as Oprah Winfrey, Tiger Woods, and him? Did his success show the importance of not stoking the racial guilt of whites? Before Klein could get the words out, Obama answered:

> There's a core decency to the American people that doesn't get enough attention. Figures like Oprah, Tiger, and Michael Jordan give people a shortcut to express their better instincts. You can be cynical about this. You can say, "It's easy to love Oprah. It's harder to embrace the idea of putting more resources for young black men—some of whom aren't so lovable." But I don't feel that way. I think it's healthy, a good instinct. I just don't want it to stop with Oprah. I'd rather say, "If you feel good about me, there's a whole lot of young men out there who could be me if given the chance."[12]

The Audacity of Hope put it more politically, recalling a former Illinois state senate colleague who was prone to charge racism when people voted the wrong way. A white liberal colleague remarked to Obama: "You know what the problem is with John? Whenever I hear him, he makes me feel more white." Obama, characteristically, started with a one-handed defense of his former black colleague, noting the difficulty of finding the exact tone that is angry enough but not too angry. Then he switched to the other hand: "Still, my white colleague's comment was instructive. Rightly or wrongly, white guilt has largely exhausted itself in America; even the most fair-minded of whites, those who would genuinely like to see racial inequality ended and poverty relieved, tend to push back against suggestions of racial victimization—or race-specific claims based on the history of race discrimination in this country."[13]

"Rightly or wrongly" was a telling caveat. Obama taught civil rights law at the University of Chicago. He is an expert on the entrenchment of white supremacy in American society—a structure of power based on privilege that presumes to define what is normal in society. At its extreme, white supremacy is about bigots wearing sheets and scrawling hate messages. More commonly it is a structure of power that reflects and favors white culture. If you live in this society without being constantly reminded of your race, and don't have to worry about representing your race, and can worry about racism without seeming self-interested, and don't have to worry about being targeted by police because of your race, you are a beneficiary of white supremacy. Its privileges are your daily bread and environment. If race were no longer a structure of power conferring privileges on some in American society, we would not need civil rights lawyers to fight discrimination cases against corporations, trade unions, and the government, and law schools could relegate civil rights law to a historical sideline.

Obama would never say that. However, he did say it in his way, pressing the point that the problem is entrenched in white attitudes and social structures. The organized political Right has obviously battered the cause of racial justice, Obama observed; however, the cause is losing for a larger and more important reason, the "simple self-interest" of most white Americans: "Most white Americans figure that they haven't engaged in discrimination themselves and have plenty of their own problems to worry about." No measure aimed at helping racial minorities will get more than short-term support from whites, he warned. Moreover, no measure bearing high costs for whites will be supported for any period. Since white guilt is largely exhausted in America anyway, those who care about racial justice need to talk about the common good, not racial justice.[14]

Obama supported affirmative action, but he preferred to talk about universal programs that help minorities, such as expanding access to health care and creating better schools. He understood why the civil rights establishment keeps racial discrimination on the front burner, preserving what he calls the "old" thinking about racial justice. But race is a more fluid category for Obama than it is for the civil rights establishment, and he suggested that the "old" thinking is a deterrent to moving forward as a multiracial society. It matters, Obama argued, that in the past generation the black middle class has grown fourfold and the black poverty rate has been cut in half. Hispanics have made comparable gains. Most blacks and Latino/as have already climbed into the middle class or are on their way, despite the barriers thrown in their way.[15]

Obama presented himself as an advocate of helping others get there. He stressed work and opportunity, not racism. As a state senator during the Clinton years he had been a Clinton liberal, not the kind that lived, as he put it, by "old habits." He supported welfare reform, fought for day-care provisions, and advocated work requirements for welfare recipients. In his telling he understood, better than many white liberals, that a majority of African Americans supported Clinton's overhaul of the welfare system.

Did that make Obama an advocate of postracial politics? To many journalists, voters, and political professionals, the answer was obviously "yes." Obama subsequently played down the race issue as much as possible in his presidential campaign, which gave rise to more claims that he represented the advent of postracial politics. But that was not what he said on the rare occasions that he addressed the issue. In *The Audacity of Hope*, Obama explicitly denied that he was a symbol or champion of postracialism.

To think clearly about race, he argued, Americans must view their nation on something like a split screen, holding in view the just, multiracial society that they want and the reality of an America that is not yet a just society. On the second screen, race remains a major marker of inequality and social privilege. As long as the two screens are so glaringly different, you cannot have a genuinely postracial politics, but America has moved considerably in that direction: "I have witnessed a profound shift in race relations in my lifetime. I have felt it as surely as one feels a change in the temperature. When I hear some in the black community deny those changes, I think it not only dishonors those who struggled on our behalf but also robs us of our agency to complete the work they began. But as much as I insist that things have gotten better, I am mindful of this truth as well: Better isn't good enough."[16]

That had perfect pitch for the massive audiences that turned out for Obama's book tour. *The Audacity of Hope* set off an overwhelming flood of public adulation. White audiences pleaded with Obama to run for president; blacks polled on the subject feared that he would be killed; some of Obama's black friends resented the pressure to run, protesting that white liberals underestimated the danger that Obama would be assassinated. Senate majority leader Harry Reid surprised Obama by telling him it was pointless to wait for a better moment. The presidency was reachable, and he was not cut out for the slow-paced Senate anyway. Obama, revising his timetable, sought assurance on one point: Was he being too audacious? Was it unseemly to run for the presidency so soon? His friends, Illinois senator Richard Durbin and former Senate majority leader Tom Daschle, told him to stop worrying about it. His lack of Senate experience was an asset, since he had fewer votes to defend than would be the case by 2012 or 2016. Obama's political handler David Axelrod told him in November 2006 that he would never be hotter and that he was the ideal antidote to George W. Bush.

In January 2007 Obama decided to go for it and started building his team. If he could win the Iowa caucus, he believed, he could win the nomination. If he lost Iowa, the whole thing was just a dream.

A Campaign Movement

Three moments stand out in Obama's drive for the White House, not counting the sublime moment of Grant Park on November 4, 2008, and putting off, in this chapter, the veritable beginning of his presidency six weeks before the election, when crashing and bailing commenced on a stunning scale and Obama learned what his presidency would be about. The first moment was January 3, 2008, when he won the Iowa caucus and soared to the top of the Democratic field. The second was the "race speech" of March 18 in Philadelphia, when Obama rescued his presidential candidacy and laid the groundwork for his separation from Jeremiah Wright Jr. The third was his triumphant speech at the Democratic convention in Denver, on the forty-fifth anniversary of the March on Washington.

Everything was at stake in Iowa. Obama realized that he had one chance to leap to the front of the field—at the beginning. If he won Iowa, a virtually all-white electorate, his numbers would pop everywhere, and African Americans would stop hedging against disappointment and move to his camp. To beat Hillary Clinton, Obama had to end her front-runner status before her superior organization built up momentum. Heading into caucus day, nobody knew where the race stood. The Obama team's final pre-caucus poll had him finishing third—before anyone had an inkling that 239,000 caucus-goers would show up, nearly twice as many as in 2004.

Obama's victory speech was carefully written, delivered with consummate polish despite not having been practiced, and singularly unleashed in feeling:

You know, they said this day would never come. They said our sights were set too high. They said this country was too divided, too disillusioned to ever come together around a common purpose. But on this January night, at this defining moment in history, you have done what the cynics said we couldn't do. . . . We are one nation. We are one people. And our time for change has come!

The opening riff was an echo of Martin Luther King Jr. The appeal to "our time" was an echo of Jesse Jackson's presidential campaigns. Both were fashioned into a story about America realizing itself. To claim a "defining moment in history" for the outcome of a mere caucus vote would have been ludicrous for any other candidate in any contest, evoking ridicule for grandiosity. On this night, Obama took the risk of appearing grandiose to those who did not share the exultant feeling that history had changed.

For Obama in Des Moines, to claim a defining moment in history was to avow his promise-and-fulfillment relation to the civil rights movement and to invite *all* others to take part in redeeming King's dream for America. Reaching this far, rhetorically, was for special occasions only; Obama wanted the votes of people who had limited tolerance for such talk. But this was a special night not to be wasted. Thus Obama called Americans to a freedom movement for all people in the cadences of the civil rights movement. The Obama campaign, like King's dream, was an extension of America's struggle for freedom from tyranny, British imperialism, Axis fascism, and the part of American history that reeked of bondage and exclusion:

> Hope is what led a band of colonists to rise up against an empire; what led the greatest of generations to free a continent and heal a nation; what led young women and men to sit at lunch counters and brave fire hoses and march through Selma and Montgomery for freedom's cause. Hope—hope is what led me here today.[17]

This idea that the bridge in Selma led to Obama's campaign was always there, although Obama played it down most of the time. It was no easy thing, even for someone of Obama's shrewdness and disciplined temperament, to find the balance that worked best. From the beginning of his campaign in February 2007 he wanted to give a big speech on the race issue, but he and his advisers kept judging that the moment for it had not arrived, and perhaps never would. The issue was there all the time anyway, and much of his following liked that he didn't say much about it. After the primary season began, and Obama's campaign took off, Shelby Steele tried to influence public perceptions by publishing a best-selling book, *A Bound Man: Why We Are Excited about Obama and Why He Can't Win*. Steele, a prominent black conservative writer, contended that Obama could not win because he tried to have it both ways on the race issue, he had no idea who he was, and winning was impossible anyway.[18]

In Steele's telling, Obama was caught in the historic double bind between African American bargainers and challengers. Bargainers bargained for acceptance in white America by not presuming that white Americans are racist, while challengers challenged white Americans to prove themselves innocent of racism. The leading bargainers in American society, by Steele's reckoning, were Bill Cosby, Colin Powell, and Oprah Winfrey; the leading challengers were Al Sharpton and Jesse Jackson. Had Steele written his book a few months later, undoubtedly Jeremiah Wright would have played a larger role. As it was, Steele's timing was perfect; Wright got less than a page without being named, but a huge controversy over Wright gave ballast to Steele's book as it hit the bookstores.

The bargainer/challenger debate, Steele argued, takes place between and within the races, setting guilt as impotence against innocence as power. America needs to be delivered from this sorry either/or, which is why Obama generated so much excitement. However, Steele claimed, Obama was too hopelessly bound by the social forces behind these categories to find a voice of his own. Obama was a racial cipher, not an actualized individual. He had a talent for inauthenticity that made him good at fashioning a racial persona, which was not the same thing as achieving selfhood. According to Steele, Obama constantly negotiated the either/or in a vain attempt to grant racial innocence to white Americans at the same time that he withheld it from them. Thus, like the fictional Tod Clifton in Ralph Ellison's *Invisible Man*, Obama had not achieved visibility as an individual. Since he lacked a real self, it was not clear that he had any real beliefs. This was why Obama could not win, Steele argued. If Obama bargained zealously, he could not win black majorities. If he opted for challenge, making himself black enough, he could not win a majority of any other group. Since winning was impossible anyway, Steele advised Obama to give up trying. Obama would do better to find out who he was, which would at least put him on the path to finding some integrity.

Steele was insightful in describing parts of his subject. He noted that challengers are granted distinct roles on special occasions to arbitrate who is racist and what racism looks like, and he rightly stressed that bargainers often have to hide their anger at whites for fear of wrecking the bargain. But his attack on Obama's personal character was absurd, a Swift Boat operation of spinning strength into weakness. *Dreams from My Father* was the most compelling memoir written by any American politician of the past century, and Obama was merely a political aspirant when he wrote it. The reflective, searching, and emotionally complex author of this work had no sense of self, even as he perceptively recounted his struggle for an identity? The disciplined, thoughtful candidate who conducted an unprecedented march to the White House was a cipher projecting the illusion of personhood? Steele was wrong about Obama and his political prospects, which caused Steele to misconstrue the upshot of his own thesis. Obama succeeded at the very thing that Steele claimed was most needed to move the country forward—transcending the morality play of challengers versus bargainers. Obama's success at this endeavor proved not that he was a fraud, as Steele claimed, but that Steele got Obama wrong, and his electoral prospects, and the futility of trying.

All of that, however, was very much at issue in the early going. Obama's campaign was mortally threatened on March 13, 2008, when ABC's *World News Tonight* broadcast select video clips of Jeremiah Wright's sermons. If the Wright controversy had exploded two months earlier, the Obama campaign would not have survived it. As it was, the primary season was more than two months old when clips of Wright's most dramatic riffs in the pulpit were broadcast over network television and instantly rocketed across cable television and the Internet. Remarkably, Obama's team was unprepared for this disaster, even though Obama had caused a stir in February 2007 by disinviting Wright from delivering an invocation at the news conference in Springfield announcing Obama's candidacy.

Just before Obama launched his campaign, he learned of a forthcoming article on Wright by Benjamin Wallace-Wells in *Rolling Stone* magazine. Wallace-Wells admired Wright, noting that Wright was very important to Obama and that Wright was amazingly radical. In fact, Wright was at least as close to Malcolm X as to Martin Luther King Jr., which made him the most radical mentor that any significant American political figure has ever had. Sealing his point, Wallace-Wells quoted some zingers from a Wright sermon:

> Racism is how this country was founded and how this country is still run! . . . We are deeply involved in the importing of drugs, the exporting of guns and the training of professional KILLERS. . . . We believe in white supremacy and black inferiority and believe it more than we believe in God. . . . We care nothing about human life if the ends justify the means! . . . And. And. *And!* GAWD! Has GOT! To be SICK! OF THIS SHIT![19]

Obama's aides David Axelrod, David Plouffe, and Robert Gibbs, reading these quotes, pictured a nightmare campaign launch in which Wright became the story and Obama became an asterisk. They pleaded with Obama to disinvite Wright from the program; if Wright went onstage, they warned, the campaign might explode before it began. Obama was reluctant to humiliate his friend and spiritual mentor. He admired Wright, was grateful to him, and realized that Wright's pride would be injured. If Obama had to hold a seminar on the role of jeremiads in black church preaching, he was up for doing so. His aides prevailed, however, and Michelle weighed in that she had never liked Wright; moreover, in her view, the quotes that Wallace-Wells unearthed were damaging and repugnant. Obama called Wright, telling him apologetically that his sermons were sometimes "kind of rough," not the sort of thing that one could readily explain at a news conference launching a presidential run: "*Rolling Stone* has got ahold of one of your sermons, and, you know, you can kind of go over the top at times." Wright agreed to join the Obamas privately and stay off the stage, although he made no secret to mutual friends of feeling snubbed.[20]

The Obama campaign knew enough to be panic stricken at the prospect of a disastrous campaign launch. A year passed, however, before anyone dug into the story. The Clinton team carried out opposition research on Wright but balked at using it. In the early going they expected to coast to victory; afterward they feared that they could not feed it to a reporter without being found out and accused of racism. The following March, after the Wright problem exploded in the media, Obama was furious with his staff for not having discovered the Wright tapes that nearly torpedoed Obama's candidacy. But Obama himself did not foresee the problem because he had never heard Wright speak in full-jeremiad mode. Wright was an every-week preacher of enormous accomplishment and spiritual conviction. Trinity Church had sold videos of Wright's sermons for years from its gift shop. Even an ardent opposition researcher could have listened to hundreds of hours of Wright's sermons without hearing anything like the snippets that instantly became notorious in March 2008, rocking Obama's campaign. ABC journalist Brian Ross, asked by the producers of ABC's *Good Morning America* to look into Wright, watched sermons for days before striking a gusher—Wright's sermon of September 16, 2001, the Sunday following 9/11.

On that Sunday Wright delivered a jeremiad on anti-imperial blowback. Americans have far more experience with terrorism than that of being victimized by it, Wright admonished. Americans have dished out a great deal of terrorism of their own: "We bombed Hiroshima. We bombed Nagasaki. And we nuked far more than the thousands in New York and the Pentagon—and we never batted an eye!" America supported state terrorism against Palestinians and black South Africans, Wright continued, "and now we are indignant because the stuff we have done overseas is now brought right back into our own front yards." The very things that Americans thought nothing of doing to others were now blowing back. Reprising Malcolm X's famous utterance after President John F. Kennedy was assassinated, Wright exclaimed: "America's chickens! Are coming home! To roost!"

Another clip showed Wright calling out, "The government gives them the drugs, builds bigger prisons, passes a three-strike law and then wants us to sing, 'God Bless America.' No, no, no! God damn America, that's in the Bible for killing innocent people! God damn America for treating our citizens as less than human!" The latter statement reprised William James's condemnation of American imperialism in the Philippines. Wright's method of reprising famous sayings, especially from the Bible, might have gotten more play had the ABC report not included a clip of Wright endorsing the urban legend that the U.S. government invented the HIV virus to destroy people of color. By the following day Wright was famous, as cable outlets played the clips repeatedly and Fox News played them constantly.[21]

Obama was shocked by the clips, grasping immediately that they mortally threatened his candidacy. He had heard Wright rail on occasion, but never like this, and in truth, he had rarely attended services at Trinity after his daughter Malia was born in 1998. But he could not say that after playing up, for years, his near-family connection to Wright and his membership at Trinity Church. Obama had already begun to apologize for Wright before the issue exploded, telling a Jewish group that Wright was like an uncle that the family still treasured despite his penchant for occasionally saying things that embarrassed the family. The ABC report, however, was potentially lethal, not merely embarrassing. Obama declared that he "vehemently" disputed and "strongly condemned" the "inflammatory and appalling remarks" that Wright had apparently uttered from the pulpit. His campaign announced that Wright had been dropped from its African American Religious Leadership Committee. Four days later, Obama amplified his "eccentric uncle" tack in a stirring address at the National Constitution Center in Philadelphia.[22]

Everything was at stake in Philadelphia, where Obama pointedly noted that the American experiment in democracy was launched across the street by a group of farmers, scholars, and statesmen who insisted on being free. The founders produced a remarkable document that founded a nation, he observed, but it was stained "by this nation's original sin of slavery." Words on a parchment proved not to be enough to deliver African Americans from slavery or a subsequent century of segregation, even though the Constitution held the answer to America's terrible problem—the ideal of equal citizenship before the law.[23]

Obama appealed to two authorities—the American Constitutional order of liberty and justice, and his own experience. The ideal was in the Constitution, but it took a succession of freedom movements to narrow the gap between the ideal and America's reality, and there was still a gap. Obama declared, "I chose to run for the presidency at this moment in history because I believe that we cannot solve the challenges of our time unless we solve them together—unless we perfect our union by understanding that we may have different stories, but we hold common hopes." He believed in this struggle because he was an

American *and* because he had an unusual American story. Retelling his story, Obama stressed that his family included people "of every race and every hue, scattered across three continents." For as long as he lived, "I will never forget that in no other country on Earth is my story even possible."[24]

His story would not have been possible for anyone of Reverend Wright's generation, Obama suggested, which helped to explain Wright's fixation with the sins of white America. Repeating his condemnation of Wright's "incendiary language," which denigrated "both the greatness and the goodness of our nation" and which threatened to widen the racial divide in America, Obama addressed the questions of the moment: Yes, he had realized that Wright was sometimes a "fierce critic of American domestic and foreign policy." Yes, he had heard Wright make statements of this sort in church. No, he had never agreed with many of Wright's political views; he had "absolutely" disagreed on many points; and he had never thought that anyone had to agree with one's pastor about politics. Wright was wrong, and something worse, Obama remarked, his pastor was divisive, "at a time when we need unity." But disowning Wright was out of the question; it was on a par with disowning the black community or Obama's beloved white grandmother, "a woman who helped raise me, a woman who sacrificed again and again for me, a woman who loves me as much as she loves anything in this world, but a woman who once confessed her fear of black men who passed by her on the street, and who on more than one occasion has uttered racial or ethnic stereotypes that made me cringe. These people are part of me. And they are a part of America, this country that I love."

Obama took a brief pass at conveying to white Americans that black Americans have favorite places for conveying their resentment, notably barbershops and churches. The fact that so many white Americans were shocked to learn that Wright said angry things from the pulpit confirmed that Sunday morning remains the most segregated part of the week in American society. This anger is many-sided and not always constructive, Obama allowed, "but the anger is real; it is powerful; and to simply wish it away, to condemn it without understanding its roots, only serves to widen the chasm of misunderstanding that exists between the races."[25]

Moreover, anger in the white community is similarly intense and problematic, Obama acknowledged. Most working-class and middle-class white Americans have little or no tolerance for any talk about white supremacy. They deny that being white gives them any privileges in society, and they resent having to deny it. They also resent any insinuation that their fear about crime smacks of racism. White Americans see their jobs being shipped overseas and their pensions dumped after decades of labor, they hear of minorities getting preferential treatment through affirmative action, and they feel pushed aside by immigrants for jobs they might have gotten. All of that, Obama explained, makes white Americans ripe for the politics of the Republican Right: "Like the anger within the black community, these resentments aren't always expressed in polite company. But they have helped shape the political landscape for at least a generation. Anger over welfare and affirmative action helped forge the Reagan Coalition."[26]

Obama understood the resentments of angry blacks and whites; he respected the humanity of angry souls on both sides, plus the humanity of racial groups left out of this conversation; and he opposed the angry politics of reaction: "This is where we are right now. It's a racial stalemate we've been stuck in for years." Contrary to what was often said about him, he did not believe that America's racial division could be healed by his success. But he did believe that America was much less racist than it used to be, even if Wright did not believe it: "The profound mistake of Reverend Wright's sermons is not that he spoke about racism in our society. It's that he spoke as if our society was static; as if no progress has been made." Obama asked Americans to consider the wonder of his campaign, which rested on a coalition "of white and black, Latino and Asian, rich and poor, and young and old." America is bound to its tragic past, Obama allowed, but its true genius is its immense capacity to change, a capacity that Wright grievously underestimated.[27]

Having shown his sympathy for the resentments of white voters, and his willingness to criticize Wright, Obama asked white Americans to recognize that the grievances of black Americans are based on terribly real things belonging not only to the past. Recognition, in this case, called for specific deeds, not merely words of aspiration or self-defense. It called for investments in schools and communities, enforcing the civil rights laws, demanding fair treatment in the criminal justice system, and ensuring equal opportunity for all Americans. America rises or falls together, Obama urged. What really mattered in the election of 2008 was whether it would be about the distractions that divided Americans or the common interests that really matter. Every form of the politics of division was a distraction from the common good that American politics should be about. Obama exhorted, "Let us find that common stake we all have in one another, and let our politics reflect that spirit as well."

Obama knew he could not win an election that turned ugly. To succeed, he had to be the candidate of hope who did not scare away or otherwise alienate independent voters. He implored Americans not to fall for another round of bread-and-circus distractions. If the nominating process came down to Wright's eruptions, or to ridiculous speculation about Obama's secret agreement with Wright's opinions, or to allegations that a Clinton staffer played the race card, what mattered would be squandered. Nothing would change; wedge issues would drive this election, just like the others. Obama urged Americans, or more immediately, Democratic primary voters, to come together and say, "Not this time." This time the election had to be about crumbling schools that stole the future of America's children of all races, emergency rooms filled with people lacking health insurance, and the ravages of escalating inequality.

Obama ended with his currently favorite story, which he had told at Martin Luther King Jr.'s home church, Ebenezer Baptist in Atlanta, on MLK's birthday. Ashley Baia was a twenty-three-year-old white woman who worked for Obama's campaign in Florence, South Carolina, a mostly African American community. One day she took part in a roundtable discussion where campaign workers told their stories. Ashley recounted that when she was nine years old her mother got cancer, lost her job, and thus lost her health care. The family filed for bankruptcy, and Ashley, trying to help her mother, convinced her that her favorite meal was a mustard and relish sandwich—the cheapest way to eat. Ashley ate mustard and relish sandwiches for a year until her mother got better. Years later, telling this story, Ashley said that she joined the Obama campaign because she wanted to help other children who needed to help their parents.

Obama reflected that Ashley could have made a different choice. She could have blamed her family's poverty on blacks living high on welfare or Hispanics stealing precious jobs. Instead she joined the struggle for social justice. In any case, after Ashley finished her story, she asked the workers to explain why they had joined the Obama campaign. All gave their reasons, sometimes with a story; many cited a specific issue. Finally their attention turned to an elderly black man who had not spoken. Asked why he had joined the campaign, the man did not mention health care, the economy, education, the war, or even Barack Obama. He did not mention any issue. He said only, "I am here because of Ashley."

Obama repeated this tellingly powerful line—"I am here because of Ashley." This single moment of recognition between a young white woman and an old black man, he remarked, does not, by itself, provide health care or a job to anyone in need: "But it is where we start. It is where our union grows stronger."[28]

America was overdue for a political leader who dared to treat Americans as adults in talking about race. Obama presumed to speak for all sides, capitalizing on his capacity to understand and represent different perspectives. This capacity was the key to his appeal and his success, which showed in the outpouring of reaction to what was usually called "the race speech." Liberals and moderates overwhelmingly praised the speech as historic and a breakthrough; many compared it to King's "I Have a Dream" speech. A smattering of political conservatives lauded the speech in similar terms while rejecting Obama's politics. Mike Huckabee, a contender in the Republican presidential race, judged that Obama handled a difficult topic and situation "about as well as anybody could." John McCain, also running for president, commended Obama for an "excellent" speech that was "good for all of America to have heard." Republican columnist Peggy Noonan aptly noted that it was a speech "to think to, not clap to" and that it would be remembered "as the speech that saved a candidacy." Conservative social scientist Charles Murray, a controversial figure in research about race, called the speech "just plain flat out brilliant—rhetorically, but also in capturing a lot of nuance about race in America. It is so far above the standard we're used to from our polls."[29]

Very few Democrats criticized the speech, even as the Democratic primaries rolled on. Former mayor of New York Ed Koch was a notable exception, blasting Obama for making his white grandmother the moral equivalent of Wright's "hateful statements." Hillary Clinton edged as far as she dared in that direction, condemning Wright's remarks and criticizing Obama's judgment: "He would not have been my pastor. You don't choose your family, but you choose what church you want to attend. . . . Hate speech [is] unacceptable in any setting. . . . I just think you have to speak out against that."[30]

It mattered that Republican presidential candidates and Obama's chief Democratic rival felt obliged to treat this issue gingerly, especially as the speech was lavished with praise. However, the Right pundits with the biggest audiences—Rush Limbaugh, Glenn Beck, and Sean Hannity—blasted the speech and the reaction to it as ridiculous. In their telling, Obama's choice of pastor and lingering affection for Wright disqualified him for the presidency, and Obama abused his white grandmother to obscure the real issue. Neoconservative columnist Charles Krauthammer put it tartly, describing Obama's speech as "a brilliant fraud" that distracted attention from what it was supposed to be about, namely, Obama's reprehensible devotion to Wright. The race speech, Krauthammer declared, was a brilliant piece of sophistry, elegantly fashioned to mask Obama's own "scandalous dereliction" in supporting Wright's ministry.[31]

On the political left, especially the academic left, and in black church circles where Wright was revered, there were bruised feelings and outrage of another sort, although publication on this topic was usually eschewed. Houston A. Baker Jr., a scholar of African American literature, broke the publication taboo, protesting that Obama staged a flag-draped embarrassment reminiscent of the Parthenon scene in Robert Altman's movie *Nashville*: "A bizarre moment of mimicry, aping Martin Luther King Jr., while even further distancing himself from the real, economic, religious and political issues so courageously articulated by King from a Birmingham jail. In brief,

Obama's speech was a pandering disaster that threw, once again, his pastor under the bus." Cornel West, who shared the Left critique of Obama, yet also campaigned hard for his nomination and election, later told me, "It was a *very* delicate moment. That was a daily tightrope with perils on all sides."[32]

I walked that tightrope in speeches to academic, religious, and political gatherings and in interviews with reporters. For several weeks, friends of mine who prized Obama *and* Wright—West, James A. Forbes, James Cone, Obery M. Hendricks Jr., Melissa Harris-Perry, and Michael Eric Dyson—tried to prevent an outright break between them. But on April 28 Wright gave a cantankerous performance at the National Press Club that showed his lack of interest in helping Obama. Obama was devastated by Wright's tone of derision and contempt, which felt like a deliberate attempt to sabotage his candidacy. The next day, campaigning in Winston-Salem, North Carolina, Obama repudiated Wright's "divisive and destructive" remarks and denied that Wright accurately represented the black church. He was finished with Jeremiah Wright, whom, he said, he had apparently misjudged. For the next week the Obama team fretted that Wright's performance destroyed their shot at winning the Democratic nomination. Obama took solace in gallows humor, joking to aides that he could always fall back on making speeches for a living. On May 6, however, Obama won North Carolina by fourteen points, which put him on a straight path to the nomination. The superdelegates started to drift in his direction, and Obama pulled further ahead of Hillary Clinton, although Clinton made him fight for the nomination, which made him a stronger candidate.[33]

At the Democratic convention in Denver, very bitter grievances between the Obama and Clinton camps were held in check, and the Democrats made a strong case for ending eight years of Republican rule. Obama, rehearsing his convention speech, had a rare moment of emotional overflow. The last night of the convention was on August 28, 2008, the forty-fifth anniversary of the March on Washington. That day, rehearsing at a Denver hotel, Obama tried to say that forty-five years ago, Americans from every corner of the land were drawn by the promise of freedom to come to the Washington Mall "to hear a young preacher from Georgia speak of his dream." But Obama could not get through the words "forty-five years ago," which caught in his throat. He fought back tears. "I gotta take a minute," he told aides, calming himself with a stroll around the room. "This is really hitting me. I haven't really thought about this before really deeply. It just hit me. I guess this is a pretty big deal." His speechwriter, Jonathan Favreau, later reflected that he had seen Obama get this emotional only once before—in Iowa, when Obama spoke to a group of young volunteers who were new to political caucusing.[34]

That night Obama won his sizable convention gamble. Only Obama, in full audacity mode, would have staged the convention's final night at Invesco

Field, where, fortunately, it did not rain, Obama did not look egotistically inflated at his Greek temple, and he did not prove unable to hold the attention of a stadium audience. He gave a powerful, though list-oriented, speech watched by 40 million viewers that looked as impressive as it sounded. Obama worked a typical Obama theme, this time calling it "the American promise" of opportunity and responsibility for all. This time, however, he was tougher and more specific than in his stump speech. Stressing the struggles of working people, he called for tax cuts for the nonrich and higher taxes on corporations that ship jobs overseas. He made a strong case for strengthening the middle class, investing in renewable energy, universalizing health coverage, and repairing America's international image. He amplified Bill Clinton's skillful convention summary of the miserable economic situation and John Kerry's forceful convention summary of John McCain's retreat to Republican establishment orthodoxy. He stressed his differences with McCain and gave a clear picture of what an Obama presidency would be about.[35]

Except that Obama's candidacy represented something magnificent that his campaign, and then his convention, assiduously played down, and a global financial catastrophe soon turned the campaign into disaster management. To the end, Obama ran a decidedly postracial campaign, talking about racial justice as little as possible and requiring his workers not to discuss publicly the racial antagonism that they encountered while campaigning for him. Since most white Americans have a low threshold for anything smacking of racial grievance, Obama reasoned, better not go there in a political campaign. Better not evoke the civil rights movement in prime time at the convention; confine that material to the daytime speeches. The blogosphere lit up with charges that Obama was a proud type with overweening self-regard, which called up centuries of violence against "uppity" blacks. Obama forbade his campaign aides from mentioning the racial subtext, let alone complaining about it.

Then Wall Street crashed the economy. The case for ending the rule of the Republicans was awfully strong heading into September 2008; afterward it was unarguable. Building up to the Democratic convention, 70 percent of Americans said that the Bush administration had done a bad job. Approximately the same percentage said the same thing about the incumbent Republican administration's handling of the economy and the war in Iraq, two things that went together, given the staggering costs of the war.

In a normal election year, any one of these three issues would have been enough to dispatch the incumbent party, and the watershed elections of modern times were two-for-three affairs. 1932 was a referendum on a disastrous economy and a failed presidency, but no war. 1968 was about a disastrous war and a failed presidency, but the economy grew anyway. 1980 put Jimmy Carter's presidency and economic performance on trial, but it was mere piling-on to claim that Carter botched the Cold War and Iran. 2008 marked the first legitimate three-for-three election of modern times, and Democrats knew that they could not miss cleaning up, except, perhaps, at the top of the ticket.

The possibility that Democrats would lose the presidential race despite their enormous advantages scared many of them throughout the summer. I heard it constantly on the lecture trail. "Do you really think Obama can win?" anxious liberals asked me, especially academics. Often the question was not "Will he win?" it was "Do you really think it's even possible?" Some were convinced that the polling data were meaningless because the Bradley effect (named after former L.A. mayor Tom Bradley, who won fewer white votes than he polled) was worth up to fifteen points. Many braced themselves against disappointment, muttering quietly, "You know he's going to lose, don't you?"

The Republican field, the weakest in memory, had only one candidate, John McCain, who had any chance of winning the presidency, but the Republicans lucked into nominating him. If the Democrats had nominated one of their usual bland, white male, career politicians—think Walter Mondale, Al Gore, or John Kerry; or in 2008, Joe Biden or Christopher Dodd—they would have cruised to victory with no summer anxieties. Hillary Clinton would have led by a smaller but still sizable margin by August 2008.

Obama had a much steeper mountain to climb, even among Democrats. On the eve of the Democratic convention, 27 percent of Hillary Clinton's supporters reported that they were not willing to switch to Obama, and according to a mid-July New York Times/CBS News Poll, 30 percent of white Americans held a favorable view of Barack Obama and 24 percent viewed Michelle Obama favorably. These pitiful numbers were the yield, to that point, for the Obamas among white Americans after two years of overwhelmingly favorable news coverage, countless magazine cover stories, and dozens of primary and caucus campaigns that ended with a soaring victory speech.

The Democratic convention helped a great deal with both problems, as Hillary and Bill Clinton spoke up for Obama; Michelle Obama gave a luminous address; and the Democrats stressed that the election was about something more than Obama's background, his personality, his race, his politics, his oratory, his church, his newness, his inexperience, his family, his primary victories, his victory over the Clintons, and his rock star tour of Europe. It was about salvaging a decent society and playing a better role in the world.

Grant Park

The beginning of the Obama administration is inseparable from the crash of September/October 2008; thus, chapter 4 begins with the crash. But for a moment we peek ahead to November 4, 2008, in Grant Park, Chicago. It was sunny and cool in Chicago on election day. By nightfall, over 100,000 people were heading to Grant Park in a festive mood. People sang and danced in anticipation of victory; hip-hop blared from speakers across Michigan Avenue; reporters reached for analogies to the feeling and moment. Perhaps the best analogous moment was November 9, 1989—the night the Berlin Wall came down. After Obama's election was announced, the crowd of 140,000 joined in a boisterous recitation of the Pledge of Allegiance. Oprah Winfrey clutched a stranger, weeping joyfully. Jesse Jackson cried too, despite his mixed feelings about Obama.

Then Barack and Michelle Obama strode onto a blue stage adorned with American flags. Obama projected deep seriousness and gratitude. "I know you didn't do this just to win an election and I know you didn't do it for me," he declared. "You did it because you understand the enormity of the task that lies ahead. For even as we celebrate tonight, the challenges that tomorrow will bring are the greatest of our lifetime—two wars, a planet in peril, the worst financial crisis in a century. Even as we stand here tonight, we know there are brave Americans waking up in the deserts of Iraq and the mountains of Afghanistan to risk their lives for us. There are mothers and fathers who will lie awake after their children fall asleep and wonder how they'll make the mortgage, or pay their doctor's bills, or save enough for college. There is new energy to harness and new jobs to be created; new schools to build and threats to meet and alliances to repair."[36]

To Americans who did not vote for him, Obama declared that he heard their voices and needed their help. To America's enemies who wanted to destroy America, he promised, "We will defeat you." And to all who had wondered if America's beacon still burned brightly, "tonight we proved once more that the true strength of our nation comes not from the might of our arms or the scale of our wealth, but from the enduring power of our ideals: democracy, liberty, opportunity, and unyielding hope." In that mood he took on the greatest economic crisis since the 1930s before he took office.

Notes

1. Parts of this opening section adapt material from Gary Dorrien, "Hope or Hype?" *The Christian Century* (May 20, 2007).

2. See Colin L. Powell, *My American Journey* (New York: Ballantine, 1995).

3. Barack Obama, *The Audacity of Hope: Thoughts on Reclaiming the American Dream* (New York: Three Rivers Press, 2006), 18.

4. Obama, *The Audacity of Hope*, 3–4.

5. Obama, *The Audacity of Hope*, 4.

6. Obama, *The Audacity of Hope*, 7.

7. John Heilemann and Mark Halperin, *Game Change: Obama and the Clintons, McCain and Palin, and the Race of a Lifetime* (New York: Harper Perennial, 2010), 58; Richard Wolffe, *Renegade: The Making of a President* (New York: Three Rivers Press, 2010), 47.

8. Text reprinted in David Remnick, *The Bridge: The Life and Rise of Barack Obama* (New York: Vintage Books, 2011), 447–448.

9. See Bill Glauber, "War Protestors Gentler, But Passion Still Burns," *Chicago Tribune* (October 3, 2002); cited in Remnick, *The Bridge*, 346–347.

10. Obama, *The Audacity of Hope*, 38.

11. Obama, *The Audacity of Hope*, 240.

12. Joe Klein, "The Fresh Face," *Time* (October 15, 2006).

13. Obama, *The Audacity of Hope*, 247.

14. Obama, *The Audacity of Hope*, 247.

15. Obama, *The Audacity of Hope*, 248.

16. Obama, *The Audacity of Hope*, 233.

17. Barack Obama, Iowa victory speech, January 3, 2008, youtube.com, accessed March 8, 2011; see Mary Frances Berry and Josh Gottheimer, *Power in Words: The Stories behind Barack Obama's Speeches, From the State House to the White House* (Boston: Beacon Press, 2010), 134; Heilemann and Halperin, *Game Change*, 1–8.

18. Shelby Steele, *A Bound Man: Why We Are Excited about Obama and Why He Can't Win* (New York: Free Press, 2008). This section on Steele adapts material from Gary Dorrien, "Visible Man Rising," *Religion & Ethics Newsweekly* (September 2, 2008).

19. Ben Wallace-Wells, "Destiny's Child," *Rolling Stone* (February 22, 2007); David Plouffe, *The Audacity to Win* (New York: Penguin, 2010), 40.

20. Plouffe, *The Audacity to Win*, 40; Remnick, *The Bridge*, 468–470; Heilemann and Halperin, *Game Change*, 235.

21. Brian Ross and Rehab El-Buri, "Obama's Pastor: God Damn America, U.S. to Blame for 9/11," ABCNews.com, March 13, 2008.

22. Barack Obama, "On My Faith and My Church," *Huffington Post*, March 15, 2008, huffingtonpost.com; Heilemann and Halperin, *Game Change*, 235.

23. "Text of Obama's Speech: A More Perfect Union," *Wall Street Journal* (March 18, 2008), http://blogs.wsj.com/washwire; for another text, see Obama, "A More Perfect Union," *Los Angeles Times* (March 19, 2008), www.latimes.com/news/nation-world.

24. "Text of Obama's Speech," 2.

25. "Text of Obama's Speech," 5.

26. "Text of Obama's Speech," 5.

27. "Text of Obama's Speech," 5–6.

28. "Text of Obama's Speech," 8.

29. Jake Tapper, "Huckabee Defends Obama . . . and the Rev. Wright," ABC News, March 19, 2008, http://blogs.abcnews.com/politicalpunch; John McCain, "Interview with Chris Matthews," *Hardball College Tour at Villanova University*, April 15, 2008, http://hardblogger.msnbc.msn.com; Peggy Noonan, "A Thinking Man's Speech,"

Wall Street Journal (March 21, 2008); Charles Murray, "Have I Missed the Competition?" *National Review Online* (March 18, 2008), http://corner.nationalreview.com.

30. Ed Koch, "Why Obama's Speech Was Unconvincing," March 25, 2008, www.realclearpolitics.com; Mike Wereschagin et al., "Clinton: 'Wright Would Not Have Been My Pastor,'" *Pittsburgh Tribune-Review* (March 25, 2008).

31. Charles Krauthammer, "The Speech: A Brilliant Fraud," *Washington Post* (March 20, 2008), www.washingtonpost.com; see Howard Kurtz, "Media Notes: A Complex Speech, Boiled Down to Simple Politics," *Washington Post* (March 20, 2008); Berry and Gottheimer, *Power in Words*, 180–181.

32. Houston A. Baker Jr., "What Should Obama Do about Rev. Jeremiah Wright?" Salon, April 29, 2008, www.salon.com/opinion ; T. Denean Sharpley-Whiting, ed. *The Speech: Race and Barack Obama's "A More Perfect Union"* (New York: Bloomsbury, 2009).

33. See Remnick, *The Bridge*, 531–533.

34. Remnick, *The Bridge*, 538.

35. This section adapts material from Gary Dorrien, "Yes We Can . . . Change the Subject?" Public Broadcasting System, *Religion and Ethics Newsweekly: One Nation*, August 26, 2008.

36. "Full Transcript: Senator Barack Obama's Victory Speech," ABC News, November 4, 2008, http://abcnews.go.com/Politics.

4

Saving Capitalism from Itself

B Y NECESSITY, THE OBAMA PRESIDENCY BEGAN EARLY, nearly two months before Obama was elected and four months before he was inaugurated. This was unfortunate for Obama and the nation. Had Obama not helped to push through the Bush administration's obsequious bailouts of September/October 2008, he might have been less obsequious when his turn came. Had the financial system crashed in December instead of September, Obama might have demanded tougher treatment of the firms that caused the crash, which might have led to stronger policies of his own—assuming his election. As it was, Obama was co-opted before he began, and he stayed on that path after he took power, even as he pushed through the biggest, most ambitious, and most far-reaching domestic spending bill in forty years.

Comparisons to Franklin D. Roosevelt in 1933 are telling and inevitable. Roosevelt and Obama both stepped on the Keynesian gas, battled Republicans, and refused to nationalize the banks, although in Roosevelt's case, the banks in question were small. In Obama's case, the banks were colossal and got more so after getting their bailouts, which made them far too powerful—enough to prevent real reform. The crucial political difference between 1933 and 2009, however, was that America was deeply into a depression when Roosevelt took office, whereas Obama's job was to prevent a depression from occurring. Obama helped to pull the economy out of its death spiral, but not in a way that inspired much gratitude.

It was daunting to assume power at a time when the economy was shrinking by nearly 6 percent annually. When Obama's economic team met in Chicago in December 2008 to form its strategy, it reeled at the news that already frightening job loss figures for September and October had been revised upward. The United States lost 1.9 million jobs in the last four months of 2008 and 2.6 million for the year, the highest loss total since 1945. November and December were horrible, racking up job losses of 584,000 and 524,000, the first time that the U.S. economy had ever lost more than 500,000 jobs in consecutive months. The numbers got even worse during Obama's first four months in office, totaling 741,000 jobs lost in January 2009, 681,000 in February, 652,000 in March, and 519,000 in April. In October 2009 the unemployment rate peaked at 10.1 percent. Dealing with that overshadowed everything when Obama took office.[1]

By the end of Obama's first summer in office the job loss figure was down to 201,000 jobs. In November the economy registered its first job gain in two years. In March, April, and May 2010 the economy registered job gains of 208,000, 290,000, and 413,000. But Obama won little credit for averting a depression, and he backed away from a second stimulus focused on transportation and infrastructure jobs. He saved or created more than 3 million jobs, but that left 14 million Americans out of work, which made him disinclined to tout the jobs that he saved.

Obama was hamstrung before he started, coping with a free-falling economy and the necessity of doing something as fast as possible. The time factor militated against the spending project that he wanted most—a "smart grid" of transmission lines for electricity. There were similar problems with big infrastructure proposals, and the crisis in the labor market turned out to be worse than his team expected upon entering office. Pushing for a big stimulus, he got less than he wanted from Congress, and he decided not to return for a second round of employment spending, after round one launched the Tea Party. If Obama fails to win a second term, he will rue, more than any decision he has made, the one to back off on Keynesian gas.[2]

Crashing and Bailing

The case for ending the rule of the Republicans was awfully strong when they held their convention in St. Paul, Minnesota, from September 1–4, 2008. The mortgage crisis had begun in August 2007, when BNP Paribas, France's biggest bank, halted redemption on three investment funds backed by mortgage bonds. Bush officials spent the succeeding year claiming that the big banks contained the crisis with write-downs and capital raises, but by September 2008 the mortgage meltdown in the United States was enormous, totaling $2.5 trillion of lost value.

In the first eight months of 2008 the economy lost 605,000 jobs, which seemed horrendous at the time. Bear Stearns, a storied investment bank, had gone down in March, snapped up by JPMorgan Chase with taxpayer money after drowning in its own hyperleveraged excess. At its peak in 2007, Bear Stearns was valued at $20 billion; a year later it was down to $236 million. In public, Bush officials treated Bear Stearns as an isolated case, even as Merrill Lynch, Citigroup, Washington Mutual, and Wachovia reeled from staggering losses, and the failure of IndyMac Federal Bank in July yielded the first pictures of anxious depositors lining up to withdraw their money.[3]

John McCain's top economic adviser, Phil Gramm, a former champion of deregulation in the Senate, blasted "whiners" for criticizing the bad economy; Gramm opined in July that the economy's losers suffered only from "mental depression." This view polled very badly, and McCain, heading into the Republican convention, realized that he had no good issues, except voter unease with Obama. McCain did not want his convention to fixate on unhelpful issues, and he realized that his party had a serious morale problem. So he revved up the party's base by choosing a spectacularly unfit running mate, Sarah Palin, whom he had met a single time.[4]

Most speakers at the convention said nothing about mortgage foreclosures, job losses, or George W. Bush; even the word *Republican* was rarely heard at the Republican convention. Former presidential contestant Rudy Giuliani, warming up the crowd, tossed out red meat about terrorism and radical Democrats. Former presidential contestant Mitt Romney won the prize for red meat, declaring that even the Roberts Supreme Court was liberal, like the rest of "liberal Washington." Former presidential contestant Fred Thompson, revising Gramm, explained that only Democrats complained about economic distress. All skipped past the fact that the U.S. economy, needing to create at least 100,000 jobs per month to keep up with a growing population, lost jobs in every month of 2008.[5]

The Bush administration's ideological refusal to regulate the mortgage industry was a factor in the mortgage meltdown, but McCain had the same ideology. The Bush budget deficits were similarly enormous and self-inflicted, but McCain would have made the deficits worse by cutting corporate taxes, eliminating the alternative minimum income tax, ramping up military spending, and extending Bush's tax cuts. Obama took aim at the latter issue, stressing the fiscal damage and sheer unfairness. McCain's only idea for cutting the budget deficit was to cut earmarks; Obama noted that if earmarks were eliminated, the savings would total only $19 billion per year.

Obama was happy to acknowledge that McCain once had a sensible position on the Bush tax cuts, which he dropped to make himself competitive in

Republican presidential primaries. Similarly, McCain had once aspired to be known as a green conservative, and he opposed offshore drilling on the grounds that the environment matters. But on his way to the nomination he dropped environmentalism and deliberately avoided voting on all eight attempts to pass a bill that would have expanded America's wind and solar industries. McCain, savoring his remaining dissent from Bush-style oil politics, still opposed drilling in the Arctic National Wildlife Refuge. But then he picked a far-Right running mate who chanted, "Drill, baby, drill!" and made no exception for ANWR.

Briefly the postconvention campaign threatened to be about lesser things, such as who first used the phrase "putting lipstick on a pig." Coming out of the Republican convention, McCain led in some polls by 3 to 4 percent. Then crashing and bailing commenced.

On the morning after Palin thrilled the Republican convention with a feisty speech, Treasury Secretary Paulson told Bush that they had to take over Fannie Mae and Freddie Mac, the congressionally chartered companies that owned or guaranteed half the nation's $12 trillion mortgage market. In one year Fannie Mae's common share price had dropped from $66 to $7.32, and net losses for the two companies stood at $5.5 billion. Paulson and Federal Reserve Board chair Ben Bernanke persuaded Bush that seizing both companies simultaneously was the only alternative to a global meltdown, since nearly every American home mortgage lender and Wall Street bank relied on these companies to facilitate the mortgage market, and foreign investors led by Japan, China, and Russia held more than $1 trillion of the debt issued or guaranteed by the two companies.

Allowing Fannie Mae and Freddie Mac to crash would have left major economic powers feeling betrayed and expropriated. On September 7 Paulson and Federal Housing Finance Agency chair Jim Lockhart took Fannie Mae and Freddie Mac into conservatorship, wiping out common and preferred shareholders, protecting debt holders, and providing up to $100 billion to each company to backstop capital shortfalls. Paulson vowed to downsize both companies once the crisis had passed, restructuring them as normal utilities; somehow he talked as though he had years remaining as Treasury secretary. Later he recalled, "We had, I thought, just saved the country—and the world—from financial catastrophe."[6]

But the week of reckoning had just begun, and the trio of Paulson, Bernanke, and New York Federal Reserve president Timothy Geithner had already set a sorry precedent for what was coming, in the Bear Stearns rescue. Bear Stearns, having been deemed too big to fail, was bailed out by the Federal Reserve pending its sale to JPMorgan, which offered $2 per share for a firm that, a year previously, had traded at $170 per share. A week of controversy over JPMorgan's lowball offer ensued, threatening the deal. Bear Stearns shareholders would have come out with nothing if not for the government; as it was, the Federal Reserve's $30 billion loan got Bear Stearns through the week, and Bear Stearns shareholders eventually got $10 per share, thanks to the Bush administration and some adept campaigning in the media. Paulson had made a fortune during his years as chief executive of Goldman Sachs, where he helped to build the casino economy. Now he shuddered at cutting bailout deals. He worked for a Republican president who couldn't believe, either, that his presidency was ending this way. These misgivings had everything to do with what happened to Lehman Brothers, which was unlucky for being next in line.[7]

The crisis escalated immediately after the Fannie Mae and Freddie Mac takeover. Lehman Brothers screamed for rescue; Merrill Lynch and Washington Mutual were drowning too; and General Electric CEO Jeffrey Immelt told Paulson that GE couldn't sell its commercial paper, a frightening sign that a systemwide liquidity crisis had begun. Lehman had $600 billion of assets, which made it thirty times bigger than Bear Stearns had been at its peak. If Bear Stearns was too big and interconnected to fail, Lehman was more so. But Lehman had bad timing and a fateful combination of capital and liquidity problems, which scared off potential buyers. According to Credit Suisse, Lehman's assets were worth $20 billion less than the value at which they were carried, creating a huge capital hole, which caused anxious counterparties to flee, creating a huge liquidity problem. Lehman had virtually no cash left. Paulson understood that a crash by Lehman would probably set off a global meltdown. He also believed, however, that the Bush administration and both parties in Congress would not stand for any more bailouts, and in his telling, he insisted to potential buyers of Lehman that the government had no legal authority to inject capital into Lehman or to commit any public money to a deal.

Whether or not Paulson made the latter claim at the time, or only stressed it later, is disputed. Legally, the government had to find a financial institution to act as a conduit for government loans to Lehman, as JPMorgan had been in the Bear Stearns deal. But the problem that made a difference was the political one, not a legal objection. Section 13(3) of the Federal Reserve Act allows the Fed to finance or seize control of financial firms and insurance companies under "unusual and exigent circumstances." That could have covered almost anything that Paulson grappled with in September 2008. Paulson and Geithner rescued Bear Stearns under this provision, and two days after Paulson let Lehman go bankrupt, he and Geithner engineered a Section 13(3) bailout of American International Group (AIG).

What mattered about Lehman was that it fell between these precedents, on the weekend of September 13–14. Paulson and Geithner, assembling the

Wall Street CEOs at the New York Federal Reserve, implored them to save Lehman on their own, with government help. Repeatedly Paulson insisted that there was no political will in Washington to save Lehman. It was up to the Wall Street bankers to save the world and themselves from an economic meltdown. Somebody had to buy Lehman, and the others had to create a fund to facilitate the deal, though Paulson half expected to seal the deal with government largesse.

Vikram Pandit of Citigroup protested against focusing exclusively on Lehman. If they didn't deal with AIG too, the group would be back the following weekend for that. Geithner replied that they had to focus on Lehman. Lloyd Blankfein of Goldman Sachs protested against holding the assembled group responsible for anybody else's balance sheet. If Wall Street rivals rescued Lehman, AIG and Merrill Lynch would expect to be rescued too. If each company were responsible for the others, all investment houses would be more vulnerable. It didn't help that Lehman chief executive Dick Fuld was unpopular in this group, but in the end, the CEOs came up with $30 billion to facilitate a deal for Lehman, which didn't matter because Paulson could not find a buyer.[8]

Paulson wanted Bank of America to buy Lehman, which estimated that it would have to unload $70 billion of bad Lehman assets to make a deal. Bank of America's CEO Ken Lewis, it turned out, preferred to own Merrill Lynch's army of retail stockbrokers, whom he bought for $50 billion on the same day that Lehman went down. Paulson's last refuge for Lehman was the British bank Barclays. For a moment he thought he had pulled off a rescue by getting Bank of America to buy Merrill Lynch and Barclays to buy Lehman. But Barclays' regulator, the Financial Services Authority, deemed at the last minute that Britain had no business swallowing Lehman's mountain of debt and toxic assets. Paulson had entered the weekend believing that saving Lehman was the key to averting a global meltdown. Then he learned that there was no key. He could not find a buyer for Lehman; he believed that the Federal Reserve had no legal authority to guarantee an investment bank's trading book or its liabilities; his boss was ready to let a big firm go down; and Paulson spent much of the weekend learning that AIG's problems dwarfed those of Lehman Brothers.

AIG was the poster child of the derivatives fiasco. A corporation of U.S.-based insurance companies claiming assets of $1 trillion, its financial products unit bankrupted the conglomerate by trafficking in derivatives tied to subprime mortgages. AIG's derivatives unit was a huge casino selling phantom insurance for credit-default swaps with no backing aside from the value of dubious mortgages. The company financed long-term mortgages with short-term paper, which required more promissory notes every time the mortgages lost value, and it took huge losses in its securities lending program by lending out high-grade bonds for cash. Doug Braunstein, AIG's financial adviser from JPMorgan, told Paulson that AIG's books were marked "aggressively." What did that mean? Braunstein replied, "The opposite of conservatively." Paulson later recalled, "It gave me a chill to think of the potential impact of AIG's problems. The firm had tens of millions of life insurance customers and tens of billions of dollars of contracts guaranteeing 401(k)s and other retirement holdings of individuals."[9]

AIG was the epitome of systemic risk, being connected to hundreds of companies and financial institutions. If AIG went down, the process of unwinding its contracts would take many years, destroying countless lives and businesses. Letting AIG go down was unthinkable, even as the world learned on September 15 that Lehman Brothers had filed for bankruptcy; Paulson pushed Securities and Exchange chairman Christopher Cox to push Lehman's board to get it over with. Paulson was more distraught than Bush about failing to save Lehman because he understood better what was likely to happen. He told Bush that perhaps they would get lucky. For a couple of hours on Monday, September 15, Paulson tried to be optimistic. But earlier that morning, in his telling, Paulson gazed at mid-Manhattan and wondered "if anyone out there on the streets could possibly imagine what was about to hit them."[10]

On that day the Dow Jones index fell 504 points, AIG fell by 60 percent, and credit markets tightened. Off camera, Paulson stuck to his story that he had no legal basis to save Lehman; in public, he didn't say it because doing so might have caused a run on Morgan Stanley or Goldman Sachs. Sarah Palin admonished Paulson not to go soft on AIG because the American people hated bailouts; Paulson told her that he didn't like bailouts either, but a failure by AIG would be catastrophic for the American people. On Tuesday the commercial paper market froze and AIG exploded. Paulson, Geithner, and Bernanke rushed to save AIG with an $85 billion bridge loan, rationalizing that AIG was different from Lehman because it was strictly a liquidity problem, not a capital problem. That turned out not to be true, but the rationale mattered on September 16, the same day that a stampede began for Treasury securities paying 0.10 percent. President Bush, stunned at bailing out AIG, asked how an insurance company could be so systemically important. Paulson explained that AIG was an unregulated holding company of regulated insurance companies. Bernanke described it as a hedge fund sitting atop an insurance company.

Wednesday was even worse, as the AIG bailout did nothing to calm the credit and stock markets, and short-sellers brought Morgan Stanley to its knees. The Dow lost another 449 points, and Bernanke told Paulson that the time had come to bail out Wall Street as a whole, not just a few firms. On Thursday Bernanke and Paulson took that message to President Bush and key congressional leaders, warning that a full-scale financial panic was underway. Withdrawals from money market funds topped $400 billion overnight ($5 billion was normal), and the yields on short-term Treasury bills fell below zero. Bernanke warned that if Congress did not pass a whopping bailout called the Troubled Asset Relief Program (TARP), "we may not have an economy on Monday." The economy they had was teetering on the brink of an abyss. On Friday Bernanke and Paulson made that plea to Congress; Paulson's aide for legislative affairs, Kevin Fromer, picked a right-sounding number out of the air, $700 billion. The public probably would not hate $700 billion more than $500 billion, Fromer reasoned, but anything closer to $1 trillion would be at risk of being rejected by the House and Senate.[11]

Meanwhile, in the race for president of the United States, McCain had a very bad week, and Obama emerged as the candidate fit to be president. Obama kept in close contact with Paulson, who told friends there was no comparison between Obama's understanding of the economic crisis and McCain's. Obama supported Paulson's proposal, working with House Speaker Nancy Pelosi to deliver Democratic support. McCain was erratic at best. On September 15 he announced, "The fundamentals of our economy are strong," a much-quoted howler that stuck to him. The following day McCain declared on NBC's *Today* show that there should be no bailouts for AIG or anybody else. The day after that he pulled back from this position, realizing the gravity of where it led, but the next day he called for the firing of Christopher Cox with no explanation of why he was singling out Cox. McCain's friend Senator Lindsey Graham warned Paulson that McCain was leaning toward leading the opposition to TARP.

Then McCain announced that he would suspend his campaign in order to return to Washington to help solve the economic crisis. Paulson was appalled; nobody knew if McCain would support the TARP bill or rally Republicans against it. At the moment, McCain didn't know either. On September 25, the day that Washington Mutual went down, the biggest bank failure in U.S. history, until Wachovia started to crash the next day, Bush convened a meeting of Republican and Democratic leaders at the White House at McCain's request. Bush began the meeting by observing, "If money isn't loosened up, this sucker could be going down," referring to America's economy. Bush had little else to say, and Paulson asked the Democrats to speak. Obama, speaking for the Democrats, ranged over the issues in detail, supported the TARP idea, showed that the only alternative being floated by some Republicans—a mortgage insurance scheme—was unworkable and irrelevant, and asked for McCain's view.

McCain was irked by Obama's showy display of knowledge, and he hadn't made up his mind about what to say. He declined to speak, explaining that he had come only to listen. That floored everybody. McCain had called for this meeting; everyone had come to learn what the Republican candidate for president believed. Many Republicans opposed any bailout, but most were not quite ready to defy Paulson. House Democrats accused McCain of blowing up a deal, which in fact did not exist. Obama had come to the meeting worried that McCain and Bush were setting a trap for him. Now he realized that McCain had no plan; he was winging it from moment to moment. Finally McCain said that both sides had legitimate concerns, and he hoped they could work out an acceptable compromise. Asked if he supported Paulson's plan, McCain said that he wasn't sure because he had not read it.

McCain had not read the three-page plan to spend $700 billion that the entire country was talking about. The meeting ended badly. House Republican Spencer Bachus, a lonely pro-Paulson Republican trying to cut a deal with the Democrats, claimed Republican credit for TARP's taxpayer protections, which Pelosi and other Democrats heatedly denied. Barney Frank, the leading House Democrat on financial issues, demanded to know from McCain what the Republican Party proposed to do. McCain sat stone-faced. A shouting match ensued between Republicans and Democrats. Vice President Dick Cheney laughed at the chaotic brawl taking place until Bush stood up to announce, "Well, I've clearly lost control of this meeting. It's over."[12]

The Democrats, meeting in the Roosevelt Room, plotted their next move. Paulson rushed in, fell on his knees before Pelosi, and begged her not to blow up the plan. Pelosi laughed at the spectacle of a Christian Scientist on his knees before her, but Frank, normally on good terms with Paulson, ripped him for begging the wrong party. Three times Frank screamed, "Fuck you, Hank!" Frank had jeopardized his party standing by working so closely with Paulson on an unpopular proposal. In the heat of the moment he couldn't stand any suggestion that Democrats were any part of the problem. Obama played peacemaker, urging Paulson to get the Republicans on board. Paulson agreed, apologetically, that that was what he had to do. Leaving the White House, Obama told his aides by speakerphone that now he realized that McCain had no business being president: "We have *got* to win. It was crazy in there. Maybe I shouldn't be president, but *he* definitely shouldn't be!"[13]

Obama's heightened self-confidence showed, the next day, in the first presidential debate, just as 80 million voters who had not taken part in the primaries began to tune in. By then McCain had decided not to come out against TARP. To his credit, McCain stuck to that position through the election, even as he fell behind Obama in the polls and realized that his only chance of closing the gap was to attack Paulson's scheme as a betrayal of capitalism and Americanism. On Monday, September 29, the House of Representatives rejected the TARP bill by 228 to 205. Four days later the House passed it by

263 to 171, with 91 favorable Republican votes. In between the crisis struck hard in Europe, sending markets in a drastic turn downward and pushing European banks to the edge of collapse. That got the attention of reachable no voters, as did pleas from Obama and McCain. Paulson later recalled that for the first time, on the day of the first House vote, he saw Obama lose his cool, resembling Paulson's own constant state of agitation. Paulson realized that his nightmare of a global economic meltdown was occurring. He had to make the public understand how bad it was without setting off an all-out panic.

Nationalizing the banks was out of the question for Paulson, since Socialism was anathema to him and nearly all the big banks were in trouble. It wasn't a question of taking over parts of the financial sector that the government could swallow; the pillars of the financial system itself were in jeopardy. At first Paulson planned to spend the TARP money buying toxic assets at market prices. But the stock market kept falling, market prices for bad debt were frighteningly low, credit remained nearly frozen, and the crisis spread to Europe and the rest of the world. Numerous European officials, appalled that Paulson let Lehman Brothers go down, declared that they would not allow a similar crash. British prime minister Gordon Brown half-socialized Britain's banking sector, declaring that he opposed mere giveaways to the parties that created the mess. Brown, however, was in that group, having been a major facilitator of deregulation and derivatives as chancellor of the exchequer in Tony Blair's Labour government from 1997 to 2007. Other European nations followed Brown's lead.

Paulson half-agreed, changing his mind. Brown had the right idea, Paulson decided, by injecting billions of pounds of capital into the system instead of targeting illiquid assets. The crucial thing was to strengthen the banks before the entire system crashed. But Paulson shuddered at the rest of Brown's prescription—nationalizing the Royal Bank of Scotland and HBOS, firing the top executives of banks, taking seats on bank boards, freezing bonuses for bank executives, and imposing a 12 percent dividend on preferred stock. Admittedly, House and Senate Democrats were making a fuss about executive compensation, to which Paulson was sympathetic to some degree. But the compensation issue was unwieldy, and to Paulson, the rest of the British plan was out of bounds ideologically, except for the essential thing, capitalizing the banks.[14]

The United Kingdom's strongest banks—HSBC, Barclays, and Standard Chartered—turned down the capital because they didn't want public representatives on their boards, and they wanted nothing to do with caps on executive compensation. Paulson was determined to prevent JPMorgan's Jamie Dimon and Wells Fargo's Richard Kovacevich from similarly refusing to play. Paulson wanted all of America's megabanks to accept his plan to give them billions of dollars, and he knew what they would not swallow, even when faced with extinction. He knew that his American banking brethren always overestimated their capital strength, and they loathed any government restrictions on their freedom to do whatever they wanted to do—which was, mostly, to gamble on derivatives and pay huge bonuses.

On October 13, the same day that Brown unveiled his plan, Paulson met with the chief executives of eight financial powerhouses. Earlier that day he told General Motors chief executive Rick Wagoner that TARP was only for financial companies, not for essential companies in crisis that made things. Even if the TARP bill (the Emergency Economic Stabilization Act of 2008) said no such thing, Paulson took it that way. He reasoned that financial firms tended to die quickly, while industrial firms could always stretch out their suppliers for a while. The essential thing was to save the banks. Along with Bernanke, Geithner, and Federal Deposit Insurance Corporation (FDIC) chair Sheila Bair, Paulson told the bankers that he was recapitalizing them with billions of dollars and guaranteeing new unsecured senior debt. Citigroup, JPMorgan, and Wells Fargo headed the list at $25 billion each; Bank of America got $15 billion; Goldman Sachs, Merrill Lynch, and Morgan Stanley received $10 billion each; Bank of New York Mellon got $3 billion; and State Street Corporation got $2 billion. The following week the Federal Reserve announced that it would spend $540 billion to purchase short-term debt from money market funds, but on November 12 Paulson scrapped his plan to buy toxic assets, opting to spend the remaining TARP money on recapitalizing more banks. Five days later the Treasury dispensed $33.6 billion to twenty-one banks, notably Sun Trust and Capital One, each for $3.5 billion. The following week there were taxpayer infusions for twenty-three more banks.[15]

Paulson reasoned that the banks would start lending again if he gave them money. But this approach did not satisfy either part of Brown's objection. Paulson's arrangement *was* a mere giveaway, overpaying for preferred stock with no control rights, and it went to the very people that created the crisis. It did nothing about the compensation issue, and it did not get the banks to start lending again. Had Paulson given the banks tangible common equity instead of preferred stock (which is essentially a loan) and told them to invest it in the real economy or write off their toxic debt, they would have had to do so. As it was, they didn't know what their assets were worth, so they sat on the taxpayers' money, not being required to do anything else with it.

Citigroup, within weeks of receiving its first $25 billion gift from taxpayers, got another $20 billion of TARP money on November 24 and a whopping $306 billion guarantee (2 percent of America's gross domestic product), all with no public stake, no management changes, and no annoying demands to do anything for the public with the public's money. Treasury and Fed officials managed not to take an equity stake in Citigroup by structuring the deal like an insurance program, which concealed the amount of risk that taxpayers took on. Bank of America got a similar deal just before the Obama administration took office, receiving a fresh $20 billion capital injection and a guarantee of up to $118 billion in losses on toxic assets. AIG, Paulson's greatest headache, consumed four bailouts totaling $175 billion and doled out $165 million of bonus payments without finding a bottom to its sinkhole of toxic debt exceeding $1 trillion.[16]

Smaller institutions socked away their TARP money, too, or used it to repay short-term loans from the Federal Reserve. Some of them used taxpayer money to buy rival banks. Wells Fargo acquired massive exposure to California mortgage failures by taking over Wachovia, and JPMorgan Chase took on similar liabilities by taking over Bear Stearns and Washington Mutual. When Obama took office, half the $700 billion TARP money was spent, it was spread among 257 financial institutions in forty-two states, and only a trickle of it was getting invested in a disintegrating economy.[17]

The Troubled Asset Relief Program probably saved the financial system from completely collapsing in the last months of 2008, and most of the banks repaid their bailouts and infusions within a year. But the program was seriously flawed, beginning with its stupendous unfairness. Its basic terms were obsequious to the banks, asking them only to issue preferred shares to the Treasury, participate in the FDIC's guaranteed debt program, and modify the terms of residential mortgages "as appropriate." Under the Paulson plan banks still got tax exemptions for mergers, and banks taking taxpayer money still paid generous dividends, all the while sitting on their taxpayer bailouts. McCain was furious that the program took a light pass at the mortgage problem while rewarding the banks so lavishly. Obama agreed in a cooler voice, adding that Paulson missed an opportunity to do something about excessive executive compensation. Had McCain lashed out publicly at Paulson in late October, he might have closed the gap on Obama. Obama, anticipating a late barrage, promised Paulson that he would stick to a reactive quid pro quo: He would criticize Paulson or restrain himself exactly to the extent that McCain did so.

After the election, Obama stopped calling Paulson, although Paulson had some of the worst days of his tenure in November and December. AIG, Citigroup, and Bank of America came back for more bailing out, and the public raged against all of it. Paulson took so much criticism from all sides that at times he fell into despair and self-doubt, needing Geithner to buck him up. But two weeks after the election, Obama gave Paulson the strongest endorsement imaginable by choosing Geithner to be his Treasury secretary. Amid all the criticism, Paulson fully appreciated what it meant that Obama chose Geithner to be his successor. Whatever Paulson might have gotten wrong, he must have gotten the big things right, because Obama chose his partner to carry on the approach they had taken.

That was a fair reading and an omen. Geithner was the regulator closest to Wall Street when its gambling binge wrecked the economy. He was comfortable with the system and his respected place in it. He believed that mergers between big banks are desirable and to be encouraged; thus he played matchmaker for them. Obama, realizing that Treasury secretary would be his most important cabinet selection, seriously considered only Geithner and former Treasury secretary Larry Summers, an architect of the Clinton administration's deregulation policies.

Summers, a former child prodigy at MIT and Harvard and the nephew of legendary economist Paul Samuelson, was only two years removed from his rocky five-year tenure as president of Harvard University. Invariably described as brilliant, egotistical, and quarrelsome, Summers was the exception to the no-drama rule in Obama's inner circle. In various parts of his career Summers's aggressive personality counted against him, but not on Wall Street, which prized his cocksure analytical performances, his favors during the Clinton administration, and the sheer fact that he prized his high standing on Wall Street. During his Harvard presidency Summers consulted for Taconic Capital Advisors, even as he admonished faculty underlings against moonlighting. In 2008 he made more than $5 million consulting one day per week for a hedge fund, D. E. Shaw and Company. Summers and Geithner became friends in the 1990s during their time together at Treasury; Geithner's standing rose as he became known for his willingness to clash with Summers over policy.

By considering only Geithner and Summers for Treasury, Obama had already made his most important decision—to stabilize the existing system. After he settled on Geithner, Obama asked Summers to be his senior adviser on economics, with daily access. Summers, disappointed at not getting Treasury, said no. If he couldn't have Treasury, he wanted the National Economic Council, which at least had a staff. In Washington, one has no power if one has no staff. Clinton had created the National Economic Council as an economic analogue of the National Security Council. Under Clinton and Bush, the NEC chair was a neutral broker of economic policy views in the executive branch and the field as a whole; Clinton's second Treasury secretary, Robert Rubin, pioneered the position. Obama had already promised the position to a former Clinton budget director, Jack Lew, but Summers was insistent, even though he had no intention of merely brokering the views of others. Summers told Obama that he would be willing to filter, for him, the range of pertinent policy perspectives, but he would also push his own views. Obama said that was fine with him; he wanted Summers and he didn't need a broker, since intellectual brokering was his specialty. Obama would be his own broker.

There would not, however, be much brokering to do between the economic advisers who helped Obama win the Democratic nomination and those who joined later, because the later group routed the early one. Obama's early team included Paul Volcker, University of Chicago economist Austan Goolsbee, Brookings Institution economist Jason Furman, investment guru Warren Buffett, Republican former SEC chair William Donaldson, Republican former Bush Treasury secretary Paul O'Neill, UBS Americas president and CEO Robert Wolf, and two former chairs of the Council of Economic Advisers, University of California, Berkeley business professor Laura D'Andrea Tyson and Columbia University economist Joseph Stiglitz. This group was short on Rubin protégés, even though most of the Democratic braintrust in this area consisted of people that Rubin mentored during his years at Goldman Sachs, Treasury, and/or Citigroup. Rubin epitomized the melding of Wall Street and the government, plus the prominence of one firm, Goldman Sachs, in melding together the two career tracks. Most of his protégés supported Hillary Clinton and had backgrounds in the Clinton administration; among Obama's early team, only Furman was a Rubinite. After Clinton conceded the nomination, however, Obama appointed Furman as head of his economic team, and the Rubinites streamed to Obama. Summers entered Obama's circle through Furman, eventually convincing Obama that he needed Summers's purported brilliance. When Obama won the presidency, he hired many Rubinites, notwithstanding that by then, Rubin was politically toxic for his recent role as chair of Citigroup. The Rubin protégés in Obama's administration included Summers, Geithner, Furman, Peter Orszag, Michael Froman, Philip Murphy, Gene Sperling, Jack Lew, Gary Gensler, Diana Farrell, Lewis Alexander, Lael Brainard, and David Tipton.[18]

This surge of Clinton veterans swept away most of the team that had guided Obama's campaign, except Furman and Goolsbee. During the campaign Obama relied on his friend Wolf to keep him informed about the financial meltdown. Afterward Obama decided that appointing a top Wall Street operative to a senior post would provoke more wrath in the aftermath of the bailouts than it was worth. Prominent liberals were bound to cause problems too, Obama judged, so he excluded them. Stiglitz and Paul Krugman, besides being too eminent with Nobel prizes, were likely to rattle the market with impolitic remarks, as was former labor secretary Robert Reich, who clashed with Rubin and Summers during the Clinton administration. Even middle-roaders like Tyson and Donaldson, who blasted the housing debacle, were ruled out. The key, negatively, to the appointment derby was Volcker, who contented that Obama needed to recreate the old Reconstruction Finance Corporation, treat the banks to tough love, and rebuild the wall between commercial and investment banking. According to Volcker, the banks were overdue to clear out the clutter and find a bottom. According to Geithner and Summers, Volcker needed to get his clock fixed. Reviving the banks and preventing a depression were more important than reforming the banks, at least for Obama's first year.[19]

Obama liked brainy, cosmopolitan, Ivy League, nonideological, no-drama types who reminded him of himself. As soon as he met Geithner, a few weeks before the election, he liked him for all these reasons. Geithner grew up mostly in Zimbabwe, Zambia, India, and Thailand; his father, Peter Geithner, ran the Ford Foundation's Asia program. On one occasion Peter Geithner, directing Ford's microfinance program in Indonesia, met Ann Dunham Soetoro; Obama loved that story. Timothy Geithner, by studying at Dartmouth, continued a family tradition, after which he earned a master's degree in international economics at Johns Hopkins. For three years he worked for Kissinger Associates before making the leap to government work in 1988, joining the International Affairs division of the Treasury Department. In the latter part of the Clinton administration, Geithner worked under Rubin and Summers and thus counted both as mentors.

Under the guidance of Geithner and Summers, Obama expected to play a cautious hand in the financial arena. For Obama, sneers about "Government Sachs" were off base and not funny. He respected the sharp intelligence of Geithner's circle and its sophisticated models of financial analysis, such as VaR (value at risk), which uses statistical ideas and probability theories to quantify portfolio risks as a single number. Analysts prize the ostensible ability of VaR to picture short-term trends by measuring normal probabilities. The big firms measure VaR every day. On the one hand, Obama realized that these models provided a false assurance of safety for firms that should have used common sense about packaging bad mortgages and getting leveraged by 30 to 1. On the other hand, he respected Wall Street's capacity to finance making things in the real economy, and he identified with the brainy achievers who rose to the top. Wall Street obviously had to be regulated better, and the proliferation of dark markets had to be curtailed. The system had to be reformed, a task that Rubin's protégés were eager to carry out, sometimes for redemption.

But the banks that Paulson and Geithner stuffed with taxpayer money had no interest in reforming, and by setting his sights too low, Obama missed a precious opportunity—to reduce Wall Street to the role it had in American society before it fell in love with securitizations and derivatives.

House of Cards

For twenty years securitizations and derivatives were great at concocting extra yield and allowing the banks to hide their debt. It seemed a blessing to get a low-rate mortgage. It was a mystery how the banks did it, but you trusted that they knew what they were doing. Your bank resold the mortgage to an aggregator, who bunched it up with thousands of other subprime mortgages, chopped the package into pieces, and sold them as corporate bonds to parties looking for extra yield. Your mortgage payments paid for the interest on the bonds. This scheme was ingenious for creating value and charging fees at every link in a chain of selling, packaging, securitizing, and reselling. It was ingenious, that is, as long as housing values always went up and there was no reckoning for the trashy assets held with borrowed money on which the whole casino was built.[20]

Broadly speaking, a derivative is any contract that derives its value from another underlying asset, such as buying home insurance. More narrowly and pertinently, it is an instrument that allows investors to speculate on the future price of something without having to buy it. Derivatives were developed to allow investors to hedge their risks in financial markets—in essence, to buy insurance against market movements. In each case they quickly became major investment options in their own right, allowing executives to claim "earnings" for contracts in which money exchanged hands only at a designated, sometimes far-off future date.

Option trading—paying for the right to exercise an option in the event that prices move in a set direction—soared in the 1970s, aided by the growth of computers, which helped to gauge the volatility of assets. The more that prices move, the more that buyers exercise their options. Currency swaps, and then interest-rate swaps, emerged in the 1980s. Currency swaps exchange bonds issued in one currency for another currency, enabling both parties to seek lower interest rates; interest-rate swaps pair variable-rate borrowers with borrowers on a fixed rate, as both parties try to manage their risk exposure.

From there it was a short step to the credit-default swaps pioneered in the late 1990s, in which parties bet on, or insured against, defaults. Credit-default swaps are private contracts that allow investors to bet on whether a borrower will default. Until the financial reform bill of 2010, this market was completely unregulated. In theory, credit-default swaps are a form of insurance because sellers guarantee to pay investors if their investments go bad. In reality, the credit-default mania of the 2000s was pure gambling exempted from standard insurance reserve requirements and state gaming laws. Credit-default sellers were not required to set aside reserves to pay for claims, and in 2000 the Commodity Futures Modernization Act exempted credit-default swaps from state gaming laws and other forms of regulation.

For ten years credit-default swaps were fantastically lucrative. In 1998 the total value of credit-default contracts was $144 billion; by 2008 it was $62 trillion and at the very heart of the financial crash. The derivatives market as a whole was equally spectacular and concentrated. In 2003, seven banks owned 96 percent of the derivatives in the U.S. banking system, which had a total value of $56 trillion; by 2008 the market was estimated to be $520 trillion. Alan Greenspan, Federal Reserve chair from 1987 to 2006, was a major proponent of derivatives, contending that the big banks and financial firms, being highly leveraged, needed a market vehicle to transfer their risks. An ardent libertarian, Greenspan worried when he took the Federal Reserve post that he would clash with Fed professionals who believed in regulation. To his delight he found that the Federal Reserve governors shared his strong opposition to most forms of regulation, and he took pride that the derivatives market exploded on his watch.[21]

But these instruments offered dangerous incentives for false accounting and made it extremely difficult to ascertain a firm's true exposure. By design, they generated huge amounts of leverage in which investors controlled assets far exceeding the original investment, and they were developed with virtually no consideration of the broad financial consequences. Securitization, contrary to what it sounds like, practically ensured unaccountability by creating new types of information asymmetries. Mortgage bundlers knew more than the buyers about what was in the bundles, but nobody knew very much, which left nobody responsible for what happened to them. Essentially, securitization allowed banks to set up off-balance-sheet vehicles to hide their debt. If financial institutions could parcel out their risk, supposedly there was nothing to worry about, since housing values always went up. At every link in the chain, every time a loan was sold, packaged, securitized, or resold, transaction fees were charged and somebody's "wealth" increased. Bonuses were paid for short-term paper gains on money held up for as long as ten years.

The mania for extra yield fed on itself, blowing away business ethics and even common sense. For nine years Harry Markopolos, an investment officer with Rampart Investment Management in Boston, warned the Securities and Exchange Commission that Bernard Madoff's $50 billion investment empire had to be fraudulent because his constant high profits were impossible. But the SEC did no better with Madoff's outright Ponzi operation than it managed with Wall Street's high-yielding securitization trading. One pyramid-style breeder of paper gains and bonuses looked too much like another.[22]

Obama's early presidency was defined by the chilling briefings that he received in November and December 2008 about the country's economic collapse. He vowed that he would not preside over a Japan-like recession and decline. Summers told Obama that his goal should be to make the recession of 2008–2009 as forgettable as the recession of 1982, which American history textbooks already passed over. Summers had no concept of changing the system; he had only a strongly Keynesian plan to get it running again. Obama selected an ideal chief of staff for deal making that pushed things through Congress—Rahm Emanuel, a voracious operator, political pragmatist, former senior adviser to President Clinton, and, at the time, U.S. House representative from Illinois. Emanuel vowed to line up a big stimulus bill to be signed on the first day of Obama's presidency. That was a daunting task for pre-appointees lacking offices, so Obama and Emanuel settled on a slightly less ambitious date—February 16. Obama wanted Republican support, but by moving so fast, he signaled that he was ready to roll over Republicans that wanted no part of the new New Deal.

Stabilizing the System

The Obama campaign had called for a $150 billion stimulus package, matching Bush's stimulus of the previous February. By early December that figure was not even a starting point, and on December 16 Obama's economic team assembled in Chicago. Geithner, Summers, Orszag, and Goolsbee were key players; Christina Romer, a UC Berkeley economist, turned out to be the crucial player. Romer was a prominent advocate, along with her husband and Berkeley colleague David Romer, of "New Keynesian" theory, which argues that prices and wages do not always adjust to changes in economic conditions. Because prices and wages are "sticky," government has a key role to play in using fiscal policy or monetary policy to attain efficient macroeconomic outcomes. Romer's doctoral dissertation focused on Franklin Roosevelt's skittish approach to social investment, contending that Roosevelt failed to spend enough to lift America out of the Depression, and in 1937 he reduced employment spending, which sent unemployment soaring. In her later work, on which Romer collaborated with David Romer, she focused on the impact of tax policy on economic growth.[23]

Romer had played no formal role in the campaign, aside from sending an occasional message to Goolsbee, but in Chicago she immediately accepted Obama's offer to be his chair of economic advisers. She had supported the Obama for President campaign before it existed, watching his 2004 Boston convention speech repeatedly. In the spring of 2008 Romer's career plans had suffered a blow when Harvard president Drew Gilpin Faust vetoed Romer's invitation from the economics department to teach at Harvard. The factional politics at Harvard were brutal. In this case, however, Faust's controversial decision did not diminish Romer's standing in the academy. Romer later recalled that in building up to the December 16 briefing, David Axelrod told her that this meeting needed to be a "holy shit moment." Romer, drawing on the lessons of her research, was willing to provide it, telling Obama, "Things are grim and deteriorating fast. This is horrible."[24]

The burning question was how big the stimulus needed to be to avert a depression. New York senator Chuck Schumer, in a television interview, declared that Obama might need to ask for $300 billion. Orszag, who had just served as director of the Congressional Budget Office and was gearing up to be Obama's budget director, thought that Schumer's figure sounded about right, though perhaps it needed to be higher. Romer told the group it would take at least $800 billion to prevent a depression, and she favored asking for $1.2 trillion. It was pointless to ask for less than half of what the country needed: "We have to hit this with everything we have." Summers concurred that Romer had the range right. Emanuel grimaced at the prospect of getting that much out of Congress. The rest of the group concurred at the lower end, agreeing to ask for something between $700 billion and $800 billion. Obama stressed that he wanted the most important decision of his early presidency to be based on an expert estimate of what the country needed, not on politics, although most of his team assumed that Paulson was right about the maximal figure; anything over $1 trillion would never get through. As it was, to get an $800 billion stimulus on top of Paulson's TARP bailout meant that Obama would begin his presidency $1.5 trillion in the red, not including the $9 trillion in guarantees from the Federal Reserve and FDIC that the Bush administration racked up in its final eighteen months.[25]

All of this, plus the second half of the TARP money, had to be proposed and fought for before Obama took office. On January 10, 2009, Romer, now as the nominee designate to be chair of the Council of Economic Advisers, and Jared Bernstein, an aide to Vice President Elect Joe Biden, made a case for a stimulus of $775 billion featuring a middle-class tax cut, business investment incentives, state fiscal relief, food stamp and unemployment insurance increases, and large investments in infrastructure, education, health, and energy. The goal was to stimulate enough economic activity to save or create at least three million jobs by the end of 2010. Romer and Bernstein acknowledged that tax cuts and fiscal relief to states create fewer jobs than direct increases in government purchases. However, there was a limited supply of shovel-ready projects, and speed was crucial; thus, tax cuts and state relief had to play a key role. They urged Congress to aim for a balance between infrastructure and energy spending that favored the construction and manufacturing sectors and the more general measures that created jobs in all sectors of the economy. Fatefully, not realizing that the worst was still to come in monthly job losses, Romer and Bernstein predicted that without a big stimulus, unemployment would peak at 9 percent, and with a stimulus, it would stay under 8 percent. Though Romer had the sky-is-falling role among Obama's advisers, even she badly underestimated the extent of the financial crash on the labor market.[26]

Aides to Obama lacking offices and appointments fanned out across the Congress in early January, lobbying for the second half of the TARP money— which Bush requested but did nothing to attain—and a new stimulus bill. The sums were staggering and the pace was ferocious. Romer suspected that the blue-chip business economists were underestimating the crisis, but she felt pressure not to be far out of line with their estimates, and she knew that nobody was working with adequate numbers. Struggling not to seem alarmist, she guessed too low. Obama spent a big piece of his political capital getting the new Senate to approve the release of the second half of Bush's bailout fund, which occurred five days before he was inaugurated. It helped that Geithner was willing to apologize for (usually unspecified) things that he and Paulson got wrong; Geithner understood the political value of humility. But a week before the inauguration, it was revealed that Geithner had failed to pay his self-employment taxes during his years at the International Monetary Fund. Geithner immediately repaid $42,702 and apologized for not paying sufficient attention to his taxes.

This problem would have eliminated any other cabinet appointment; in Geithner's case, the tax evader in question was slated to run the Treasury Department, which houses the Internal Revenue Service. But Obama stuck with Geithner, even though doing so dragged out the vetting process for other nominees, and even though Geithner took a daily roasting in the media for designing the hated bailouts. America needed a Treasury secretary on day one, and Geithner had become indispensable to Obama.[27]

Normally a transition is about lining up a new team. Obama, lining up his team in an abnormal time, realized that he had to have a first-rate White House Office of Legislative Affairs to get his agenda through Congress. Thus, he picked top operatives from the current or former staffs of Joe Biden, Max Baucus, Tom Daschle, Ted Kennedy, and Henry Waxman, respectively: Ron Klain, Jim Messina, Pete Rouse, Melody Barnes, and Phil Schiliro. Democrat presidencies had a tradition of downgrading congressional relations. That ended with Obama, who told his team that everything was at stake in working effectively with Congress, at least the Democratic majority.

In a bad poker move, Obama announced at the outset that he wanted $300 billion in tax cuts, which failed to lure Republican support and left him short of bargaining chips. Over Axelrod's objection, Obama stuck with Paulson's refusal to attach any significant conditions about compensation or lending to the bailouts, another move that Republicans should have liked, but Obama got no credit for giving up Democratic principles in this area too. Geithner and Summers persuaded Obama that going easy on Wall Street egos and interests was essential at this stage.

From the beginning of Obama's presidency, Senate minority leader Mitch McConnell and House minority leader John Boehner committed the Republican Party to obstruction. Politics trumped everything else. If Obama succeeded, he would get the credit; if he failed, Republicans would clean up. What mattered was to make Obama a one-term president. In the Senate, Republicans Arlen Specter, Olympia Snowe, and Susan Collins worked with Democrats to shape the stimulus package. Three other Republican senators wanted to work on the bill—George Voinovich, Lisa Murkowski, and Mel Martinez—but McConnell scared them off, threatening retribution. Boehner, leading a very conservative Republican bloc in the House, had an easier time keeping his group in line, though after the midterm elections Boehner had the harder job. On February 13, the $787 billion American Recovery and Reinvestment Act of 2009 passed without a single House Republican vote.

Obama was stunned by this outcome. He told friends that he had expected to deal with fierce partisanship, but this was something else: a total lack of responsibility for governing. McConnell and Boehner urged their colleagues to oppose the bill before it existed. Obama wasted precious time and substance trying to win Republican support, refusing to believe that House Republicans were universally on board for letting the economy suffocate. He grasped belatedly that his only chance of winning Republican support (aside from the three Republican senators) was among Republican governors such as Arnold Schwarzenegger (California) and Charlie Crist (Florida), who had responsibility for governing.

The Recovery Act, though smaller than it needed to be, was a huge achievement. It was actually seven landmark bills rolled together. It contained the largest tax cut for the middle class since the Reagan administration ($288 billion); the biggest infrastructure bill since the Interstate Highway Act of 1956 ($105.3 billion); the biggest education bill since the Johnson administration ($100 billion); the biggest antipoverty and job training bill since the Johnson administration ($82.2 billion); and equally historic investments in clean energy ($27.2 billion), housing ($14.7 billion), and scientific research ($7.6 billion), plus a miscellaneous expenditure of $10.6 billion. The tax cut included a $15 billion expansion of the child tax credit and a $4.7 billion expansion of the earned income tax credit, which did more to help the working poor than any bill in two decades. The infrastructure investment included $27.5 billion for highway and bridge projects and $8 billion for rail projects. The education bill provided $53.6 billion to prevent layoffs and cutbacks in schools across the country and made a $5 billion down payment on Obama's signature education reform, "Race to the Top," which rewards states that invest in successful charter schools. The antipoverty bill included $40 billion to provide extended unemployment benefits and $19.9 billion for the food stamp program. The clean energy bill, the biggest in America's history, contained $6 billion for renewable energy technology and $5 billion for weatherizing homes.[28]

Had Obama pushed these projects separately, he would have gotten more credit for achievements on the scale of the New Deal and the Great Society. The antipoverty measures in the tax cut and the aid to unemployed and low-income workers were especially overlooked. By expanding the eligibility requirements for the earned income tax credit, the Recovery Act prevented millions of families from being pushed into poverty, although the final bill was less generous on this count than the House bill, mainly because the three Republican votes in the Senate were tremendously expensive—almost $150 billion. The bill that passed the House was very close to the Obama team's proposal, but in the Senate, Republicans attained major increases for the elderly and the wealthy at the expense of working-class taxpayers and the stabilization fund for states. For Obama, getting any Republican support was worth the cost. Moreover, he believed that getting the package passed as soon as possible was more important than getting credit for the things in it.

Originally, Obama wanted to do more for small businesses than the stimulus eventually provided ($15 billion in new loans from the Small Business Administration), and he wanted a big piece of the stimulus to build a network of national transmission lines for electricity—"the smart grid." The latter was to be his signature engine of growth for the new economy, the equivalent of the interstate highway system in the 1950s and the Internet in the 1990s. But it was hard to justify investments that carried a high risk of not paying off or that merely gave cheaper loans to small businesses that would have secured the capital anyway. Above all, the ferocious pace was his enemy on the thing he wanted most. Approximately 250 state and local regulators would have to approve any plan to modernize America's transmission lines. That would be a slow process, even with a Supreme Court that believes in eminent domain. Obama settled for an $11 billion down payment on the smart grid and relinquished his hope of a hugely visible legacy investment.

Having opted for the low end of the range that Romer and Summers wanted, Obama had to hope that he was not repeating the Japanese mistake of the 1990s, spending just enough to avert the worst but not enough to end the recession. A year earlier, Paul Krugman had blasted the Bush stimulus for pointlessly handing out $300 to middle-class taxpayers who would not spend it. Krugman pleaded that an intelligent stimulus goes to people who need it more, thereby doing double duty—alleviating the hardships of people living from paycheck to paycheck and pumping up consumer spending. A year later, Krugman appreciated the strong antipoverty dimensions of Obama's plan, and he was careful not to get personal in his critiques, as he and Summers were longtime friends and sparring partners. But he warned that Obama's stimulus was not big enough; in fact, it needed to be twice as big.[29]

The cost of an effective stimulus is less than the headline cost, Krugman stressed. The point of increasing government spending is to increase the gross domestic product, and economists generally agree that the multiplier effect is 1.5. A fiscal injection of $100 billion raises GDP by $150 billion. Moreover, assuming a marginal tax rate of 33 percent, $50 billion of the injection comes back in additional revenue; thus, the increase in GDP per dollar of added debt is 3, not 1.5. Romer and Bernstein assumed, with most economists, that $150 billion of spending (which constituted 1 percent of GDP) generates one million jobs. That comes out to $50,000 per job, Krugman noted—a very good investment for a suffocating economy. By contrast, the multiplier of a tax cut is 0.75, half that for public investment, and the increase in GDP per dollar of added debt is only 1. Krugman implored Obama and the Democrats not to repeat the Japanese mistake: "I don't know about you, but I've got a sick feeling in the pit of my stomach—a feeling that America just isn't rising to the greatest economic challenge in 70 years."[30]

Obama replied that critics like Krugman didn't have to hustle for votes in the U.S. Senate. His administration did the best that it could with Congress. Summers, Romer, and Bernstein told Obama that from an economic standpoint, there was no danger of doing too much stimulus. A bigger stimulus would have bigger multiplier effects. In late 2009 Romer and Bernstein wanted another round of stimulus spending, which yielded one speech calling for a $50 billion transportation infrastructure bill and nothing else. Obama judged, in the face of the Tea Party explosion, that congressional leaders had no more stomach for employment spending. Bernstein and Romer lamented that the same thing was true of Obama. Instead of pushing for an infrastructure bill modeled on the New Deal's Works Progress Administration, Obama backed off the Keynesian gas. Romer later recalled, after resigning from the administration, that Obama made a premature exit from trying to break the unemployment spiral: "I remember that fall of 2009 as a very frustrating one. It was very clear to me that the economy was still struggling, but the will to do more to help it had died."[31]

Summers agreed with Krugman that the stimulus should have been over $1 trillion. In his telling, however, the administration tried hard to get $900 billion; it was simply untrue that Obama settled for less than what was politically achievable. The administration took as much as it could get from the sixtieth Senate vote. Plus, Krugman was a contrarian anyway. Summers explained that Krugman always criticized whoever was president or Treasury secretary, and he always gravitated to "opposition and dramatic policy." Krugman blasted the early Clinton administration from the right, he savaged the Bush administration from the left, and now he blasted Obama from the left, said Summers: "The only politician I remember him praising in the last sixteen years is John Edwards." Krugman, in reply, allowed: "When things go crazy, my instinct is to go radical on policy, and Larry's is to be a little more cautious."[32]

Caution prevailed on employment spending, which saved or created more than three million jobs in the summer of 2010, and on taking care of the banks, where Summers felt vindicated by the recovery of the megabanks. The banking system was paralyzed when Obama took office because the banks had $2 trillion worth of toxic assets that they refused to resolve or, often, even to acknowledge. The big private equity funds and hedge funds refused to pay more than 30 cents on the dollar for the mortgage bundles, and the banks were afraid to book such huge losses on their holdings. The banks held out for at least 60 cents while sitting on their bailouts. Obama judged that to break the deflationary spiral, his administration had to dispose of the toxic debt. The big bankers, however, having lived with phony balance sheets for their entire careers, had other priorities.[33]

One option for the Obama administration was Paulson's original plan, which Krugman aptly dubbed "cash for trash," this time with more public accountability. A second option that Geithner briefly considered was to ramp up the insurance approach, "ring-fencing" bad assets by providing federal guarantees against losses. But these were more-of-the-same options that coddled the banks and did not solve the valuation problem. A third option, the "bad bank" model, created transitional banks to soak up bad debt. Here the risk of getting prices wrong was daunting, assuming that assets were valued immediately. If the government overpaid for toxic securities, taxpayers were cheated; if it did not overpay and the banks took mark-to-market prices, many were sure to fail. In theory, a bad bank could have stalled on the price issue, waiting until values rose, but Geithner and FDIC chair Sheila Bair judged that that smacked too much of alchemy, floating assets into ether.

For two months Geithner made convoluted proposals and Summers tore them apart; Geithner got frustrated that it never worked the other way around, since Summers made no proposals. For a while, Summers and Romer leaned toward taking over a couple of big banks to put the fear of nationalization into Wall Street and to ward off excessive risk taking in the future. Geithner called this "the Old Testament option," sacrificing a bank or two to appease the nation's wrath. Krugman and Stiglitz pushed hard for selective nationalization, but Summers feared that it might cause a run on the banks; also, he disliked Stiglitz. Finally on March 15 Obama told his economists to agree on something, and they settled on Geithner's "Aggregator Bank," which blended the original Paulson plan with some elements of the bad bank topped off with an auction scheme to find private buyers for the toxic debt. Geithner called it the Public-Private Investment Partnership plan. The centerpiece of the plan was, and is, a $1 trillion public-private investment fund run by the FDIC and Treasury Department. The government is teaming up with hedge funds and private equity firms, subsidizing up to 95 percent of deals partnered with them, to buy up bad loans and toxic securities. The FDIC holds auctions and does most of the partnering work.[34]

So far it isn't working very well, although the program is so opaque that it's hard to monitor. The Geithner plan is the most cumbersome and non-transparent of the main options. It is obsequious to Wall Street. It coddles the banks and showers shareholders with taxpayer-funded gifts. It offers a taxpayer guarantee to hedge funds and private equity firms that they won't lose money if they get in. Essentially, it is a scheme to bribe private investors to buy the bad loans and toxic securities for more than they're worth. The big banks are balking at it anyway because they want to rebuild the casino without being hampered by government restrictions.

In the early months of the Obama administration the FDIC created a pilot program featuring cheap financing for investors to buy up bad assets, which it cancelled in June 2009 after the banks proved unwilling to book losses on their holdings. The previous month, the Federal Reserve stress-tested nineteen banks, and only one needed another cash infusion to survive the summer. This was a milestone achievement that vindicated much of Geithner's and Paulson's handiwork. But the banks passed the tests by putting off their day of reckoning. The bailouts saved them from crashing, which made the banks feel better, which made them averse to dealing with the root cause of their illness—their phony balance sheets. Somehow it is never quite time to get their house in order.[35]

And so the two best chances to cut the banks down to size came and went, with a third still to come, also not taken. The best opportunity was in September 2008, but Henry Paulson passed on it. The second opportunity was in the spring of 2009, but Obama opted for continuity. The third opportunity came with the debate over the financial reform bill a year later, but Obama preferred the Volcker Rule, which passed only in a gutted form.

Notes

1. U.S. Department of Labor, Bureau of Labor Statistics, "Employment Situation Summary," December 2008, www.bls.gov; "U.S. Job Losses Hit Record in 2008," *BBC News*, January 9, 2009; Laura A. Kelter, "Substantial Job Losses in 2008: Weakness Broadens and Deepens across Industries," *Monthly Labor Review* (March 2009), 20–26.

2. U.S. Department of Labor, Bureau of Labor Statistics, "Employment Situation Summary, April 2009," and U.S. Department of Labor, Bureau of Labor Statistics, "Employment Situation Summary, November 2009," www.bls.gov; Kelter, "Substantial Job Losses in 2008," 24–26; Rex Nutting, "Job Losses Accelerate to 263,000 in September," *Wall Street Journal: Market Watch* (October 2, 2009), www.marketwatch.com.

3. For a detailed account of the fall of Bear Stearns, see William D. Cohan, *House of Cards: A Tale of Hubris and Wretched Excess on Wall Street* (New York: Anchor Books, 2010).

4. Andrew Malcolm, "Phil Gramm's 'Whiners' Comment Causes John McCain a Headache," *Los Angeles Times* (July 10, 2008), http://latimesblogs.latimes.com.

5. Gary Dorrien, "Back to the Subject," Public Broadcasting System, *Religion and Ethics Newsweekly: One Nation*, September 9, 2008.

6. Henry M. Paulson Jr., *On the Brink: Inside the Race to Stop the Collapse of the Global Financial System* (New York: Business Plus, 2010), quote 18.

7. See Cohan, *House of Cards*, 56–154.

8. Andrew Ross Sorkin, *Too Big to Fail: The Inside Story of How Wall Street and Washington Fought to Save the Financial System—and Themselves* (New York: Penguin Books, 2010), 299–307; Paulson Jr., *On the Brink*, 171–221.

9. Paulson Jr., *On the Brink*, quotes 205, 204; Sorkin, *Too Big to Fail*, 339–340.

10. Paulson Jr., *On the Brink*, quote 222.

11. Paulson Jr., *On the Brink*, 222–270; Sorkin, *Too Big to Fail*, 376–450; Bernanke quote, "The Reckoning—As Crisis Spiraled, Alarm Led to Action," *New York Times*, www.nytimes.com/2008/10/02/business.

12. Paulson Jr., *On the Brink*, 285–299; Sorkin, *Too Big to Fail*, 490–493; Jonathan Alter, *The Promise: President Obama, Year One* (New York: Simon & Schuster, 2010), 3–10.

13. Alter, *The Promise*, quotes 13; see Paulson Jr., *On the Brink*, 299–300.

14. Paulson Jr., *On the Brink*, 338–356; Joe Nocera and Edmund L. Andrews, "Running a Step Behind as a Crisis Raged," *New York Times* (October 23, 2008), A1, 20; Gary Dorrien, *Economy, Difference, Empire: Social Ethics for Social Justice* (New York: Columbia University Press, 2010), 156–157.

15. "Bailed-Out Banks," n.d., CNNMoney.com; Rick Newman, "The Best and Worst Bailed-Out Banks," *U.S. News and World Report* (June 9, 2009), USNews.com; Paulson Jr., *On the Brink*, 360–364.

16. See Nocera and Andrews, "Running a Step Behind," A1, 20; Edmund L. Andrews, "U.S. Plans $800 Billion in Lending to Ease Crisis," *New York Times* (November 26, 2008), A1, 20; Michael Lewis and David Einhorn, "The End of the Financial World as We Know It," *New York Times* (January 4, 2009), 9–10; Eric Dash, Louise Story, and Andrew Ross Sorkin, "Bank of America to Receive $20 Billion More," *New York Times* (January 16, 2009), B1, 6.

17. Edmund L. Andrews and Eric Dash, "Deeper Hole for Bankers: Need Keeps Growing for Funds in Bailout," *New York Times* (January 14, 2009), A1, 22; Eric Lipton and Ron Nixon, "A Bank with Its Own Woes Lends Only a Trickle of Bailout," *New York Times* (January 14, 2009), A1, 24; David M. Herszenhorn, "Senate Releases Second Portion of Bailout Fund," *New York Times* (January 16, 2009), A1, 16.

18. See Alter, *The Promise,* 28–29; Ron Suskind, *Confidence Men: Wall Street, Washington, and the Education of a President* (New York: HarperCollins, 20110), 27–28, 133–158.

19. See Louis Uchitelle, "Glass-Steagall vs. the Volcker Rule," *New York Times* (January 22, 2010); "Former U.S. Treasury Secretaries Endorse Volcker Rule in *Wall Street Journal,*" *Bloomberg BusinessWeek* (February 21, 2010), www.businessweek.com.

20. This section adapts material from Gary Dorrien, *Economy, Difference, Empire,* 152–154.

21. See Alan Greenspan, *The Age of Turbulence: Adventures in a New World* (New York: Penguin, 2008), 366–373; Peter Coy, "Are Derivatives Dangerous?" *Business-Week* (March 31, 2003), www.businessweek.com, accessed December 1, 2008; see R. Batra, *Greenspan's Fraud: How Two Decades of His Policies Have Undermined the Global Economy* (New York: Palgrave Macmillan), 2005; Gary Dorsch, "Weapons of Financial Mass Destruction," Financial Sense University, October 8, 2008, www .financialsense.com, accessed October 30, 2008; "A Nuclear Winter?" *The Economist* (September 18, 2008), 12.

22. See Thomas Zambito and Greg B. Smith, "Feds Say Bernard Madoff's $50 Billion Ponzi Scheme Was Worst Ever," *Daily News* (December 13, 2008), 2; Thomas L. Friedman, "The Great Unraveling," *New York Times* (December 17, 2008), A39; Lewis and Einhorn, "End of the Financial World," 9–10.

23. See Christina and David Romer, *Do Tax Cuts Starve the Beast? The Effect of Tax Changes on Government Spending,* Brookings Papers on Economic Activity, Spring 2009; Christina Romer and Chang-Tai Hsieh, "Was the Federal Reserve Constrained by the Gold Standard During the Great Depression?" *Journal of Economic History* (March 2006); Christina Romer, "The Great Depression," *Encyclopaedia Britannica* (December 2003); Christina Romer, "The Nation in Depression," *Journal of Economic Perspectives* (Spring 1993).

24. See Shan Wang, "Faust Vetoes Tenure Decision," *Harvard Crimson* (May 22, 2008); David Warsh, "Old Embers, New Flames," *economicprincpals.com: an independent weekly* (June 15, 2008), www.economicprincipals.com/issues/2008, accessed March 21, 2011; Alter, *The Promise,* "holy," 88; Richard Wolffe, *Revival: The Struggle for Survival Inside the Obama White House* (New York: Crown Publishers, 2010), "things," 177.

25. Alter, *The Promise,* quote 88; Lawrence Summers, "Obama's Down Payment: A Stimulus Must Aim for Long-Term Results," *Washington Post* (December 28, 2008), www.washingtonpost.com/wp-dyn/content; Suskind, *Confidence Men,* 152–54.

26. Christina Romer and Jared Bernstein, "The Job Impact of the American Recovery and Reinvestment Plan," January 10, 2009, http://krugman.blogs.nytimes .com/2009/01/10.

27. See Brian Wingfield, "Geithner's Tax Troubles Are Serious," *Forbes* (January 13, 2009), www.forbes.com; Byron York, "Geithner Can't Explain His Failure to Pay Taxes," *National Review Online* (January 19, 2009), www.nationalreview.com.

28. Recovery.gov—Tracking the Money, www.recovery.gov, accessed March 25, 2011; Kimberly Amadeo, "The Economic Stimulus Package," About.com, March 2,

2011, http://useconomy.about.com; "American Recovery and Reinvestment Act of 2009," *Wikipedia*, http://en.wikipedia.org/wiki; "ARRA of 2009: Questions and Answers," www.womenof.com/ARRA.

29. Paul Krugman, "Stimulus Gone Bad," *New York Times* (January 25, 2008); Paul Krugman, press conference, Willamette University, January 30, 2009, quoted in Aliza Earnshaw, "Krugman: Stimulus Needs to Be Twice as Big," *Portland Business Journal* (January 30, 2009), www.bizjournals.com/portland/stories.

30. Paul Krugman, "Bang for the Buck (wonkish)," Krugman blog, "The Conscience of a Liberal," January 13, 2009, http://krugman.blogs.nytimes.com/2009/01/13; Krugman, "Failure to Rise," *New York Times* (February 13, 2009), quote, www.nytimes.com/2009/02/13.

31. "Coulda Woulda Shouldas from White House Alumni," *New York* (July 11, 2011), 18, 20; see Frank Rich, "Obama's Original Sin," *New York* (July 11, 2011), 14–22; Suskind, *Confidence Men*, 353–354.

32. Benjamin Wallace-Wells, "Paul Krugman's Lonely Crusade," *New York* (May 2, 2011), 24–27, 86–87, quotes 86; see Wolffe, *Revival*, 179.

33. Shamim Adam, "Obama's Economic Stimulus Program Created Up to 3.3 Million Jobs, CBO Says," *Bloomberg News* (August 24, 2010), www.bloomberg.com/news.

34. U.S. Treasury Department, "The Public-Private Investment Partnership," Track the Stimulus: All You Want to Know About the Economic Stimulus Plans, http://trackthestimulus.com; Edmund L. Andrews, Eric Dash, and Graham Bowley, "Toxic Asset Plan Foresees Big Subsidies for Investors," *New York Times* (March 21, 2009), A1, B4; Alter, *The Promise*, 206.

35. Jim Puzzanghera and E. Scott Reckard, "Bank 'Stress Test' Results Hint at Economic Recovery," *Los Angeles Times* (May 8, 2009), A1; Graham Bowley, "Two Banks Cited in Stress Tests Find Investors," *New York Times* (May 9, 2009), B1; Edmund L. Andrews, "Plan to Help Banks Clear Their Books Is Halted," *New York Times* (June 4, 2009), B3; Gretchen Morgenson and Don Van Natta Jr., "Even in Crisis, Banks Dig in for Battle Against Regulation," *New York Times* (June 1, 2009), A1, 13.

5

Timidly Bold Obamacare

THE IRONIES OF OBAMA ARE NOWHERE THICKER than in his campaign to achieve national health insurance. Shortly after he pushed through the stimulus package and decided to save America's automobile industry, Obama rolled the dice on national health insurance—an act of astonishing boldness and ambition.

History and the current politics were forbidding. Eight presidents before him—Theodore Roosevelt, Franklin Roosevelt, Harry Truman, Lyndon Johnson, Richard Nixon, Gerald Ford, Jimmy Carter, and Bill Clinton—had tried and failed in this area. The polling data were unfavorable. All of Obama's top officials and advisers were opposed to taking on health care in his first year. From the outset Obama described health care reform as a "herculean lift" politically; later he bemoaned that it was also a "Rubik's Cube" of interrelated puzzles. No nation has ever reformed something as huge and unwieldy as the U.S. health system. Obama took for granted that pursuing national health insurance would cost him 10 to 15 points in popularity. Then he went for it in a cautious, political, piecemeal, and uninspiring way—and achieved more reform than anybody before him except Johnson.[1]

The ironies began with the fact that Obama was not ardent in this area when he began his presidential campaign. Hillary Clinton had a more ambitious health care plan than did Obama, one featuring mandated coverage that he opposed, and she spoke with greater passion about it. Obama played up his opposition to requiring individuals to buy health insurance. Later he stuck to this position while competing against McCain. But somewhere on the campaign trail, the stories that people told Obama about losing their health insurance after they got sick, losing their home to pay for medical treatment, and losing their health coverage upon losing their job changed his thinking and feeling about this issue.

In the later campaign he spoke every day, and with greater feeling, about the necessity of overhauling the health care system. He changed the way that he viewed his prospective presidency, becoming someone who was willing to risk everything for health care reform. With some prodding by his campaign staff, Obama told audiences that he remembered keenly the heartbreak that he felt at watching his mother struggle with medical bills as she lay dying of cancer. Ann Dunham died in November 1995, two months after Obama launched his first campaign for elected office. She had health insurance that paid her hospital bills directly but was denied disability coverage for her uncovered expenses. On the campaign trail, Obama did not distinguish between medical coverage and disability insurance, suggesting, wrongly, that his mother had been denied medical coverage. But the memory of his mother's anguish was real, as was her exclusion from disability coverage based on a preexisting condition. Running for president, Obama told audiences that help was on the way. He would abolish the worst practices of the insurance companies and get (nearly) everybody covered. Usually he added that doing so was an economic imperative, not just a moral one. America had to get control of its Medicare and Medicaid costs; otherwise the country was going to drown in debt when the Boomer generation retired. By the time that he took office, Obama had changed his mind about mandating coverage because he had converted to the view that the only way to reform the system and convince insurers to extend coverage to everyone was to give insurers the largest possible pool of healthy customers.[2]

National Health Insurance: The Backstory

That was an American way of conceiving the issue; elsewhere it is usually about the right of citizens to medical care whether or not they have the money for it. In the 1880s, Otto von Bismarck established the world's first system of national health insurance, in Germany. In 1911, Britain took a similar path, covering most workers and their dependents, and by 1913 ten European nations had adopted some form of compulsory health insurance. After World War II, most European nations either adopted or strengthened universal health insurance systems. In 1948 the General Assembly of the United Nations, in phrases ringing of European social democracy, declared in its Universal Declaration of Human Rights that access to health care is a basic economic right:

Everyone has the right to a standard of living adequate for the health and well-being of himself and of his family, including food, clothing, housing and medical care and necessary social services, and the right to security in the event of unemployment, sickness, disability, widowhood, old age or other lack of livelihood in circumstances beyond his control.[3]

Eleanor Roosevelt, chairing the U.N. Human Rights Commission, was the principal force behind the Declaration of Human Rights. Sadly, her nation's government did not ratify its sections on social and economic rights, including the right to health. But the USA did not lack movements contending that no one should go broke because of an illness. Theodore Roosevelt's Bull Moose Party campaigned in 1912 for health insurance for industrial workers. Between 1916 and 1920, fifteen state legislatures introduced health insurance bills, and in 1917 the social insurance committee of the American Medical Association (AMA) called for serious study of various forms of social insurance.[4]

However, public interest in health insurance faded after the United States entered World War I, partly for its association with foreign radicalisms, and the AMA called for no more experiments in it. In 1934 the New Deal resurrected the idea of health insurance at the national level, responding to the crisis of hospitals battered by the Depression. Franklin Roosevelt's Committee on Economic Security debated whether to include national health insurance in its proposal for Social Security. Roosevelt, believing that he could get health insurance in a subsequent bill, decided not to jeopardize the Social Security Act of 1935 by including health care. After Social Security passed, a second group of New Dealers—the Technical Committee on Medical Care—pushed for a program of compulsory health insurance at the state level partly supported by federal subsidies. This initiative would have allowed states to decide whether to participate in the program. But by then the AMA had become a lobbying powerhouse. It protested that government health insurance would strip physicians of their autonomy; Republicans opposed any expansion of the New Deal; and Southern Democrats joined forces with Republicans, protesting that health insurance would lead to racially integrated hospitals.[5]

Government health insurance, by 1938, was an orphan of the New Deal, signaling that the creative phase of the New Deal was over. The failure to fold health insurance into Social Security spurred employers and hospitals to develop private health insurance alternatives. Before the 1920s there were numerous attempts to develop private insurance schemes at local levels; in 1929 Baylor University Hospital in Texas made a breakthrough, founding the first Blue Cross plan for hospital care. By 1945 about one-fourth of the American population had some kind of private health insurance, usually a Blue Cross plan for hospitalization and/or a Blue Shield plan for physician services. By

1950 slightly more than half of Americans had private health insurance, as employers got federal tax breaks for providing insurance plans, plus healthier workers.[6]

Meanwhile Roosevelt had not given up on getting everyone covered. During World War II, he told aides that he wanted to resurrect national health insurance as soon as the war ended, as part of an economic bill of rights. The Wagner-Murray-Dingell Senate bill of 1943 offered a prototype, proposing a national system of comprehensive health insurance operating as part of Social Security. Reformers were finished with the small ambitions and dubious politics of state-based proposals. Three months after World War II ended, Roosevelt's successor, Harry Truman, made the Wagner-Murray-Dingell proposal the centerpiece of his Fair Deal agenda—a single insurance system covering all Americans that allowed doctors and hospitals to choose their method of payment.

The Fair Deal got off to a rocky start, as Truman struggled to make the transition from a wartime economy and Republicans won control over both houses of Congress in 1946. Truman fought back in the election of 1948, campaigning against Republicans for opposing national health insurance, which helped him retain the presidency and regain Democratic control of Congress. But the very forces that blocked national health insurance in the late 1930s were better organized in the late 1940s, and they benefited from a spike in public fears about Communism. Republicans and the AMA railed against "socialized medicine," Southern Democrats still loathed government health insurance as a threat to segregation, the private health insurance industry resisted competition from the government, and the trade unions split over it. Some unions, such as the United Auto Workers, believed they could do better by bargaining with their deep-pocketed employers.[7]

National health insurance smacked too much of European Socialism, if not Communism, to vast sectors of the American electorate. In 1957 young John Dingell, having taken over his father's congressional seat two years earlier after the elder Dingell's death, reproposed his father's health insurance bill. Afterward, Dingell began every session of Congress by putting the bill in play; when Obama took office in 2008, Dingell was eighty-two years old and still memorializing his father's belief in the right to health care.

The creation of a middle-class economy in the 1950s and 1960s caused reformers to trim their sails on health insurance, aiming at parts of the issue that employer-based coverage did not address—the elderly and the poor. The Kerr-Mills Act of 1960 provided federal grants to states to cover health costs for the elderly poor, but by 1963 only twenty-eight states participated in the program, and many states did the minimum to qualify for it. John F. Kennedy, in 1962, advocated legislation establishing hospital coverage for seniors—Medicare—but Southern Democrats in the House of Representatives killed it.

That set the stage for the major U.S. health reform of the twentieth century, the establishment of Medicare and Medicaid in 1965. The AFL-CIO pressed hard for Medicare, describing it as a public Blue Cross program that unions could not provide for retirees. Lyndon Johnson, upon winning the presidency in his own right, pushed a three-layered bill through Congress: Medicare Part A (for hospital and home health care), Medicare Part B (for physician care), and Medicaid (a separate program providing limited coverage for the poor and disabled). Part A was the Democrats' longstanding hospital insurance proposal; Part B refashioned a Republican proposal for voluntary insurance subsidized out of general revenue; Medicaid was tacked on at the last minute; and Medicare and Medicaid were incorporated into the Social Security Act.

This victory, though monumental, left millions of Americans under the age of sixty-five with no health coverage. It set off a sharp increase in health care costs, which rose from 4 percent of the federal budget in 1965 to 11 percent in 1973, contributing to the inflationary spiral of the early 1970s. And it created a new political problem for advocates of national health insurance—the existence of a large class of beneficiaries that no longer had a stake in providing coverage for everyone.[8]

In 1971, Senator Ted Kennedy, taking aim at the first and second problems, proposed a universal single-payer plan to be financed entirely through payroll taxes. President Richard Nixon, countering Kennedy's Health Security Act, offered a plan of his own in 1971 and expanded it in 1974 as the Comprehensive Health Insurance Plan (CHIP). Nixon's plan called for universal coverage and voluntary employer participation, with employers contributing 65 percent of the premium cost. Others proposed plans with variable financing schemes. Kennedy, recalculating the politics, teamed with Wilbur Mills in 1974 to propose a comprehensive plan featuring an employer mandate and personal cost-sharing. The new Kennedy plan relied on private insurers, as in Nixon's scheme, giving up on single-payer simplicity, but Kennedy required employers to participate, and he financed his plan with a payroll tax.

In the spring of 1974 it seemed likely that Congress would pass one of these bills or a conflation of them. The House and Senate still had moderate Republicans; the U.S. Chamber of Commerce supported Nixon's plan; the AMA toned down its opposition to the whole business; and Democrats split over supporting the Kennedy-Mills bill or waiting for a larger Democratic majority in the next Congress to pass a stronger bill. If not for the Watergate scandal that ended Nixon's presidency, some version of national health insurance might have passed in the summer of 1974. As it was, Nixon self-destructed, a spectacle that consumed Congress through the summer. President Gerald

Ford briefly supported Nixon's health insurance plan, and other compromise bills were proposed. But the political moment to do something big and bipartisan had passed. Ford dropped comprehensive health insurance, opting for a fiscal austerity agenda that he called Whip Inflation Now, and Kennedy hoped for a Democratic president who would revive the issue.

Instead he got Jimmy Carter, who supported comprehensive national health insurance while campaigning for president in 1976 and dropped it shortly after entering the White House. Carter focused on containing health care costs, arguing that national health insurance had to wait for cost reforms and a stronger economy. Kennedy countered with a comprehensive plan in which private insurers competed for customers. Carter responded with a plan featuring a basic package of benefits provided by businesses, an expansion of public coverage for the poor and elderly, and a new public corporation that sold coverage to everyone else. In some ways this proposal to create a public corporation was actually bolder than Kennedy's plan, although Carter projected a distant launch date for it, 1983. None of it mattered because neither of these plans had any chance of passing the post-Watergate Congress. Congressional committees were decentralized, health reform was parceled out to four committees in the House, and any member on the House floor could amend a bill. More importantly, the stagflation of the Carter years—a deadly combination of recession and inflation—killed the issue for years to come and paved the way for the presidencies of Ronald Reagan and George H. W. Bush.[9]

Reagan and Bush racked up record federal deficits and buried the dream of national health insurance, although Bush, dealing belatedly with the deficits, broke his vow not to raise taxes, which helped to make him a one-term president. Twelve years of Reagan and Bush fueled record disparities between the lower and upper classes, while middle-class wages remained stagnant. This toxic combination revived national health insurance as a national issue. By 1991, nearly 40 million Americans had no health insurance, and more than 22 million were underinsured. That year Harris Wofford won a special election for the U.S. Senate in Pennsylvania by advocating Kennedy-style health care reform, which set off an explosion of proposals for play-or-pay employer mandates, single-payer plans, managed competition approaches, and expanding private plans. National health insurance was emphatically back in play. Even Bush, running for a second term in 1992, was forced to come up with a reform plan revolving around health care tax credits and purchasing pools. Bill Clinton, running against Bush, held out for a managed competition approach and urged Americans to summon the courage to change.

In January 1993, a few days after Clinton was inaugurated, he announced that he was appointing Hillary Rodham Clinton to direct a task force on national health reform that would submit a plan to Congress in one hundred days. Like other national policy-making councils in previous administrations, this group would meet in private until the plan was unveiled. Hillary Clinton and Clinton aide Ira Magaziner conferred with thirty-four working groups comprising over 600 experts, aides, and officials before devising a plan that closely resembled the managed competition model on which Bill Clinton had campaigned.

A few things were wrong with this proposal, and many things went wrong. The timeline was too ambitious, overreaching to match Franklin Roosevelt's fabled first one hundred days, and Clinton had no strategy for what would happen after he introduced the plan to Congress. By appointing his spouse to head up the task force, Clinton invited a barrage of antifeminist, anti-Hillary vitriol from the Right, which ensued immediately, and he set off charges of nepotism from a wider range of critics. Clinton tried hard to appease the insurers, large employers, doctors, and hospitals, but these groups fought against aspects of the plan that conflicted with their interests. Early in the process, one of Clinton's aides, fretting that Clinton's boat was overloaded with unfriendly interest groups, warned that "our boat may sink from its own weight." That was dead on. Moreover, by tying himself so closely to his spouse's proposal, Clinton ensured that he and Hillary would be blamed for every problem that the reform plan encountered. Clinton sacrificed crucial negotiating space by identifying unequivocally with the plan. Clinton aide Paul Starr later confirmed that this was not merely a public posture, as the Clinton health plan was emphatically the work of both Clintons. In any case, delivering a finished product to Congress was not very political. New York Democratic senator Daniel Patrick Moynihan, who chaired the Senate Finance Committee, gave a preview of what the Clinton plan was in for by opining that America had no health care crisis and that the Clintons should have consulted with him before hatching a colossal solution to small problems.[10]

In retrospect, the Clinton plan had no chance of passing. Yet for all its problems, it seemed to have a real chance when Bill Clinton presented it to a joint session of Congress on September 22, 1993. The basic idea of the plan was to build a public-private partnership between government agencies and the existing health insurance companies. It called for universal coverage, employer and individual mandates, competition between private insurers, and government regulation to keep costs down.[11]

The early polls and Democratic response were mostly favorable. The Clintons were widely lauded for devising a market-based reform that achieved nearly universal coverage without hurting the insurance companies. Hillary Clinton, testifying to Congress for several days on the scope and mechanics of the plan, gave a commanding performance and was showered with praise. The Clinton presidency, after nine months of turbulence and extremely hostile accusations, seemed to have turned a corner.

Rumors about Clinton's sexual infidelities were already part of his public persona when he assumed office, and they escalated in December 1993 when David Brock published a salacious piece in the *American Spectator*, based on the gossip of Arkansas state troopers, that depicted Clinton as a promiscuous sociopath and Hillary as a foulmouthed harpy who cared only about power. Brock's article rocketed far beyond the Right's echo chamber of Clinton bashing, inspiring many imitators and ending Clinton's first year in office very badly. Clinton had started his presidency badly, by blundering into a new policy on gays and lesbians in the military, Don't Ask, Don't Tell. Then the Republican Right recycled an erroneous story that had withered during the campaign, charging that the Clintons exploited their relationship with a savings and loan operator, Jim McDougal, in a fraudulent real estate deal in Arkansas. There was never anything to this story about Whitewater property, but Clinton's enemies stoked it until the day before his last day in office, when he and Hillary were cleared of all wrongdoing. Legally, Whitewater opened the door to all the subsequent Clinton scandals. In July 1993, when associate White House counsel Vincent Foster committed suicide, right-wingers upped the ante on Whitewater, claiming that Clinton and/or Whitewater drove Foster to suicide or that Clinton had him killed. Christian Right leaders Pat Robertson and Jerry Falwell, radio superstar Rush Limbaugh, and *New York Times* columnist William Safire pursued the Foster story relentlessly and often ghoulishly.[12]

In August Clinton pushed through a historic deficit reduction plan that laid the foundation for his later budget surpluses. Clinton increased tax revenue by $240 billion by raising taxes on the wealthiest 1.2 percent of Americans and by exacting a 4.3 cent federal gas tax. This package cut the deficit in half in one year and set off the private investment wealth explosion of the 1990s. In 1993, however, the plan won zero votes among the 167 House Republicans and zero votes among the 44 Senate Republicans. Republican leaders declared that Clinton's budget was a disaster that would set off a recession. Texas Republican Phil Gramm warned that its impact would be "devastating," and Georgia Republican Newt Gingrich claimed that Clinton's tax increase, besides leading to a recession, would increase the deficit too.

At the time that Clinton proposed to reform health care, he was already besieged, personally and politically—tagged by the Right as a left-wing con man with a shrewish wife from hell, neither of whom belonged anywhere near the White House, and by much of the Left as a slick opportunist who cared only about his career. Clinton's vindication had to wait until after the midterm elections of 1994, in which House and Senate Democrats were routed mainly because of a health care debacle, the gun issue, and a gusher of Clinton bashing.

Very briefly, Clinton's health reform plan sparked a premature hope of a break in this narrative of illegitimacy and disaster. Even Clinton-haters admitted that both Clintons were gifted policy wonks. But the Clinton plan was exceedingly complex and bureaucratic, running 1,342 pages. It was very much a creation of the White House and the president himself. It was proposed by a president who had won 43 percent of the popular vote and who thus lacked adequate leverage to achieve anything this big. It was delivered to a Congress that resented having been excluded from the bill's authorship. And it evoked inspired opposition, especially from neoconservative activist Bill Kristol, the National Federation of Independent Businesses, the Health Insurance Association of America, and Gingrich's House Republicans, plus liberals who held out for single payer.

Kristol, in a much-quoted series of policy memos faxed to Republican leaders, made the case for outright obstruction, urging Republicans to oppose all health care proposals "sight unseen." The National Federation of Independent Businesses warned that an employer mandate would be deadly for small businesses. The Health Insurance Association of America spent $30 million on television ads depicting a fictional middle-class couple, Harry and Louise, who fretted over the dire consequences of health reform. "This plan forces us to buy our insurance through those new mandatory government health alliances," Louise complained. "Run by tens of thousands of new bureaucrats," Harry added. "Having choices we don't like is no choice at all," Louise replied. In unison, "They choose, we lose." These immediately famous ads drowned out the $150,000 spent by the Democratic National Committee, which countered that Harry and Louise were in no danger of losing anything and that covering 40 million Americans in need would be something worth doing.[13]

As it was, the Health Security Act of 1993 died in the Senate Finance Committee, where Moynihan, with an eye on history, explained that by saying there was no health care crisis, he had not meant to say there was no insurance crisis. Certainly, he allowed, there were problems with the insurance companies. However, the Clinton health plan would not work in the real world, and anyone who thought differently "doesn't live in it."[14]

Obama was a student of the Clinton health care debacle. He told aides that he would not have handed a plan carved in stone to Daniel Patrick Moynihan, and he would not have told New Jersey senator Bill Bradley that he needed no help drafting a health care bill. So Obama swung to the other extreme.

Obamacare in the Making

Obama took the opposite approach to a very similar plan. The fact that he tried to win the very thing that Clinton failed to get made him determined to pursue it differently. Two things were crucial to Obama's strategy—(1) allowing House and Senate Democrats (and, hopefully, some Republicans) to feel that they owned the bill and (2) enacting it quickly. Congress would not pass a big bill that it did not own, and speed was essential to getting anything passed. Unfortunately, these things contradicted each other, which forced Obama to decide between them. Had Obama pushed hard to get what he wanted through the Senate, he might have gotten a better bill, one containing a public option. As it was, he opted for Senate ownership and slowness, lost time, lost the initiative, lost Ted Kennedy's Senate seat, and settled for what he could get—which was far more than anyone before him for preretirement people in need.

In the early going, nobody on Obama's senior staff wanted to take up national health insurance except Melody Barnes, a legislative aide who had worked previously for Ted Kennedy. Biden and Axelrod opposed it vocally, citing the political hazards. Axelrod believed that a big education bill should be next. Obama's economists, led by Romer, argued that it was too soon to fight over health care, noting that Roosevelt did not propose Social Security until 1935. Emanuel didn't like the politics of the health care issue; he was opposed to Obama's newly expansive concept of it; and for a while he kept saying so even after Obama made up his mind that health care was next.

To get something going, Obama leaned on the only person who intersected his circle of family and close friends and his circle of close political advisers—Valerie Jarrett, who organized a White House conference of stakeholders, health care experts, and elected officials in March 2009. The expansion of the State Children's Health Insurance Program (SCHIP) had been achieved the previous month. This was the last remnant of the Clinton health care initiatives, which Bush had vetoed twice. Obama's advisers wanted to trumpet the SCHIP expansion and move to something else, warning that failing at health care reform would derail his entire agenda. Obama, reprising his campaign stump speech, told the March conference that getting people covered and getting health care costs under control were necessities for American society; the risk looked different if one recognized that America had to do it.

Medicare for everyone was off the table, Obama stipulated, and so was any plan that contributed to the deficit. The health insurance companies had to be part of the solution, and health reform had to pay for itself. All other reform proposals were in play. Obama made it clear that he wanted Republican support and that he was willing to fall short of achieving universal coverage. On other topics he tired of having to say the same thing over and over, but in this area, he was willing. He wanted as much as he could get, and he was willing to settle for it. He would not make the perfect the enemy of the good, unlike what he called his "bleeding heart liberal" friends. He was a big believer in partial victories that made a large difference.[15]

When Social Security was established, it covered less than 40 percent of senior citizens. It did not cover retired domestics, state employees, and farm-workers, and thus it covered very few African Americans. But it was worth establishing, contrary to Roosevelt's left-wing critics, and it got stronger in every succeeding decade. In 2009, health care reform had been dead for fifteen years. Obama was determined to win a major breakthrough on his watch, and he knew that he would never have more political capital than he held at that moment.

So Emanuel and Nancy-Ann DeParle, director of the White House Office of Health Reform, threw themselves into getting something done as quickly and pragmatically as possible. First they cut deals with health insurance companies, drug companies, and hospitals, co-opting a big piece of the coalition that defeated the Clinton plan. It helped that some major players in the industry were ready to position themselves as pro-reform, at least for a while, if only to forestall a public option (which scared them) or a single-payer system (which would put the health insurance companies out of business).

Obama persuaded some health industry officials to sponsor television ads endorsing health care reform. He spoke at the AMA convention and announced that he was open to negotiating about malpractice reform. He cut a breakthrough deal with the drug companies, which agreed to cut the cost of drugs by $80 billion over ten years and spend $150 million on television ads supporting health care reform. For a while, as the discounts and rebates piled up, it appeared that the very interest groups that had killed the Clinton plan would finance the implementation costs of the Obama plan. The Pharmaceutical Research and Manufacturers of America pledged $80 billion, hospitals pledged $150 billion, and the insurance industry pledged $100 billion. The AMA, breaking its nearly century-long tradition of opposing health reform, supported Obama's proposal to provide health insurance to most of the nation's uninsured, improve competition and choice in health care insurance, and promote prevention and wellness. This breakthrough was possible because the AMA had changed during the sixteen-year interval between the Clinton and Obama proposals. The old AMA was overwhelmingly male and Republican, demanding fee-for-service medicine and favoring doctors who worked for themselves. The new AMA was increasingly female and liberal, as doctors took salaried jobs in hospitals, criticized fee-for-service medicine, and gave priority to public health concerns. Most of the health care industry still opposed any reform, but Obama bought six months of breathing room by cutting divide-and-conquer deals that improved the industry's image.[16]

Meanwhile the U.S. Congress, despite being controlled by Democrats in both houses, proved more difficult to manage. Part of the problem was that Congress was long out of practice at actually making legislation. Both houses were habituated to precut deals that eliminated having to spend much time making arguments on the House and Senate floors. Health reform was huge, unwieldy, and messy, and it nearly died in the same place that it died previously, the Senate Finance Committee.

Max Baucus, a Democratic senator from Montana, chaired the Senate Finance Committee. He was a Democratic survivor in a red state who had nearly lost his seat in 1994 after supporting Clinton's 1993 crime bill, which included a ban on assault weapons. Baucus had played a key role in helping George W. Bush enact tax cuts for the wealthy, and he took pride in his good relations with conservative Republicans, especially Iowa senator Chuck Grassley and Wyoming senator Mike Enzi. He told Obama's aides that supporting health care was the hardest thing he had done in politics since taking on the National Rifle Association.

Baucus was committed to getting health reform through the Senate, in the absence of Kennedy, who was ailing with a brain tumor. When Obama took office, Baucus floated one of the better national health insurance proposals, stressing the necessity of getting control of costs and improving quality. Both of these goals, Baucus argued, were out of reach lacking a "new public plan option, similar to Medicare." In his scheme, the public option would offer the same level of benefits as private plans, but it would use its administrative advantages over private plans to hold down costs. After Obama announced that health reform was next, Baucus worked hard at crafting a bill, but he missed a May deadline, and he failed to produce one in June and July too. Obama, though frustrated, stuck with Baucus, who insisted that no bill was worth having that lacked Republican support.[17]

Inside the Senate Finance Committee, Grassley was slow-walking the bill to its grave. He wanted to support something called health reform, but only if it attracted significant Republican support. The two Republican senators from Maine, Olympia Snowe and Susan Collins, were plausible Republican votes in support of health care reform; Pennsylvania senator Arlen Specter had switched to the Democratic Party in April; Grassley was unwilling to be one of three Republican supporters. He was afraid of McConnell and his own base.

Baucus worked on Grassley, as did Obama, inviting him to the White House six times. Grassley asked Obama to say that he would sign a bill not containing a public option. Obama *was* willing to sign a bill lacking a public option, but he was not willing to say so at the time, since saying it would sell out the Democrats who regarded the public option as essential to real reform. In August, Obama asked Grassley if he would support the bill if all his specific demands were met. Grassley replied that probably he would not. Very few Republicans were willing to consider any bill that added more than three million people to the insured camp, and Grassley was not willing to oppose 90 percent of his party, even though he was already on bad terms with much of his state party. Baucus asked Obama for more time to work on Grassley, but Grassley broke away, playing the fear card.

Addressing a town meeting in August, Grassley declared that Obama's plan would set up "death panels" that "pulled the plug on Grandma." In 2003, the Medicare prescription drug bill had provided counseling on end-of-life issues and care. It passed with the votes of 204 Republican House members and 42 Republican Senators, including Grassley. Now Grassley was describing the same provision in the emerging health care bill as a plot to execute Grandma. At first, Baucus indulged his friend's fearmongering as red meat for the Republican base. But Grassley went on to stoke a national uproar over "death panels" and the very idea of health reform, claiming that "Obamacare" was an unqualified disaster that would negate individual rights and destroy the health care system. Baucus was stunned that Grassley chose to inflame public hysteria, attacking core features of the plan that Grassley had previously accepted in committee proceedings. For Baucus and Obama, the dream of a bipartisan deal was finally dispelled. Both had wasted precious months courting Republican allies, although for Obama, it was mostly a question of indulging Baucus.[18]

Baucus seemed to be stuck. He prized his moment and was not willing to yield his leadership role, yet he failed to push forward. In September, Obama's aides drafted their own bill and threatened to post it on the White House website, which forced Baucus's hand. A month later the Senate Finance Committee finally had a bill, winning one Republican vote in committee (Snowe), the same result that it could have achieved four months earlier. Meanwhile the country had erupted in a frenzy over death panels and socialized medicine, and the Senate champion of universal health care, Kennedy, died of a brain tumor. In early November the House adopted a reform bill with a weak version of the public option, attaining a victory margin of five votes and a single Republican supporter. On Christmas Eve morning, the Senate approved health reform by a vote of sixty to forty, with zero Republican supporters and no public option. There was some talk of cutting a reconciliation bill immediately after Christmas and passing it by January 5, but the White House pleaded exhaustion, so vacations were taken.

There was a $200 billion difference between the House and Senate bills. In early January the Democrats debated what to do about it. House Speaker Nancy Pelosi drove a hard bargain, telling Senate Democrats: "Here's our proposal. We don't have one. Our proposal is our position." House leaders were not interested in shrinking the bill or dumping the public option. Senate Democrats objected that the House bill topped the tripwire figure of $1 trillion over ten years; they also complained that House leaders were too stubborn to make deals or even to know how to go about it.[19]

They were still arguing on January 19, when the state of Massachusetts shock-ingly elected a Republican, Scott Brown, to replace Kennedy, and the Demo-crats lost their ability to muster a filibuster-proof sixty votes in the Senate. Many pundits declared that health reform was dead; always they noted the irony that losing Kennedy's vote killed it. For a while they seemed to be right.

Fearing Public Efficiency

The basic elements of so-called Obamacare had a long history in Democratic and even Republican politics. Republican stalwarts Bob Dole and Howard Baker had espoused them in the 1990s, and in 2009 these former Senate leaders took pride in having done so, speaking for the dream of a bipartisan reform. But by Obama's time only Democrats and progressive independents cared about people lacking health coverage, with precious few exceptions. Some plans recycled the Kennedy-Dingell Medicare for All Act of 2006 or California representative Pete Stark's AmeriCare Health Care Act of 2007, both of which focused on expanding Medicare. Other proposals featured strong or weak versions of the public option, and some got closer than others to universal coverage.[20]

The chief exception to the "Democrats only" rule, Mitt Romney, had to wear the exception as an albatross in the 2008 Republican presidential primaries. In 2006 Romney and the Massachusetts legislature adopted a near-universal coverage plan at the state level with a program featuring an individual mandate and government subsidies to make coverage affordable. The Massachusetts plan extended coverage to 98 percent of the state's popu-lation, and, overruling Romney's veto, it mandated employer responsibility for health care coverage. In these three respects the Massachusetts plan was a prototype for Obama's reform plan, but it did nothing to control costs—a fatal flaw from the Obama team's perspective.

By midsummer 2009, certain things were clear about the emerging health care bill. It would cover 30 million to 34 million out of the 47 million uninsured. It would compel employers and employees to buy insurance, offer subsidies to help the uninsured buy policies on new insurance exchanges, institute Medicare cuts and industry rebates for cost control, provide incentives for preventive care, and impose new regulations on the insurance companies, including bans on dropping people when they got sick and discriminating against people with preexisting conditions. That left three main issues to fight over: How should the government pay for implementing the reforms, which were estimated to cost between $700 billion and $1 trillion? How should the long-term costs of the reforms be contained? And should there be a public option?[21]

The third issue was more structural and ideological than the others, but it was crucial for dealing with the second issue. Public health insurance is more efficient than private health insurance. Public plans have lower administrative costs than private plans, they do not require profit margins, and they have greater ability than private plans to bargain for lower service costs and drug prices. For these reasons, public plans have a better track record than private insurance of holding down long-term costs, despite the fact that public plans are far more inclusive, treating the poorest and sickest customers that private insurers don't want. Obama affirmed that Medicare outperforms private insurance in limiting costs and in providing access. He supported the public option for these reasons. But he did not fight for it.

The public option, a plan designed by Yale political scientist Jacob Hacker in 2005 when Hacker taught at Berkeley, was formulated as a realistic alternative to the single-payer model. It offers a public plan that competes with private plans in national or regional purchasing pools. Since public insurance is more efficient than private insurance, the existence of a public plan would force private plans to become more efficient to be competitive. The public option is a hybrid approach that builds on the best elements of the existing system—Medicare and large group plans in the public and private systems. In theory, it does not lead to a universal Medicare program. However, if it were instituted, it might lead to a universal program. To progressives like me who support single payer, that is a point in favor of the public option. In 2009, however, the long-term logic of the public option was a frightening spectacle to the insurance industry, which did not want to compete with a government plan and which foresaw that a good government plan might very well put the private insurance companies out of business.[22]

Single payer basically means Medicare for everyone, without the co-pays and deductibles of the existing Medicare system. It is not socialized medicine, as in England or Spain, where doctors and hospitals work for the government. It does not violate the Takings Clause of the 5th Amendment, which bars the government from taking private property for public use without appropriate compensation, since it does not nationalize any private firms. The single-payer plan is a system of socialized health insurance similar to that of Canada, Australia, and most European nations. Essentially it is an extension and improvement of the Medicare system in which government pays for care that is managed and delivered in the private sector.[23]

Here the position regarding private health insurance companies is straightforward: We don't need them. We don't need a system that wastes $450 billion per year in redundant administrative costs and that, until Obama, left 47 million Americans without health coverage. We could do without a system that excludes people with preexisting medical conditions and limited economic resources. We don't need a system that cherry-picks profitable clients, dumps clients when they get sick, and drives the unprofitably ill into HMOs featuring lousy care and little choice. Businesses and other employers would do better not having to provide health coverage for their employees, who often end up underinsured. We could do better than a system that ties people fearfully to jobs they want to leave but can't afford to lose because they might lose their health coverage.

The moral principle underlying the single-payer model is equally straight-forward: Health care is a fundamental human right that should be available to all people regardless of their economic resources. A society that takes seriously this principle does not relegate the poor and underemployed to second-class care or status. The United States is the only Western democratic society that has not even tried to live up to this principle. When wealthy and middle-class people have to rely on the same health system as the poor, as they do through-out Europe, they use their political power to make sure it's a decent system.

But single-payer deliverance was not on the agenda for 2009 because the insurance companies were too powerful and politically aggressive to be eliminated. In July 2009 the House bill for a system that replaced for-profit insurance companies, H.R. 676, had seventy-nine cosponsors, and the Senate bill, S. 703, had only Vermont senator Bernie Sanders. The House bill, pro-posed by John Conyers Jr., funded a universalized Medicare by maintaining current federal and state funding for existing programs and by establishing an employer/employee payroll tax of 4.75 percent, a 5 percent health tax on the top 5 percent of income earners, a 10 percent tax on the top 1 percent of earners, and a stock transaction tax of 0.25 percent. It also closed corporate tax loopholes and repealed the Bush tax cuts for the highest income earners.[24]

In 2003 Obama supported single payer, and in 2006 he was still an advocate of opening a debate on single payer in the Senate. As a presidential candidate, however, and later as president, Obama warned that single payer was politi-cally impossible. If one were starting from scratch, he sometimes mused, a single-payer system might be the best option. As it was, America's very large and dysfunctional health system made up 14 percent of the nation's gross domestic product. Reinventing something that big and politically connected had no chance of happening in 2009.[25]

The best hope for attaining equality and savings was to institute a public Medicare-like option that competed with private plans. Though Obama gave no speeches on this subject in 2008, he advocated a public option in his cam-paign position paper, "Barack Obama's Plan for a Healthy America." There he argued that no American should be turned away from *any* insurance plan be-cause of an illness or preexisting condition, and that a public plan was needed to provide coverage of all essential medical services to individuals lacking access to group coverage and to raise the efficiency standard in the health care system as a whole. One of Obama's closest political colleagues, Tom Daschle, published a book on this subject in 2008, and much of Obama's campaign team and administrative staff consisted of former Daschle aides.[26]

There was a serious momentum for a public option when Obama announced that health care was next. The Baucus plan was widely cited among policy makers, and polling data were encouraging. Nearly two-thirds of respondents from a nationwide survey of 800 likely voters were favorable or very favorable; 47 percent were very favorable. Progressives angered at Obama's escalation in Afghanistan and his acquiescence to Wall Street perked up over health care, investing deeply in the public option. Paul Krugman urged that the entire battle over health care reform rested on a crucial either/ or—whether or not reform delivered a public plan.[27]

That was not quite right. The acid test was whether reform delivered a good public plan. A good public plan would be open to all individuals and employers that want to join. It would allow members to choose their own doctors. It would eliminate high deductibles. It would allow members to negotiate reimbursement rates and drug prices. The government would run it. And it would be backed up by tough cost controls and a requirement that all Americans have health coverage.

Why should private insurers be granted an exclusive right to provide health insurance for the vast majority of American citizens? Why should ordinary citizens not be able to buy the same health insurance as their congressional representatives? If public plans are more efficient and inclusive than private insurance, why should the public option be restricted to the poor? Public insurance is more efficient because it provides benefits for less than they cost through private insurance, public plans have lower administrative costs, they eliminate the profit factor, and they are able to bargain for lower service and drug costs. Medicare's average overhead cost is 3 percent, and provincial single-payer plans in Canada average 1 percent. By contrast, the overhead costs for self-insured large companies are 5 to 10 percent of premiums; HMOs range between 15 and 25 percent; companies in the small group market average 26 percent; and individual insurance averages 40 percent of premiums. Health insurance premiums more than doubled between 1999 and 2008, during the very period that private plans slashed benefits.[28]

Defenders of the private insurance industry sometimes contend that Medicare's true administrative costs must be higher than the official figures and that Medicare does not count the costs of collecting premiums and payroll taxes. In 2006, however, the Congressional Budget Office found that administrative costs under the public Medicare plan were less than 2 percent of expenditures, while private plans under Medicare registered administrative costs of 11 percent. Hacker stressed that this CBO analysis offered a nearly perfect comparison because it compared two plans operating under nearly the same rules. Moreover, even these numbers understated the lower costs of public insurance, as the General Accounting Office reported that in 2006, Medicare Advantage plans spent 83.3 percent of their revenue on medical expenses and 6.6 percent on profits—ringing up administrative costs of 16.7 percent. Obama, upon entering office, wanted to get rid of Medicare Advantage—a giveaway to the insurance industry that supplements basic Medicare, benefiting wealthier seniors. But that was another good idea with forbidding politics. Republicans and some Democrats slammed Obama for "slashing" Medicare and aiming to kill Grandma, which yielded some bizarre protests about keeping government out of Medicare.[29]

The House bill featured a public option for the uninsured, very much along the lines that Obama's campaign plan had envisaged. This was better than nothing, though it was a far cry from realizing the game-changing potential of the public option. A plan that wasn't open to everyone or that prevented choice or negotiation would have been a plan designed to fail. It would have been like Medicaid—poorly funded and managed because its beneficiaries lack political power. Even a weak plan, however, was threatening to the insurance companies, which made at least ten Senate Democrats cool to it. From the beginning, relying on Harry Reid's head count, Obama doubted that Senate Democrats could be whipped into line to support it. Then he made a huge mistake.

Obama did not announce that he considered the public option to be dispensable, but he did not fight for it either. He viewed the public option as a desirable means to an end, not as something essential to health care reform. Some of his aides were voluble on this subject, bitterly castigating progressives for exaggerating the importance of the public option. Emanuel was always ready to cut a deal, especially on health care. He told progressives that the public option was unnecessary and that they were "fucking crazy" if they thought otherwise. How could something that nobody had heard of until recently be so important? What really mattered was to cover as many people as possible and to eliminate the predatory policies of the health insurance companies. It seemed to Obama, and especially his staff, that progressives had lost perspective on what mattered.[30]

But progressives took seriously that health care reform had to get its arms around the problem of escalating costs, and they viewed the public option, correctly, as a breakthrough for savings and equality. Even a weak version of the public option had the potential to achieve universal coverage, and a strong version would have attracted millions of middle-class Americans who would have happily dumped their policies containing high deductibles and health exclusions. Given a real choice, millions of Americans would choose a German-style approach to health care, where a mixed public-private insurance system attains better care at a fraction of the American price. A good public plan would have been a magnet for health care workers who got into their line of work to serve human needs, not to be cogs in a profit machine.

The United States spends six times as much per capita on health care administration as the average for nations belonging to the Organisation for Economic Co-operation and Development (OECD). This enormous difference is due almost entirely to the commercial marketing and underwriting costs and the myriad of billing and review practices by which American insurance companies make a hugely profitable business out of something that should be a right of citizenship. The United States could save $50 billion per year on administrative waste by adopting a public plan or upwards of $400 billion per year by establishing a single-payer system.[31]

Obama realized that his base, which got him elected, was passionate about this issue. Progressives were upset at being dismissed on other issues and were determined to make a breakthrough on this one. So Obama did not tell his progressive base that he had decided not to fight for a public option. He stalled and prevaricated, wishing not to offend his core followers, which only made them angrier. They wanted to see him fight for a major cause. Emanuel thought that progressives should be mollified by an occasional harsh word against the insurance companies, which showed how little he comprehended people who believed in something. Many progressives who worked hard for Obama the first time vowed that they would not do it again after he let the public option die in the Senate. For many of them, winning was important, but trying was even more important; Obama settled too easily for a half loaf that he could win.

Along the way, the energy swung to the Right. The angry town meetings of August 2009 featured hysteria about death panels and socialized medicine. The Affordable Care Act was packed with cost control measures that cut $500 billion from Medicare spending, which Republicans attacked as an assault on Medicare. Then Kennedy died, Obama squeaked a reform bill out of the House and Senate, and Brown's victory in Massachusetts threw the bill into jeopardy.

Democrats outnumber Republicans in Massachusetts by three to one. Obama had defeated McCain in Massachusetts by 26 points. The White House had taken Kennedy's seat for granted, somehow not noticing, until it was too late, that Brown was closing the gap on a desultory Democratic candidate, Martha Coakley. McConnell, on the day after the Massachusetts election, explained what had happened—that even Massachusetts Democrats opposed "Obamacare," which McConnell described as a government takeover of the health care system that would slash Medicare by half a trillion dollars, raise taxes by the same amount, and drive up insurance rates. This pronouncement fell on the first anniversary of Obama's inauguration. It was repeated by scores of others, sometimes without the hyperbole about a government takeover. Fox News pundit Fred Barnes declared that Obamacare was dead "with not the slightest prospect of resurrection." Many Democrats agreed, and the White House took a beating in the media.[32]

Emanuel wanted to come back with a scaled-back bill, letting go of Obama's ambitious attempt to cover 34 million uninsured people. Eliminating the worst abuses of the insurance companies would be politically popular, Emanuel reasoned; even some Republicans might vote for that. Obama replied that merely eliminating the predatory policies of the insurance companies would not work, and it was not enough. Covering as many people as possible, though controversial, was the heart of real health reform. Moreover, the smaller reforms would not work if reform itself did not deliver more customers to the insurance companies.

The answer was for the House to swallow its pride and convictions and pass the Senate bill. Then the two parties would pass a reconciliation bill under budget rules of reconciliation that required only a simple majority. For some of Obama's aides, losing the sixtieth vote in the Senate was something of a relief, as it took the pressure off the White House to deliver a stronger bill. For two months, however, while Obama and Pelosi quietly rounded up House votes for the Senate plan, liberals blasted Obama for botching a historic opportunity, and he was roasted in the media for weak leadership. Obama barely mentioned health care reform in his State of the Union address, and he had to implore angry House Democrats not to make the good the enemy of what was still attainable.

In March the begging paid off, as the House reluctantly accepted the Senate bill, ringing up 219 Democratic votes and zero Republican votes, and overcoming 34 opposing Democrats. The Affordable Care Act enacted the largest reform ever of a health care system. Obama told the news media, "This isn't radical reform. But it is major reform. This legislation will not fix everything that ails our health care system. But it moves us decisively in the right direction. This is what change looks like."[33]

That got it about right. Obama had never claimed to pursue radical reform, and he settled for less reform than he might have won had he been willing to fight for a public option. For months the White House and Democratic Senate leadership took for granted that avoiding a filibuster was more important than the gains in equality and savings that a public option would have yielded. That was wrong and hard to swallow. Even a weak public option might have attained universal coverage, an enormous moral difference from leaving 13 million people with no health coverage. People who lack health coverage end up in emergency rooms. If they are lucky, they receive expensive care that could have been avoided had they received routine care. If they are unlucky, they are turned away as though their lives don't matter.

But covering 34 million people was a colossal achievement. No one should go bankrupt because of an illness. Obama risked his presidency in order to help the poorest and most vulnerable people in American society. He knew very well that doing so would pay few political dividends and would carry a huge political downside. He took for granted that opponents would legally challenge the mandate that makes reform affordable. The health system is a highly interconnected form of interstate commerce; everyone uses health care services one way or another; and Congress holds the right to regulate the insurance markets and the markets for health care services. There may be a majority in the electoral system and the courts that are willing to ensure that poor and vulnerable people are not excluded from having the medical system work for them. And perhaps there is not. Obama has put into play the very fundamental question: What kind of country should we want to be?

Notes

1. Jonathan Alter, *The Promise: President Obama, Year One* (New York: Simon & Schuster, 2010), "Herculean," 244; Richard Wolffe, *Revival: The Struggle for Survival Inside the Obama White House* (New York: Crown Publishers, 2010), "Rubik's," 82; Obama '08, "Barack Obama's Plan for a Healthy America," www.barackobama.com.

2. See Janny Scott, *A Singular Woman: The Untold Story of Barack Obama's Mother* (New York: Riverhead Books, 2011), 335–339; Kevin Sack, "Book Challenges Obama on Mother's Deathbed Fight," *New York Times* (July 14, 2011).

3. General Assembly of the United Nations, "Universal Declaration of Human Rights," quote, Article 25, www.un.org/en/documents/udhr; see Paul Starr, *The Social Transformation of American Medicine* (New York: Basic Books, 1982), 251–253.

4. See Mary Ann Glendon, *A World Made New: Eleanor Roosevelt and the Creation of the Universal Declaration of Human Rights* (Knopf, 2000); Joseph P. Lash, *Eleanor: The Years Alone* (Norton, 1972), 55–81; R. L. Numbers, *Almost Persuaded: American Physicians and Compulsory Health Insurance, 1912–1920* (Baltimore: Johns Hopkins Press, 1978); J. G. Burrow, *AMA: Voice of American Medicine* (Baltimore: Johns Hopkins Press, 1963), 144–145.

5. Arthur M. Schlesinger Jr., *The Age of Roosevelt: The Politics of Upheaval* (Boston: Houghton Mifflin, 1960), 29–41; Catherine Hoffman, "National Health Insurance—A Brief History of Reform Efforts in the U.S.," Henry J. Kaiser Family Foundation Publication #7871, 2–3, www.kff.org; F. D. Campion, *The AMA and U.S. Health Policy Since 1940* (Chicago: Chicago Review Press, 1984), 263–270; Jacob S. Hacker, *The Great Risk Shift* (Oxford: Oxford University Press, 2006), 143–146.

6. Hacker, *The Great Risk Shift*, 144–145; Theodore R. Marmor, *The Politics of Medicare* (Chicago: Aldine, 1973); R. C. Cunningham and R. M. Cunningham, *The Blues: A History of the Blue Cross and Blue Shield System* (Dekalb: Northern Illinois University Press, 1997), 32–36; John Geyman, *Do Not Resuscitate: Why the Health Insurance Industry Is Dying, and How We Must Replace It* (Monroe, ME: Common Courage Press, 2008), 3–4.

7. R. A. Stevens et al., eds., *History and Health Policy in the United States* (New Brunswick, NJ: Rutgers University Press, 2006), 42–47; Starr, *The Social Transformation of American Medicine*, 31–41; Hoffman, "National Health Insurance," 3; Beatrix Hoffman, "Health Care Reform and Social Movements in the United States," *American Journal of Public Health* 93 (2003); Geyman, *Do Not Resuscitate*, 7–10.

8. Hoffman, "National Health Insurance," 4–5; Starr, *The Social Transformation of American Medicine*; Hacker, *The Great Risk Shift*, 145–146; Rick Mayes, "The Origins, Development, and Passage of Medicare's Revolutionary Prospective Payment System," *Journal of the History of Medicine and Allied Sciences* 62 (2006), 21–55.

9. Hoffman, "National Health Insurance," 5–6; Starr, *The Social Transformation of American Medicine*; F. J. Wainess, "The Ways and Means of National Health Care Reform, 1974 and Beyond," *Journal of Health Politics, Policy, and Law* 24 (1999).

10. Haynes Johnson and David S. Broder, *The System: The American Way of Politics at the Breaking Point* (New York: Little, Brown, 1996); Hoffman, "National Health Insurance," 7–8; Hacker, *The Great Risk Shift*, 148–149; Sidney Blumenthal, *The Clinton Wars* (New York: Farrar, Straus and Giroux, 2003), 115–123; Paul Starr, "The Hillarycare Mythology," *The American Prospect* (September 14, 2007).

11. White House Domestic Policy Council, *The President's Health Security Plan* (New York: Times Books, 1993); see Jacob S. Hacker, *The Road to Nowhere: The Genesis of President Clinton's Plan for Health Security* (Princeton: Princeton University Press, 1997).

12. David Brock, "His Cheatin' Heart," *The American Spectator* (January 1994); Brock, *Blinded by the Right: The Conscience of an Ex-Conservative* (New York: Crown Publishers, 2002); Joe Conason and Gene Lyons, *The Hunting of the President: The Ten-Year Campaign to Destroy Bill and Hillary Clinton* (New York: St. Martin's Press, 2000); Russell Watson with Mark Hosenball, "Vincent Foster's Suicide: The Rumor Mill Churns," *Newsweek* (March 21, 1994); Blumenthal, *The Clinton Wars*, 46–72; William Safire, "When an Aide Dies Violently," *New York Times* (August 2, 1993); Safire, "The 28th Piece," *New York Times* (August 12, 1993); Safire, "Foster's Ghost," *New York Times* (January 6, 1994); Safire, "What's the Charge?" *New York Times* (January 13, 1994).

13. See William Kristol, "How to Oppose the Health Plan—and Why," *Ashbrook Center* (January 1994); Johnson and Broder, *The System*; Blumenthal, *The Clinton Wars*, 117–118.

14. Quoted in Michael Kramer and Janice Castro, "The Political Interest: Pat Moynihan's Healthy Gripe," *Time* (January 31, 1994).

15. See Alter, *The Promise*, 248–251; Wolffe, *Revival*, 59–64.

16. See Alter, *The Promise*, 251–254; Wolffe, *Revival*, 64–66; Gardiner Harris, "As Physicians' Jobs Change, So Do Their Politics," *New York Times* (May 30, 2011), A1, 14.

17. Max Baucus, chairman, Senate Finance Committee, "Call to Action: Health Reform 2009," http://finance.senate.gov/healthreform2009/finalwhitepaper.

18. Sam Stein, "Grassley Endorses 'Death Panel' Rumor: 'You Have Every Right to Fear,'" *Huffington Post* (August 12, 2009), www.huffingtonpost.com; Rachel Weiner, "Grassley Voted for So-Called 'Death Panel' in 2003," *Huffington Post* (August 14, 2009), www.huffingtonpost.com.

19. Wolffe, *Revival*, quote, 79.

20. See "Medicare for All Act," S.2229, 109th Congress, 2nd Session, 2006; "Ameri-Care Health Care Act of 2007," H.R. 1841, 110th Congress, 1st Session, 2007.

21. See Baucus, "Call to Action," 3–19; Alter, *The Promise*, 258–259; Mary O'Brien and Martha Livingston, eds., *Ten Excellent Reasons for National Health Care* (New York: New Press, 2008).

22. See Jacob S. Hacker, "The Case for Public Plan Choice in National Health Reform," Institute for America's Future, 2008; Bryan Borys and David B. Jemison, "Hybrid Arrangements as Strategic Alliances: Theoretical Issues in Organizational Combinations," *Academy of Management Review* 14 (April 1989), 235.

23. This section adapts material from Gary Dorrien, "Health Care Fix: The Role of a Public Option," *Christian Century* (July 14, 2009).

24. H.R. 676, "The United States National Health Insurance Act; or, Expanded and Improved Medicare for All," introduced by Rep. John Conyers Jr., reprinted in Physicians for a National Health Program, "Expanded and Improved Medicare for All," www.pnhp.org/publications/united-states-national-health-care-act-hr-676; and as Appendix 3 in Geyman, *Do Not Resuscitate*, 235–237.

25. See Physicians for a National Health Program, "Obama to Single Payer Advocates: Drop Dead," March 3, 2009, www.pnhp.org/news/2009; David Sirota, "Obama for Single-Payer Before He Was Against It," Open Left (May 11, 2009), www.alternet.org/health.

26. Obama '08, "Barack Obama's Plan," 3–4; Tom Daschle with Scott S. Greenberger and Jeanne M. Lambrew, *Critical: What We Can Do About the Health Care Crisis* (New York: Thomas Dunne Books, 2008).

27. Paul Krugman, "Keeping Them Honest," *New York Times* (June 5, 2009); Krugman, "All the President's Zombies," *New York Times* (August 23, 2009).

28. Cathy Schoen et al., "Building Blocks for Reform: Achieving Universal Coverage with Private and Public Group Health Insurance," *Health Affairs* 27 (May/June 2008), 647; Hacker, "The Case for Public Plan Choice," 5; Kaiser Family Foundation and Health Research & Educational Trust, *Employer Health Benefits, 2008: Summary of Findings*, 1.

29. Congressional Budget Office, "Designing a Premium Support System for Medicare," November 2006, 12; Kevin Freking, "Medicare Insurers' Profits Exceed Expectations," Associated Press, December 11, 2008; cited in Hacker, "The Case for Public Plan Choice," 6.

30. Alter, *The Promise*, quote 259.

31. Hacker, "The Case for Public Plan Choice," 6; Carlos Andrisano et. al., "Accounting for the Cost of Health Care in the United States," McKinsey Global Institute,

January 2007, www.mckinsey.com/mgi/reports, 70; Commonwealth Fund Commission on a High Performance Health System, "Slowing the Growth of U.S. Health Care Expenditures: What Are the Options?" January 2007, 4.

32. Wolffe, *Revival,* quote 58.

33. Wolffe, *Revival,* quote 148.

6

Moral Empire and Liberal War

S UCCEEDING GEORGE W. BUSH ON FOREIGN POLICY was much like succeeding him on economic policy. When Obama took office he realized that it would be hard for him to do worse than Bush, even as he shuddered at the carnage that he inherited: two wars and a worldwide torrent of antipathy to the United States. Obama went to work immediately on the antipathy, knowing that this was his strong suit. On the wars he withdrew combat forces from Iraq, while keeping a noncombat force and some military bases; he escalated in Afghanistan, while claiming to have an exit strategy and no plans for permanent bases; and he started one of his own, which he partly outsourced to NATO. In foreign policy, as elsewhere, Obama is pragmatic, nonideological, predisposed to cooperation, and imbued with a Niebuhrian blend of American idealism and realism. Here, as elsewhere, his story works for and against him.

Unlike Obama's Republican opponents, most of the world does not pretend to believe that his racial identity should have no bearing on how one regards his presidency. As soon as Obama became president nearly every nation in the world registered dramatically more favorable views of the United States and its president; Israel was the only notable exception. Obama plays this advantage skillfully, having begun his presidency with a new-day-has-come speech in Cairo that will pay dividends for years to come. But that makes it very difficult for him, if not impossible, to speak truthfully about American empire. The American Right constantly accuses Obama of not believing in American exceptionalism, which is plainly false and a skillful way of playing the race card against him—plus an effective brake on any inclination that

Obama may have to speak truthfully about American empire, much less to scale it back.

Obama understands, perhaps better than any president before him, why the rest of the world perceives the United States as an empire. When he waxes about "the world beyond our borders," Obama usually begins with Indonesia and his story. Indonesia is a symbol for him of the postcolonial world's constant tensions between globalization and sectarianism, prosperity and poverty, and modernity and antiquity. Obama knew something about struggling for survival in a Third World context before he learned that Americans were supposed to believe that history does not apply to the United States. For him, everything that describes U.S. foreign policy over the past half century is a reminder of something that happened to Indonesia. The United States liberated former colonies and created international institutions after World War II, as happened to Indonesia. For forty years the United States viewed the world through the prism of the Cold War, as in Indonesia. For the past century the United States has promoted American-style capitalism and multinational corporations, zealously in Indonesia. And for the past twenty years Asian nations have become more resentful of the United States as they have grown in economic power, as in Indonesia.[1]

Until he became president, Obama readily acknowledged that America has a deeply ambiguous foreign policy record. In *The Audacity of Hope* he put it in typically two-handed fashion: "At times, American foreign policy has been farsighted, simultaneously serving our national interests, our ideals, and the interest of other nations. At other times American policies have been misguided, based on false assumptions that ignore the legitimate aspirations of other peoples, undermine our own credibility, and make for a more dangerous world." On the one hand, he contended, the United States has usually gotten the big things right. It prevailed in the Cold War, avoided a nuclear catastrophe, put an end to great power military conflict, and unleashed "an era of unprecedented economic growth at home and abroad." On the other hand, the United States has supported a long list of thuggish and thieving dictators and occasionally invaded or overthrown unnecessarily, killing a lot of people unnecessarily, always in the name of freedom and democracy.[2]

This habit of holding together America's greatness and its sins is a central predisposition that Obama shares with the American theologian Reinhold Niebuhr, whom he credits as a major influence on his thought. Niebuhr's Christian realism renewed the Augustinian roots of just war theory, upholding justice as the highest value in the social realm. Augustine taught that human communities are united by what they love in common, not by the moral rules they profess. Niebuhr, refashioning Augustine's argument, contended that the love ethic of Christ defines the highest good in the realm of personal life, but justice is the highest good in the social realm. Just war, rightly understood, is *not* a system of rules that morally validates or invalidates the waging of war, contrary to what it became in the Middle Ages. No system of rules, Niebuhr taught, can morally justify something as evil as war; morally, waging war is a tragic lesser-evil business. Everything that sinful human beings do is morally ambiguous at best. But faced with the fact that attacks upon innocent people occur, the biblical command not to kill must give way to the command of love, interpreted as the duty to protect the innocent, just as Augustine taught.[3]

Niebuhr's dialectical method of thinking, his rendering of war as a tragic necessity of attaining and upholding justice, and his emphasis on the ambiguous interrelationships of good and evil are deeply impressed on Obama's mind. Niebuhr was a chief theorist of Cold War ideology, but he qualified his ideology in this area with a strong critique of America's sentimental presumptions about itself and its denial that America was an empire. Niebuhr habitually drew out polarities and held them together, as does Obama. Niebuhr struggled constantly to hold together the love ethic of Christianity with his passionate commitment to America's national interest, as does Obama. In modern political theory and Christian ethics, Niebuhr is not merely the author of influential books; he symbolizes the very project of conjoining morality and realism. Many academics, politicians, and clergy who have never plowed through Niebuhr's works are nonetheless aware that the most prominent Christian ethicist of the twentieth century specialized in holding together the love ethic of Christianity with the things of Machiavelli. Obama, like Jimmy Carter, has actually read a fair amount of Niebuhr, which shows through in the method and spirit of his thought and, sometimes, its substance.[4]

Niebuhr was ardently anti-Republican, but Obama tries to be more two-handedly Niebuhrian in this area. Explaining his fascination with Ronald Reagan, Obama starts with the bad Reagan who, in the foreign policy area, got many things wrong: Reagan supported anti-Communist dictators, he funded the death squads in El Salvador, he supported the apartheid regime in South Africa, and he got caught in a shameful deal funneling arms to the anti-Sandinista rebels in Nicaragua. But Obama emphasizes that Reagan became a historic president by getting some colossal things right. Keeping ahead of the Soviets militarily was the sensible thing to do, even if Reagan overdid it. Reagan shimmered with pride in his country's exceptional character and history, he respected America's armed services, he had a "healthy appreciation" for the dangers to America that existed beyond its borders, and he was right to insist that there was no equivalence of evil between the United States and the Soviet Union. When the Berlin Wall came down, Obama recalls, "I had to give the old man his due, even if I never gave him my vote."[5]

For Obama, Reagan is the president to measure himself against, not Clinton. Clinton survived two terms and achieved some good things, but Reagan made history, changing the trajectory of American and world history. Obama wants to make an equally huge difference in the world in a very different time and manner.

To make history, in a good way, one must live and think creatively in the world of one's time. To Obama, George W. Bush went wrong sometime after September 11, 2001, when, instead of thinking creatively about what national security meant at the time, he resorted to "an assortment of outdated policies from eras gone by." Bush refashioned Reagan's Evil Empire as the Axis of Evil. He applied Theodore Roosevelt's updating of the Monroe Doctrine to the entire planet, reidentifying the United States with the blatant imperialism of Manifest Destiny. Even worse, in Obama's telling, the Bush administration revived the stigmatizing, binary, doctrinaire politics of the Cold War. Any American who questioned the administration's rationale for invading Iraq was accused of being soft on terrorism or of lacking patriotism. The Bush administration manufactured bad intelligence and smeared its critics as un-American. For a while, Obama recounted, all of it worked only too well; in October 2002, twenty-eight Senate Democrats joined all but one Senate Republican in handing to Bush the authorization that he sought to invade Iraq.[6]

When Obama entered the White House, he believed that the United States had gone without a coherent national security strategy since 1989. Bush, Clinton, and Bush had no guiding principles, making ad hoc decisions "with dubious results," except to the extent that the latter Bush resuscitated Cold War militarism and imperialism, which was worse. Obama had no grand strategy, either. During the 2008 campaign it was enough to say that he would get the United States out of Iraq, hunt down al-Qaeda in Afghanistan and Pakistan, and repair America's battered image by restoring something closer to a normal, diplomatic, American way of relating to the world. He was emphatic, however, that America needed some guiding principles:

> Without a well-articulated strategy that the public supports and the world understands, America will lack legitimacy—and ultimately the power—it needs to make the world safer than it is today. We need a revised foreign policy framework that matches the boldness and scope of Truman's post-World War II policies—one that addresses both the challenges and the opportunities of a new millennium, one that guides our use of force and expresses our deepest ideals and commitments.[7]

He had two starting points in this area. Returning to American isolationism was a nonstarter, even though both parties still had strong undercurrents of it, and the Truman framework was obsolete because the world it addressed no longer exists. Obama explained that the world of today lacks any serious threat of great-power warfare. Virtually all the great and emerging national powers subscribe to international rules governing trade, economic policy, and the legal and diplomatic resolution of disputes, and China is no longer an exception to this trend. The leading national powers still do not agree about liberty and democracy, Obama allowed, but disagreements in these areas rarely lead to military threats or warfare. In today's world, the threats to peace come primarily from "the margins of the global economy" where the rules of economic globalization and international cooperation have not taken hold— failed states, dysfunctional dictatorships, nations wracked by overwhelming poverty and lack of education, and chronically violent nations. Terrorism thrives in these left-out parts of the world, Obama observed, and often it has no fixed address. Thus, nation-states no longer possess a monopoly on mass violence, and increasingly, national security is about securing safety from stateless terrorism.[8]

Obama moved straight from this point to a case for refashioning America's military to concentrate more effectively on counterterrorism. He did not question the necessity of a global military empire that employs five military commands to police the world, with 750 bases in 130 nations and formal base rights in 40 nations, with an air force in each branch of the armed services and carrier battleships in every ocean, all topped off by U.S. Special Forces conducting thousands of operations per year in 170 nations. It is a good thing, Obama argued, that only the U.S. Navy patrols the entire globe, because the United States keeps the world's sea-lanes clear. Similarly, America's dominance in nuclear missiles has dissuaded Europe and Japan from entering the arms race. Obama contended that as long as Russia and China retain large military forces and rogue states behave badly, the United States must sustain its global military empire.

His caveat was that too much of this force structure is devoted to winning World War III. The official military budget in 2005, when Obama wrote *The Audacity of Hope*, was $522 billion. He noted that this figure exceeded the military budgets of the next thirty nations combined. Obama might have noted, but did not, that this official figure did not include the costs of the wars in Iraq and Afghanistan; or nuclear weapons (which are assigned to the Energy Department); or the defense expenditures of the National Defense Stockpile, Selective Service, FBI, and Coast Guard; or the State Department's security programs; or Homeland Security programs not in the Pentagon budget; or the Department of Veterans Affairs; or interest payments on the national debt related to defense spending. When these items are counted, military spending during Bush's last years in office added up to approximately $1 trillion. This figure exceeds what the rest of the world combined spends on defense—a stupendous disparity incomparable to any historical parallel.[9]

Obama passed on whether this might be too much "defense" for a nation facing a debt crisis and no great power rivals. Military spending ranked with Social Security as an untouchable election issue, and Obama planned to surround himself with moderately conservative establishment types in international affairs. His ruling idea was that America needs a "smarter balance" between the strategic force structure that polices the world and the big-scale hardware that dominates Pentagon budgets. America needs a bigger and better-equipped Army, he argued. The capacity to put American boots on the ground "in the ungoverned or hostile regions" of the world is more important than sustaining America's present overkill advantage over China or an imagined rival. The crucial thing is to restore the military's capacity to strike quickly, in sufficient numbers, with sustainable troop rotations, all of which eroded under Bush's unfunded wars.[10]

Continuity, Change, Escalation

On taking office, Obama loaded his foreign policy team with establishment heavyweights reeking of continuity and gravitas: Secretary of Defense Robert Gates, a Republican holdover from the Bush administration; Secretary of State Hillary Clinton, a vanquished rival with strong pro-Israel credentials; National Security Adviser James L. Jones, a retired Marine Corps general and former NATO commander who, being a close friend and associate of John McCain's, was surprised to be asked; special adviser for the Persian Gulf and Southwest Asia Dennis Ross, who previously directed policy planning for the State Department under George H. W. Bush and handled the Middle East for Bill Clinton; and legendary diplomat Richard Holbrooke, a special representative for Afghanistan and Pakistan whom Obama hired at Hillary Clinton's insistence. This was not "change you can believe in." This was "don't worry about Obama's inexperience, because old hands will be on deck for foreign policy and security."

Gates quickly became the leading force in Obama's cabinet, owing to his background as defense secretary and a member of the National Security Council and his many years in the CIA, which he served as director under George H. W. Bush. For that reason plus the personal factors, Obama forged a closer relationship to Gates than to any other cabinet member. Both were calm, pragmatic, analytical types who prided themselves on their businesslike approach to things and who admired each other's professionalism. Gates was usually quiet during meetings, reading Obama and the other players, until he forged a consensus. Obama's relationship with Clinton had more edge, smacking of Lincolnesque "team of rivals" governance, but they respected each other, and Clinton plunged into diplomacy with the same studious zeal that she had taken to her work in the Senate. Jones worked out a tag team with his deputy Tom Donilon, a former chief of staff in the Clinton State Department. Jones traveled extensively, drawing on his vast international experience and building relationships, while Donilon managed the everyday NSC process. Ross resumed familiar conversations with key players in the Middle East, especially in Israel and Egypt. Holbrooke, nicknamed "the Bulldozer," who forged the 1995 Bosnia peace plan, had arguably the toughest assignment, but he died suddenly in December 2010 after suffering a torn aorta. Army General David H. Petraeus also cut a large figure in the Obama administration, moving from commander of General Command to commander in Afghanistan to director of the CIA.[11]

For progressives, it was hard enough to swallow an economic team led by Geithner and Summers, though at least they were Democrats. It was harder yet to swallow a foreign policy team led by Gates and Jones, both outsiders to the Obama campaign and the Democratic Party. Obama hoped that tabbing Clinton for the State Department would deflect attention from his conservative picks for Defense and the National Security Council, but that was bitterly laughable for progressives who had lifted him over Clinton. They were not inclined to overlook that Clinton authorized Bush to invade Iraq, she defended this vote for five years, she voted for a bellicose Senate resolution against Iran, and she ridiculed candidate Obama for advocating negotiations with Iran.

Though progressives wailed about getting shut out in this area, they had special problems in it, since there is no progressive foreign policy braintrust with government experience. In this area there was nothing to compare to the prominent liberal economists that Obama bypassed. The previous Democratic administration relied on managerial types like Secretary of State Warren Christopher and National Security Adviser Anthony Lake, and its lower ranks had no figures that went on to critique America's routine practices of empire. The academy produces progressives who criticize America's compulsive expansionism, but they make little impact beyond the academy. In the foreign policy and security areas, the Democratic Party attracts managerial operators who take pride in running the American empire more smoothly than their neoconservative competition. Obama, looking over the second- and third-tier foreign policy officials from the Clinton years, decided not to bother. Here he scored more points by appointing Republicans from the party's conservative realist wing and Hillary Clinton; progressives had nowhere else to go anyway.

As a candidate in the Democratic primaries, Obama had featured his progressive credentials. He stressed that he opposed the Iraq war from the beginning, which he was committed to ending, and he advocated working cooperatively with other nations, negotiating with adversaries, closing Guantanamo Bay and the secret prisons, restoring habeas corpus, and prohibiting torture. Every day, in Obama's stump speech, he promised that his administration would lead by example. It would maintain "the highest standards" of human rights and civil liberties, restoring the rights of habeas corpus to suspected terrorists and shutting down America's recruiting poster for terrorism in Guantanamo. If Americans were ready for change, he declared, they would get it by electing him—a believer in the Constitution who had taught the Constitution to law students and who pledged to obey it as president of the United States.

Usually Obama added that he was committed to aggressive counterterrorism and to escalating in Afghanistan, positions that he played up during the general election against McCain. Afghanistan was the necessary war, not Iraq, but the Bush administration's disastrous obsession with Iraq had botched Afghanistan. At the time, Obama's progressive base mostly choked on his vow to escalate in Afghanistan, agreeing to disagree. There was also a fair amount of murmuring that Obama took little interest in Bush's vast expansion of electronic surveillance lacking court-approved warrants. After Obama appointed a decidedly old-school foreign policy team, progressives questioned whether there would be any changes to believe in.

The early answers were encouraging. In his inaugural address Obama declared that he would not "continue with a false choice between our safety and our ideals," and two days later he signed three executive orders that made a clean break with the Bush administration in this area. One abolished the CIA's use of secret prisons. Another required all interrogations to follow the Army field manual, prohibiting torture and other violent and abusive techniques. "We can abide by a rule that says we don't torture," Obama contended. "This is me following through on an understanding that dates back to our founding fathers, that we are willing to observe core standards of conduct not just when it's easy but also when it's hard." His third order fulfilled a related campaign promise, or at least tried to do so, by calling for the closure of the Gitmo prison at Guantanamo within one year.[12]

At its peak, Gitmo held 770 suspected terrorists; by January 2009 it held 248. Obama wanted the Saudi government to take the nearly one hundred Yemenis that remained, since the government of Yemen was too weak to take responsibility for them. But the Saudis declined, and the White House began to look for a place in the United States where a new prison could be built—just as the "I want my country back" rallies began to appear. The prospect that terrorists might be brought into the United States erupted as a galvanizing issue, changing the politics. Obama did not see it coming, partly because Bush and McCain had publicly supported closing Guantanamo. The firestorm over Gitmo was the first of several controversies over Obama's resolve to prosecute suspected terrorists in civilian courts in the United States. It yielded his first important defeat in Congress, in May 2009, when the Senate voted overwhelmingly to strip a war-spending bill of the funds allocated to close Guantanamo. While progressives sat back, savoring their electoral victory and opining about what Obama should do, a fear-driven backlash was building, creating a huge activism gap that widened with each month of Obama's first two years in office.

Was there a third way between prosecuting suspected terrorists in civilian courts (as progressives and civil libertarians demanded) and prosecuting them in military courts (as conservatives demanded)? Obama made a case for one, urging that the civil libertarian position was essentially correct, but that military commissions should not be ruled out for exceptional cases. Mostly he tried to defuse a contagion of alarm, unsuccessfully, without betraying the rule of law, the Constitution, and the principles on which he had campaigned. Always he lost the argument with Congress or, in one high-profile case, New York City officials. After two years of losing he gave up, agreeing in April 2011 to try accused 9/11 plotters in a military commission at Guantanamo.

Meanwhile Obama escalated unmanned drone attacks on al-Qaeda and Taliban fighters in Pakistan, authorizing 53 airstrikes in his first year in office, after Bush authorized 34 the year before. The following year Obama authorized 118 drone attacks in Pakistan, mostly on targets in the Federally Administered Tribal Areas along the Afghan border in Northwest Pakistan. The U.S. government and, usually, the Pakistani government of President Asif Ali Zardari claim that most people killed by the drone attacks are al-Qaeda or Taliban fighters and that the CIA tries hard to avoid killing civilians. A growing and very bitter civilian resistance movement in Pakistan finds both assertions hard to believe. Upon taking office, Obama instructed his security team that his number one priority was to track down and kill Osama bin Laden, an objective he achieved dramatically on May 2, 2011. And he dramatically escalated the war in Afghanistan.

Two months after taking office, Obama added 17,000 combat troops and 4,000 trainers to the United States' existing force of 37,000. By then his team had settled on its version of the salient facts in Afghanistan and Pakistan: al-Qaeda barely existed in Afghanistan; the Taliban numbered 25,000 there, up from 4,000 in 2003; the government of Afghan president Hamid Karzai was inept and deeply corrupt; the Afghan army was much like the government; the Taliban war in Afghanistan was being run from safe havens in Pakistan; the Haqqani network, in particular, had virtual immunity in Pakistan; Pakistan was the greater problem, where a powerful military and its spy agency, Inter-Services Intelligence (ISI), played a double game with the United States and the Afghan Taliban; and the situation for the United States was deteriorating in both places.[13]

Obama quickly decided that the U.S. and NATO commander in Afghanistan, Army General David McKiernan, was too cautious for the job; it didn't help that McKiernan resisted counsel from Petraeus, who was riding high from his recent success in Iraq. For the first time since Truman fired General Douglas MacArthur during the Korean War, a top American general was removed from duty during wartime. Obama replaced McKiernan with a tough-talking specialist in secret operations, General Stanley McChrystal, who had spent the past five years hunting down al-Qaeda leaders from a plywood box at Balad Airbase in Iraq.

Obama told the nation that the war in Afghanistan was going badly; thus, the surge of 21,000 extra troops was an urgent necessity. Insurgents controlled parts of Afghanistan and Pakistan, and attacks against U.S. troops and NATO allies had increased steadily. The aim of his escalation and his change of commanders was to destroy al-Qaeda in Afghanistan and Pakistan. At the time, Gates still believed that defeating the Afghan Taliban insurgency was possible, although Obama was more circumspect on this topic, reflecting the divided opinion of his advisers. He also did not say that success in Afghanistan depended upon building up a functional government and a viable army, although he acknowledged that there were special problems in this area: "Afghanistan has an elected government, but it is undermined by corruption and has difficulty delivering basic services to the people. The economy is undercut by a booming narcotics trade that encourages criminality and funds insurgency."[14]

That, at least, named part of the problem. Obama told McChrystal that he wanted American and NATO forces to clear, hold, build, and transfer. It was pointless to clear and hold any territory that they did not build into something worth transferring to Afghan leaders. Secondly, he wanted an exit strategy, insisting that he was not in for a long-term, trillion-dollar project in nation building or the next Vietnam. Obama avoided the term *counterinsurgency* for that reason, since it smacked of large and unending warfare. To McChrystal, Patraeus, and Navy Admiral Michael G. Mullen (chair of the Joint Chiefs of Staff), however, it was pointless to talk about getting out of Afghanistan when the United States had just begun to escalate. They wanted a second big escalation and an outright commitment to counterinsurgency. McChrystal told Gates that he needed at least 40,000 more troops. Gates was stunned; he was a Soviet specialist who had been at the CIA when the Soviets invaded Afghanistan with 110,000 troops. If the Soviets could not put down the Afghan resistance despite throwing out the rules of engagement, killing one million Afghans, and virtually destroying the country, how was the United States to succeed with the same number of troops?

McChrystal replied that Patraeus-style counterinsurgency changed the equation. The new American counterinsurgency doctrine (COIN), which Patraeus authored, emphasized protecting local populations and winning hearts and minds. America could not kill its way to victory in Afghanistan. But if America did counterinsurgency the right way, winning over local communities and protecting them, and building up a viable Afghan army, it could create a tolerable status quo in Afghanistan. On that basis Gates agreed to support McChrystal's request for 40,000 more troops, and the administration and military debated whether to escalate again.[15]

Obama insisted that he wanted options. The military commanders complied, sort of, using the Henry Kissinger method of providing three options, two of which they considered unlikely, undesirable, or both. All three assumed a second escalation. The fantasy option was to inject 85,000 troops for counterinsurgency across Afghanistan. That was just for show, as Obama had already made clear that he was not up for another Vietnam. The second option, for which they pressed hard, both in the White House and in leaks to the press, was a smaller version of the same thing—40,000 additional troops for counterinsurgency warfare in the south and east portions of the country, the Pashtun areas where the Taliban were strong. The third option was to add 11,000 troops to build up a professional Afghan army.

From September to early December 2009, Obama pored over these options with his military commanders, dwelling on the obvious point that each strategy drew the United States deeper into Afghanistan with no clear end in sight. Obama stressed that the mission was to destroy al-Qaeda and that he would not get hooked into nation building. But al-Qaeda was mostly in Pakistan, not Afghanistan, and Obama himself insisted that building and transferring was the key to success. That depended on building up a viable government, civil society, and professional army. The review had barely begun when someone in the military leaked a secret report by McChrystal to the Pentagon's favorite journalist, Bob Woodward, who had accompanied Jones on a recent trip to Afghanistan. Woodward disclosed in the *Washington Post* that McChrystal and the Joint Chiefs were alarmed at the deteriorating situation in Afghanistan. McChrystal used some form of the word *defeat* fourteen times, warning that America and its NATO allies could not succeed in Afghanistan "simply by trying harder." The Afghan prison system, in particular, according to McChrystal, had become a breeding ground for Taliban and al-Qaeda insurgents, who operated with relative impunity in the prisons. If the United States did not inject more forces into Afghanistan, it faced the imminent prospect of a major mission failure.[16]

Obama was furious at the leak, realizing that the military commanders were trying to steamroll him into a major escalation. He had lifted McChrystal to prominence; now, somebody in the military was using McChrystal to force Obama's hand, and a few weeks later, McChrystal made some impolitic public remarks that made it worse. Vice President Biden, pushing for option three, warned Obama that a major escalation would lock them into a replay of the Vietnam quagmire. America didn't need to have 100,000 troops in Afghanistan to kill one hundred al-Qaeda insurgents, Biden urged. (Al-Qaeda was believed to have between twenty and one hundred insurgents in Afghanistan.) Biden noted that America spent thirty times as much on Afghanistan as on Pakistan. That was skewed, he contended, because Pakistan should be the focus. Instead of pouring 100,000 troops into an unwinnable war in Afghanistan, America should step up its attacks on al-Qaeda, see if al-Qaeda and the Taliban could be separated, and distinguish among levels of the Afghan Taliban. Five or ten percent were hard-core believers that had to be defeated. A middle group of 15 to 20 percent had a grab bag of reasons for being in the fight. The rest were foot soldiers trying to feed themselves and repel foreigners from their country. The best option, Biden urged, was "counterterrorism plus," not counterinsurgency forever.[17]

Obama took Biden seriously, having entrusted him with managing America's policy and military drawdown in Iraq. He encouraged Biden to speak up at the meetings at which McChrystal, Petraeus, and others made the case for a big escalation and no case for an exit. McChrystal countered that option three was shortsighted, a prescription for "Chaos-istan." The status quo plus building up the Afghan army would not solve anything. Hillary Clinton agreed that trying to separate the Taliban from al-Qaeda was pointless; if the Taliban regained power in Afghanistan, al-Qaeda would be back in state-sponsored business. The military players were not unanimous; Army Lieutenant General Douglas E. Lute, Obama's coordinator for Afghanistan and Pakistan, told Obama that a big escalation smelled like a gamble, and he should not count on a "windfall of luck." Later he lamented that the military commanders rolled the president.[18]

Gates, mediating an increasingly tense standoff between Petraeus and Biden, scaled back his previous position that the United States should be able to destroy the Taliban. They had probably overreached in Afghanistan, Gates judged. Good governance was not going to happen, and it was not necessary for the United States to defeat the insurgency to be successful there. The goal should be to destroy al-Qaeda and to significantly degrade the Taliban. Biden asked the obvious question: If the United States committed more blood and treasure to Afghanistan, and a year later the government was still "a criminal syndicate," how would they justify having escalated? All agreed that that was the right question. The answer on which Obama settled was that out-of-control corruption was unacceptable. If the United States, by making a big surge into Afghanistan, could get the government down to a "Bangladesh level" of corruption, it would be worth doing—provided that the United States did not overstay. On that basis Obama devised a typical Obama compromise, adding 30,000 troops that he pledged would complete the mission in eighteen months and return home.[19]

Gates called this strategy "Force Option 2A" before he and Obama settled on it, though Gates's figures were 30,000 to 35,000 and an extended surge of twenty-four months. Obama reasoned that no mission of any kind could succeed in Afghanistan without destroying al-Qaeda and Afghan Taliban havens that operate in Pakistan's remote tribal regions, especially the Haqqani network and the Quetta Shura Taliban. Thus, Obama adopted and expanded the Bush administration's fourteen intelligence orders that provide the legal basis for the CIA's worldwide covert operations. The CIA operates a clandestine paramilitary army of 3,000 Afghans called the Counterterrorism Pursuit Teams that regularly conducts covert operations in Pakistan. When Obama made his decision to escalate for the second time, he told his aides that the cancer was in Pakistan, but that stopping it from spreading to Afghanistan was imperative. To get Pakistan under control, the United States had to stabilize Afghanistan. Meanwhile McChrystal got himself fired by mouthing off about senior administration officials to *Rolling Stone* magazine, and Petraeus succeeded him, technically a demotion. For Petraeus, taking over in Afghanistan was an opportunity to apply his counterinsurgency doctrine—even though Obama resisted calling it counterinsurgency.[20]

The pledge to get out in eighteen months was crucial to how Obama sold the plan to the country and himself. Somehow he convinced himself that the United States could create a viable Afghan army in that time frame and persuade a corrupt government to take an interest in governing. But none of this was possible in eighteen months. It will take years to create a professional Afghan army, and the goal of creating a functional government is so far out of reach that Obama has given mixed messages about whether it is an essential test of a successful intervention, even as he escalated America's commitment to killing and dying for the discredited Karzai government. Obama took the path of Lyndon Johnson and Mikhail Gorbachev, doubling down on a mess he inherited, just as Johnson and Gorbachev escalated in Vietnam and Afghanistan upon taking office. In both of the latter cases everything got worse, though at least Gorbachev recognized it and reversed course.

Afghanistan is a minefield of bad choices. The United States is smashing the third poorest country in the world, where Bush defense secretary Donald Rumsfeld complained that there were no hard targets to destroy, only shacks and tents. The government is corrupt from top to bottom. It barely exists outside Kabul except as an instrument of shakedowns and graft, beginning with the family of President Karzai. The Afghan army is part of the corruption plague, and, until Obama escalated the war, more than two-thirds of the economy was centered on opium traffic. Now the war is the biggest industry in Afghanistan, and the nation's economy and armed forces would likely collapse without it. Obama took the option that has "sinkhole" written all over it, pouring 51,000 additional troops into a country featuring a chronically dysfunctional government, treacherous terrain, a soaring narcotics trade, and a history of repelling foreign armies, all without spelling out how, exactly, the United States will know it has succeeded enough to get out or even to scale down.

The chief players still do not agree on what they did. Biden believes that Obama rejected the counterinsurgency option, and Patraeus believes that Obama approved a slightly scaled-down version of it. On Biden's view, Obama chose to stabilize the Afghan population centers, notably Kabul and Kandahar, to prevent the Taliban from toppling the government. Petraeus says that the American military's focus on these two cities reflects the fundamental change in counterinsurgency doctrine that he formulated. Counterinsurgency warfare is still essential to the American effort in Afghanistan, but the American military has stopped saying that it exists only to kill people and destroy things. Petraeus and Mullen, while stepping up night raids to capture or kill insurgents, emphasize that winning hearts and minds is the key to America's strategy in Afghanistan.[21]

For Obama, that approach gets the right balance. But hatred of the United States has increased in Afghanistan and Pakistan on his watch because the United States is inflicting more collateral killing in both places. The Petraeus approach rationalizes the loss of blood and treasure indefinitely without accomplishing any real progress, perpetuating a vast culture of dependency in which Afghans have no incentive to fight for a government they despise. America is never going to kill enough radical jihadists to make all Americans feel that their government has done enough for them in this department. Obama could earn his Nobel Peace Prize by pressing the point. In June 2011 he tilted in Biden's direction, promising to withdraw by September 2012 the entire escalated force of 33,000 troops and to withdraw all of America's remaining 66,000 forces by 2014. To Obama, that is the "just right" Goldilocks solution that positions him where he wants to be, as the cautious guardian of American security. But most Americans have had enough of propping up Fortress Kabul and deepening its addiction.

The American Good Neighbor

Obama doubled down in Afghanistan during the same year that he gave a stirring speech at Cairo University about Muslims and non-Muslims living together peaceably. Then he won the Nobel Peace Prize for representing the hope of an American power that practices cooperation and diplomacy. In Cairo Obama was warmly applauded every time that he said a favorable word about Islam or the Koran, which was often, and almost every time that he moralized about Muslims and non-Muslims respecting each other. He declared that he had come to Cairo to seek "a new beginning between the United States and Muslims around the world." He noted his personal connections to Islam in Africa and Indonesia, the historic contributions of Islam to civilization, and the contributions of Muslims to America's story. Obama spoke as an American who had known Islam on three continents before coming to the land of its birth and as an American president who felt an obligation to oppose every kind of bigotry. In a line that won huge applause in Cairo and a storm of right-stream objections at home, he declared: "I consider it part of my responsibility as President of the United States to fight against negative stereotypes of Islam wherever they appear."[22]

It also worked the other way around, Obama admonished. If Americans had a moral obligation to fight anti-Muslim prejudice, Muslims were obliged not to be prejudiced against the United States. That got polite applause, and Obama continued: "Just as Muslims do not fit a crude stereotype, America is not the crude stereotype of a self-interested empire. The United States has been one of the greatest sources of progress that the world has ever known. We were born out of revolution against an empire. We were founded upon the ideal that all are created equal, and we have shed blood and struggled for centuries to give meaning to those words—within our borders, and around the world. We are shaped by every culture, drawn from every end of the Earth, and dedicated to a simple concept: E pluribus unum—'Out of many, one.'"

This American song got furrowed looks and no applause, and Obama reached for a winning reference to himself: "Now, much has been made of the fact that an African American with the name Barack Hussein Obama could be elected President." The mood lightened again, with applause; Obama pressed the point that his story showed the reality of America's dream of opportunity—a dream that seven million American Muslims presently claimed for themselves. Moreover, he declared, it was worth noting that America's Muslims were bettered educated and enjoyed higher incomes than the American average.

He had points to make about seven issues. The first was that America had every right and obligation to hunt down "violent extremists" who threatened innocent people. Nearly 3,000 people were ruthlessly murdered on September 11, 2001, Obama observed, and the murderers were determined to keep killing on a massive scale: "These are not opinions to be debated; these are facts to be dealt with." The second was that America would not waver from its commitment to a two-state solution for Israel and Palestine in which the rights and legitimacy of both nations were recognized, Hamas renounced its violence against Israel, and Israel terminated its settlements in the West Bank. The third was that a nuclear arms race in the Middle East would be "hugely dangerous," but every nation, including Iran, had a right to peaceful nuclear power if it complied with the Nuclear Non-Proliferation Treaty.

The fourth was that neither democracy nor any other system of government should be imposed by one nation on any other, but all people have the right to live as they choose. The fifth was that freedom of religion "is central to the ability of peoples to live together." Islam had a rich and proud tradition of religious tolerance, Obama stressed, but among some Muslims there was a "disturbing tendency" to believe that one could not be faithful to Islam without putting down other religions. The sixth was that women should have the power of choice to be educated, to pursue careers, and to choose whether or not they lived by traditional codes. Responding to murmuring, Obama acknowledged that there was a "healthy debate about this issue" among his present audience. He allowed that a woman could choose to cover her hair without losing her equality with men, "but I do believe that a woman who is denied an education is denied equality." The last issue was economic development and opportunity. Education and innovation, Obama declared to applause, are the "currency of the 21st century." Islam was not necessarily a barrier to education and innovation, but in "too many Muslim communities," it was. He challenged his audience to invest more deeply in education, business development, and community needs, creating a new social ecology.

None of these issues would be easy to address, Obama acknowledged: "But we have a responsibility to join together on behalf of the world that we seek— a world where extremists no longer threaten our people, and American troops have come home; a world where Israelis and Palestinians are each secure in a state of their own, and nuclear energy is used for peaceful purposes; a world where governments serve their citizens, and the rights of all God's children are respected." The only way to get there was together, living by the rule of every religion to do unto others as one would have them do unto oneself.

Obama got a standing ovation in Cairo, from people that peacefully over-threw the Mubarak regime eighteen months later. The speech was widely hailed as a historic event and a perfectly pitched attempt to make a new beginning, except by critics who protested that Obama was ridiculously solicitous of his Muslim audience, he spewed nonsense about a nonexistent Islamic tradition of tolerance, he was a raving egotist with a Messiah com-plex, and he threw Israel under the bus. Charles Hurt opined in the *New York Post*, "If world peace is attained by complimenting those on the other side into submission, he made some serious progress. Obama really buttered them up in Cairo. He thanked them for everything from algebra to the pen, though he curiously failed to mention that they often throw people in prison for using it." In a similar vein, but more harshly, Fox news analyst Michelle Malkin choked on all the "pretty words" of Obama's "latest History-Making, World-Changing Speech," especially since he failed to use the words *ter-rorist* or *jihadist*. Malkin charged: "He attempted to obfuscate his explicit anti-American apologism with a mixture of disingenuousness and naiveté totally untethered to reality." Robert Spencer, in a post for *Jihad Watch* titled "Platitudes and Naiveté," agreed with Malkin that there was no evidence whatsoever for Obama's pious dictum that the violent extremists constituted a "small but potent minority of Muslims." The percentage of America-hating radical jihadists was way too high among Muslims to be described as small, Spencer assured—especially coming from the person who was supposed to keep Americans safe.[23]

Radio talk show host and former Reagan aide Hugh Hewitt blasted Obama's "deeply dishonest" omissions and dissembling: "The world is the worse for this speech because it was not honest about the situation in the Middle East, not honest about the threat from Iran, not honest about Israel's deep desire to be allowed to live in peace, and not honest about the deter-mination of Hamas, Hezbollah and Iran to destroy Israel and to gain the weapons necessary to do so in an instant." Security analyst and former Rea-gan aide Frank J. Gaffney Jr. announced, "There is mounting evidence that the president not only identifies with Muslims, but actually may still be one himself." Gaffney's evidence centered on Obama's honorific gestures, such as referring to the Koran as "the Holy Koran" and using the Muslim invoca-tion "peace be upon them." Gaffney had already suspected that Obama used coded gestures to tell Muslims that he was a Muslim; now this theme became a Gaffney hobbyhorse. Rick Moran, blogging for *American Thinker*, judged that Obama was naïve and dangerously mistaken. Obama drew the "wrong lessons" about the history of Islam, he made "false assumptions" about how America should cope with Islam, and his pieties about the greatness of Islam were falsified by the ways that Muslims abused "Christians in Iraq, the West

Bank, Egypt itself, and other Arab nations where persecution is the rule not the exception." Above all, Moran concluded, Obama was dangerously wrong to oppose American domination of the world and to parade his opposition to it in foreign countries: "Someone should have told our president that the only way the US can be prevented from dominating the world—a domination made manifest by our economic power and spread of our culture as much as our military prowess—is by subsuming our interests to those of other nations or the UN."[24]

These reactions helped to stoke impassioned rallies against the new president during his first summer as president, although the political Right also produced more thoughtful critiques. *National Review*, stepping back from a torrent of Obama-bashing, editorialized that there was a pertinent distinction between the kind of argument that a politician makes to induce a certain outcome and the kind that a logician makes to clarify a point. Obama was not in the business of telling unvarnished truths that paid no regard to consequences; at Cairo his business was to heal some of the enmity between Islam and America. This was a worthy endeavor, the editors acknowledged: "Telling historical truths and scoring historical points were not the purpose of his speech; reassuring Muslims of American goodwill was." Many Americans wanted a full-throated litany about 9/11 and jihadist terrorism, but *National Review* recognized that Obama's audience had its own litany: "A different set of grievances, from Abu Graib to NATO bombs that go astray and kill Afghan civilians, is now on the table. A myth of Christian, Western, and American hostility toward Islam has grown up." To the editors, Obama was "shockingly weak" on Iran, failing to tell Iranians to give up their nuclear program, even before an Egyptian crowd that would have cheered a strong word against Iran. On the other hand, Obama did pretty well on democracy and showcasing America's good points.[25]

Overall, *National Review* concluded, it was hard to say what good Obama might have done. His assertion that Islam and America were compatible "is either an exaggeration or a prediction." Islam as presently constituted, the editors judged, "is simply not fully compatible with the liberty that defines America politically." Something had to change before Islam and America could be compatible in actuality. *National Review*, reaching into its Roman Catholic background, recalled that American Catholics were long suspected of not being good Americans because the Catholic Church had no doctrine of religious freedom. Catholicism and America were not fully compatible until "America converted Catholics here to liberty." American Catholics, in turn, led by Jesuit theologian John Courtney Murray, helped to change Catholic teaching at Vatican Council II. For Obama's exaggeration to come true, the editors reasoned, something like this had to happen among the Muslim

Americans that he lionized. To help make it happen, Obama needed to tell American Muslims some of the "hard truths of assimilation and equality" that he diplomatically bypassed in Cairo.

The foreign reaction to Obama's speech was generally positive, usually commending Obama's evident goodwill. Marwan Bishara, senior political analyst for Al Jazeera, appreciated the difference between Obama's soft power version of normal American imperialism and the Bush version: "It was a soft imperial speech that wanted to engage. If Bush had to demonize many Muslims in order to launch the wars he did in the Islamic world, then Obama humanizes the Islamic world in order to engage." Palestinian president Mahmoud Abbas called the speech "a good start and an important step towards a new American policy," one that took seriously the suffering of Palestinians. In Israel, reactions ran true to form. Prime Minister Benjamin Netanyahu's government vaguely praised the speech as the herald of a new era of peace, stifled its opposition to Obama's statements about settlements and Palestinian statehood, and released a statement the following day reaffirming its commitment to building new settlements in the West Bank and to holding no position on whether a two-state solution could work. Defense Minister Ehud Barak weighed in with similarly calculated praise and reservations. Meretz leader Haim Oron called the speech an inspiring, optimistic, visionary "feat of enlightenment." Ofra settlement resident Aliza Herbst said that Obama's vision sounded nice but was unrealistic in a world ravaged by Muslim anti-Western hatred.[26]

In truth, every American president follows the same policy toward Israel, with an occasional creative tweak. Jimmy Carter forged a peace treaty between Israel and Egypt, and Bill Clinton broke the taboo on publicly endorsing a two-state solution, which he nearly pulled off in 2000. Obama broke another taboo in May 2011 by saying publicly what every president since Richard Nixon assumed—that the starting point for configuring the Palestinian state must be the 1967 borders plus whatever land swaps are negotiated. In 2000, however, a two-state solution with borders more or less along the Green Line was a real possibility. A decade of Israeli settlement expansion in the West Bank changed this picture, by design. Obama tried to revive a dormant peace process ahead of the United Nations timetable for a vote on Palestinian statehood, but the Israelis and Palestinians, unlike the Egyptians of Tahrir Square, are very short on creativity and surprises and so is the latest American administration.

Just War and American Order

The meaning and efficacy of the Cairo speech were still being debated in October 2009 when the Norwegian Nobel Committee announced that Obama had won the Nobel Peace Prize. He had been president for nine months, so this was very fast, even for him. In addition, the deadline for nominations was February 1, when Obama had been president for twelve days. American liberals clearly were not the only ones projecting their fondest hopes onto Obama. Explaining their decision, the Norwegian prize-givers observed that Obama had already made "extraordinary efforts to strengthen international diplomacy and cooperation between peoples" and that he was admirably committed to abolishing nuclear weapons: "Obama has as president created a new climate in international politics. Multilateral diplomacy has regained a central position, with emphasis on the role that the United Nations and other international institutions can play. Dialogue and negotiations are preferred as instruments for resolving even the most difficult international conflicts." For European believers in multilateral cooperation, the coming of Obama was the modern secular equivalent of biblical manna in the desert: "Only very rarely has a person to the same extent as Obama captured the world's attention and given its people hope for a better future."[27]

That was a nice impression, but Obama felt the absurdity of its prematurity. "Are you shitting me?" he asked, when his press secretary Robert Gibbs told him that he had won the prize. The White House went into panic mode at having to say something immediately in response. Obama knew that he did not belong in the company of the Nobel laureates that had gone before him, and he winced at winning the peace prize while contemplating a big escalation in Afghanistan. On the day of the announcement, Obama spoke with reporters in the Rose Garden before meeting with McChrystal, who spelled out the three options for an escalation of forces. To reporters Obama acknowledged that he did not belong "in the company of so many of the transformative figures who've been honored by this prize." All he could do was thankfully accept the award and try to build the kind of world that the deserving prize-winners "and all Americans" wanted to create.[28]

Normally his speechwriters, Jon Favreau and Ben Rhodes, had to prod Obama for clues about what he wanted to say as a speech deadline approached. This time it worked the other way around, as Obama announced that he wanted to write much of the Nobel speech himself. His aides compiled a 300-page binder of speeches and essays on war and peace, featuring, at his request, Niebuhr, King, Gandhi, and George Marshall; Harry Truman's announcement of the atomic bombing of Hiroshima was also included. Obama and his aides were still writing the speech on the trip to Oslo in December, just after Obama had announced at West Point that he would send 30,000 additional troops to Afghanistan.

At Oslo Obama went straight for the point that he ranked nowhere near the "giants of history" that had previously received the peace prize, notably Albert

Schweitzer, George Marshall, Martin Luther King Jr., and Nelson Mandela. Neither did he come close to the millions who struggled and suffered for justice in harsh circumstances for many years without gaining much recognition. Moreover, he came to Oslo as head of the most powerful state in the world, which was embroiled in two wars. He would not pretend that he deserved the Nobel Peace Prize, but, having received it anyway, he came to Oslo with "an acute sense of the costs of armed conflict" and a deep determination to replace war with peace.[29]

Obama plunged immediately into the concept of just war, although, contrary to what journalists nearly always said about this section of the speech, he did not explicate a Niebuhrian version of it. Obama described just war as a system of rules for the classification of hard cases, exactly as medieval theologians developed it. There is no definitive formulation of classical just war theory, but nearly all versions of it distinguish between the moral right to fight *(jus ad bellum)* and the right way to fight *(jus in bello)*, listing from seven to ten principles in each category. Regarding the moral right to fight, classical just war theory teaches that war may be waged only by a legitimate ruler; it may be waged only for a just cause; it may be fought only with a right intention in the objective and the subjective senses; the decision to go to war must be a last resort after all possible means of negotiation have been exhausted; enemies never lose the right to sue for peace; unconditional surrender is not a valid goal; international law and treaties are to be respected; the entire war must cause less harm than the harm it seeks to prevent (the principle of proportionality); and the war must be winnable.[30]

The criterion of legitimacy excludes tyrants, war by private citizens (except in emergency defense), and war by criminal gangs or privateers. For a just cause, the offense must be actual (not merely possible), intentional, of substantial importance, objective and verifiable, and unilateral (not provoked). To pass the test of right intention in the objective sense, a war must be fought only to restore peace—which rules out national honor, territorial gain, commercial aggrandizement, and weakening or destroying one's enemies as valid ends. In the subjective sense, right intention excludes hatred, vengefulness, cruelty, desire for power or fame, and material gain. Positively, subjective right intention includes love for the victims of aggression, trust in God, willingness to face risk or sacrifice, love for the enemy, humility, regret at the necessity of fighting, and in most formulations of just war doctrine, the demonstration of mercy after victory.

The second traditional category in just war theory, *jus in bello*, operates very similarly, teaching that to fight rightly, the means of war must be necessary, proportional, respectful of the immunity of the innocent, discriminating, respectful of the dignity of humankind, and not forbidden by positive law or treaties. The necessity principle rules out unnecessary killing and wanton destruction. The proportionality principle rules out any destruction greater than the damage prevented or the offense being avenged; any punishment greater than the guilt of the offender; and disproportionate violence of any kind in tactics, strategy, or use of a weapon. The immunity principle applies to all innocent persons constituting no threat, traditionally defined as children, women, the infirm, clergy, members of religious orders, foreigners, unarmed persons engaged in ordinary tasks, neutral third parties, soldiers on leave, surrendered soldiers, and prisoners. The principle of discrimination requires every weapon, strategy, and military unit to be subject to measured control. The dignity principle forbids slander, mutilation, torture, treason, perjury, lying (with exceptions), pillage, poisoning the environment, fighting on holy days or during a proclaimed truce, and profaning cemeteries or houses of worship. It also respects sanctuary and the giving of quarter to surrendered enemies.

Just war theory has theoretical and practical problems on every level, but taken seriously, it condemns nearly every war ever fought as morally unjustified. Obama, quickly summarizing the post-Augustinian "moral rules" concept of just war, made the obvious point that the stringent tests of just war theory are usually ignored when nations set out to fight, even by heads of state who claim to be guided by just war doctrine: "For most of history, this concept of 'just war' was rarely observed. The capacity of human beings to think up new ways to kill one another proved inexhaustible, as did our capacity to exempt from mercy those who look different or pray to a different God." Twice in the first half of the twentieth century, total wars between nations blurred the just war distinction between combatants and civilians. Obama made a Niebuhrian point about this development and the limitations of just war principles. Defeating Nazi Germany and the Axis powers was a transcendently just cause, Obama observed—yet more civilians than soldiers were killed in World War II.[31]

The ravages of World War II and the advent of the nuclear age convinced many anti-Wilsonians that Woodrow Wilson had been right about the necessity of building liberal internationalist organizations. Obama recalled that the Marshall Plan and the United Nations established the architecture to protect human rights, prevent genocide, and control the nuclear arms race. Many wars broke out anyway, he acknowledged, showing the limits of the architecture, but postwar liberal internationalism helped to prevent World War III, and the Cold War ended "with jubilant crowds dismantling a wall."

Twenty years later, the world was overdue to reckon with the erosion of the Truman-era architecture amid the rise of new threats. Obama noted that the world is no longer endangered by the threat of a nuclear war between rival superpowers, "but proliferation may increase the risk of catastrophe." Terrorism goes back to ancient times, but modern technology allows terrorists to kill on a massive scale. Wars between nations still occur, but wars within nations have become a greater menace, killing far more civilians than soldiers. Faced with these developments, Obama urged, we must begin to think in new ways "about the notions of just war and the imperatives of a just peace."

He had one key point about the moral right to fight, one about the moral way to fight, and three about building a just and lasting peace. "We will not eradicate violent conflict in our lifetimes," Obama cautioned. "There will be times when nations—acting individually or in concert—will find the use of force not only necessary but morally justified." Though he yielded to no one in admiring King and Gandhi, Obama was a head of state sworn to protect the American nation. Nonviolent resistance could not have thwarted the evil of the Nazi movement, and the same thing was true of al-Qaeda. Obama acknowledged that much of the world has a "reflexive suspicion" of the world's only military superpower. However, there was something to be said on this topic that completed Obama's earlier point about liberal internationalism saving the world. The Marshall Plan and the United Nations would not have existed without the United States; more importantly, Obama asserted, the world was and is fortunate that the United States is the greatest power on earth: "Whatever mistakes we have made, the plain fact is: The United States of America has helped underwrite global security for more than six decades with the blood of our citizens and the strength of our arms." From Germany to Korea to the Balkans, the United States used its power to promote peace, prosperity, and democracy, never to conquer: "We have done so out of enlightened self-interest—because we seek a better future for our children and grandchildren, and we believe that their lives will be better if others' children and grandchildren can live in freedom and prosperity."

Obama had not come to Oslo to apologize for his nation's military power or its global legacy. Though it is hard for the greatest power in history not to come off looking like an empire to the rest of the world, and he took for granted that every nation bases its foreign policy on its national interests, he was adamant that America pursues its interests in an enlightened, generous, and legitimate fashion that embraces international law—the "rules of the road." NATO is indispensable to the cause of peace in Europe, Africa, and the Middle East, and the United States is the driving force within NATO. Obama implied that national leaders recognize the legitimacy and idealism of American foreign policy even when they criticize it. When Saddam Hussein invaded Kuwait, Obama recalled, the USA rightly repelled him, in the company of a global coalition. Ten years later the world rallied to the side of the United States and supported its war in Afghanistan after al-Qaeda attacked America.

As for the just way to fight, Obama reclaimed the moral high ground: "Even as we confront a vicious adversary that abides by no rules, I believe the United States of America must remain a standard bearer in the conduct of war." This was why he had signed an order prohibiting torture, he asserted. It was why he had ordered that Gitmo must be closed and reiterated that America abided by the Geneva Conventions: "We lose ourselves when we compromise the very ideals that we fight to defend. And we honor—we honor those ideals by upholding them not when it's easy, but when it is hard."

On building a just and lasting peace, Obama advocated strengthening the institutions and sanctions of liberal internationalism, refusing to choose between realism and idealism, and promoting economic development that is ecologically sustainable. He was committed to ridding the world of nuclear weapons and to meting out stronger and more consistent punishments for governments that grossly violate the human rights of their citizens—though Obama's only word about China was that it was becoming more prosperous and open. He rejected the false binary of realism versus idealism, since there was no good alternative to dealing with the world as it really is *and* to struggling for a better world. Order and freedom go together, Obama urged. All nations pursue their own interests, and no system of order is stable if people within it are repressed. Europe found stability only after it became free. There is almost no record of democracies fighting against each other, and America "has never fought a war against a democracy." Finally, Obama implored his international audience to think creatively about global poverty, the world's ecological crisis, and the structural relationships between these two afflictions. The world must come together to feed its people and to undo the human causes of climate change: "Our common security hangs in the balance."

Obama struggled with the ending right up to the ceremony, even though the ending that he needed was obvious: a word of inspiration from King about not giving up, and a word from Obama about what that meant to him. The loving-spirited faith in human progress that King and Gandhi exemplified "must always be the North Star that guides us on our journey," Obama urged. To lose this faith is to lose our "moral compass" and our "sense of possibility." Obama cited King's Nobel Prize speech of 1964 on this theme: "I refuse to accept despair as the final response to the ambiguities of history. I refuse to accept the idea that the 'isness' of man's present condition makes him morally incapable of reaching up for the eternal 'oughtness' that forever confronts him." In the form of an exhortation, Obama summarized what King's refusal meant to him: "Let us reach for the world that ought to be—that spark of the divine that still stirs within each of our souls. . . . We can acknowledge that oppression will always be with us, and still strive for justice. We can admit the intractability of depravation, and still strive for dignity. Clear-eyed, we can understand that there will be war, and still strive for peace. We can do that—for that is the story of human progress; that's the hope of all the world; and at this moment of challenge, that must be our work here on Earth."

The audience was intently quiet through most of the speech before erupting in two thunderous standing ovations. Reactions took their usual course, although for and against were both more muted this time. Most reviewers judged that the speech was typical Obama fare. It summarized his worldview, with inspiring touches; it delivered what the Norwegian liberal internationalists wanted; and it ranked with Obama's 2004 convention speech, the race speech, his 2008 convention speech, and the Cairo speech.

Conservatives, confronted with a speech containing a fair amount of straightforward American exceptionalism, took three approaches in responding to it. A few said it was surprisingly good, and they weren't inclined to say much more; Newt Gingrich took that tack. Victor Davis Hanson, in *National Review*, still couldn't stand Obama, although he allowed that Obama said some good things. The Nobel speech, Hanson explained, contained Obama's usual tropes and foibles, including verbosity, extraneousness (even farmers rated a mention), I/me exhaustion (Obama stoked his cult of personality), the split-the-difference trope, the one-hand and the other-hand trope, veiled attacks on Obama's predecessor, Obama's insatiable fascination with his unique story, nonsense about Afghanistan the good war versus Iraq the bad war, and "the hopey-changey rhetorical flourish." Hanson's last complaint inspired a bumper sticker; mostly he stressed that Obama couldn't get enough of himself and he overprided himself on waging war differently from George W. Bush. Another conservative stalwart, Rory Cooper of the Heritage Foundation, put similar things less colorfully, with a key difference: Cooper stressed that much of Obama's speech was straight out of Ronald Reagan and George W. Bush. The bad parts of Obama's speech were terribly important to Obama, Cooper explained, because he had to make his progressive fans feel better after dousing them with American exceptionalism: "He apologized for torture and defended his undelivered promise of closing Gitmo and was unsurprisingly rewarded with one of two rounds of applause from a European audience that eats American apologies up."[32]

The reaction from left-liberal types who usually grieved at Obama's paeans to American superpower greatness was surprisingly mild. Adam Serwer, in *The American Prospect*, offered a gentle version of left-liberal dismay, describing the speech as "an unapologetic assertion of American exceptionalism, all while tying that exceptionalism to actual American behavior. It was, in short, exactly the kind of speech that one has come to expect from Obama." Undoubtedly, Serwer predicted rightly, some conservatives would be surprised that Obama defended American military intervention so vigorously, but that would show that they weren't really listening before. Obama stood for "a vision of American exceptionalism that demands certain standards of American conduct." He differed from Bush primarily in taking seriously the standards of just war and international law. John Nichols, a blogger for *The Nation*, praised the speech as "an exceptionally well-reasoned and appropriately humble address." Katrina vanden Heuvel, editor and publisher of *The Nation*, was asked why she and her magazine treated Obama's Nobel lecture so gingerly. She replied that the speech was complex, and so was America's present political situation. *The Nation*, she assured, was critical of American imperialism and the fact that Obama had embraced Bush's wars. What mattered was to build up a movement that helped Obama live up to the better parts of his vision: "He is a war president who is presiding over the escalation of a war that this country need not fight to be more secure and that may endanger his role in the world that he seeks."[33]

But on this occasion a chorus of approval drowned out Obama's Left and Right critics, as vanden Heuvel perceived. Ruth Marcus, in the *Washington Post*, lauded Obama's "brilliant" speech as "rhetoric married with a serious, comprehensive worldview—a speech not by a newcomer to the national scene or a candidate under fire, but by a president who seemed, more than ever, to have grown into the job." Joe Klein, in *Time*, enthused that Obama's "noble" speech was rigorous, balanced, "morally lucid," and wise; in short, it was so good that it justified Obama's selection for the prize. Rick Klein, for ABC News, was reminded of why Obama had swept to the presidency, seemingly so long ago, before he became an embattled rookie president. Klein suggested that Obama might be willing to trade the prize for some peace in the Democratic Party or a sixtieth vote in the Senate—but perhaps he would settle "for bottling some of the adoration and bringing it back home with him."[34]

Walter Russell Mead, a prominent foreign policy expert at the Council on Foreign Affairs, summarized the reaction, including his own: "There are no flies on our President. He could sell shoes to a snake." Mead had nothing against Obama; in fact, he appreciated that Obama inspired a surge of good feeling for the United States. But Mead pressed the point that Obama got applause for saying and doing things that differed very little from George W. Bush: "He is winding down one war, escalating a second, and stepping up the pressure on Iran. He is asserting America's sovereign right to unilateral action in self defense while expressing the hope that this right will not need to be exercised. If Bush had said these things the world would be filled with violent denunciations. When Obama says them, people purr." Mead did not mean that Obama merely put lipstick on a pig: "He gave it a makeover and sent it to charm school."[35]

Mead did not claim to know if Obama could make it work. At some level it seemed to bother him that Obama enjoyed special privileges in this area. But Obama's boasts about America's greatness did not smack of the domineering chauvinism that the Bush administration vividly conveyed. When Obama waxed about American greatness, he showed that there was some truth in America's favorite myths about itself, and he did it in a way that rejected neoconservative fantasies of "unipolar dominance." Moreover, whatever advantages Obama derived from his multicultural background, there was always a backlash to reckon with from the many who resented his emergence.[36]

The Middle East Boiling Over: Iraq, Iran, Egypt, and Libya

Obama spends fully half his time working on international affairs—presiding over a military withdrawal in Iraq, gambling on a big escalation with a tight timeline in Afghanistan, authorizing drone attacks in Pakistan, supporting democratic movements in the seething Middle East, facing off with Iran, coping with Saudi Arabia, working on a two-state solution between Israel and Palestine, dancing warily with China and Russia, responding to earthquake disasters in Haiti and Japan, maintaining military pressure on North Korea, backing Taiwan and South Korea, strengthening America's relationships with emerging powers India and Brazil, easing hostilities with Cuba, and working closely with America's European allies and Canada. That's just the top drawer.

In Iraq, Obama faced up to classic imperial dilemmas about needing to withdraw faster than it is safe to do so. In Afghanistan, Obama is trying to overlook that the Karzai government is not worth killing and dying for, and that the Afghan people will never risk their lives for it. In Iran, Obama supports the democratic opposition and briefly flirted with a game-changing deal before reverting to the Bush status quo. In Tunisia a democratic explosion occurred too suddenly for Obama to offer much help, but afterward he cautiously supported democratic upheavals in Egypt, which toppled a dictator; and Bahrain, where Saudi Arabia is determined to keep a Sunni minority in power; and Syria, where a vicious government has unleashed its repressive power; and Libya, where Obama embraced the perils of liberal war.

The irony of Iraq, for Obama, is that he has personally devoted little time to it, after riding his antiwar opposition to the Democratic nomination. From March 2005 to April 2007 the eruption of a civil war in the midst of an already ferocious insurgent war in Iraq produced huge numbers of weekly attacks and killing, averaging 2,000 attacks per month. Then casualties dropped dramatically as an escalation of U.S. forces restricted the flow of explosives into Baghdad, ethnic cleansing was completed in many areas, the anti-American

Mahdi Army suspended its attacks, and the United States co-opted Sunni insurgents by putting over 100,000 of them on the weekly payroll. The co-optation scheme was the key to the breakthrough, backed by a change in U.S. counterinsurgency strategy that emphasized protecting local populations.

But the problems that fueled the insurgency and civil war in Iraq still exist. There are serious problems with Iraqi security forces, even as they have assumed responsibility for patrolling the streets. The Iraqi military still lacks the capacity to defend its borders and airspace. And it is a perilous business to depend on buying off the insurgent opposition—the very strategy that is failing in Afghanistan.

Iraq will take decades to play out, well beyond the blink of an American news cycle. In Iraq the key players include rival groups of warlords, sectarian militias, local gangs, political and ethnic factions, a struggling unity government, and a deeply corrupted and sectarian police force. The Sunnis are enraged at being invaded, having their homes destroyed, and losing their privileged status. They are deeply opposed to the new constitution. They want a strong central government that distributes oil revenue from Baghdad. They are appalled that the United States paved the way to a Shiite-dominated government with deep ties to Iran. And they are incredulous that the United States enabled Iran to become the dominant force in the Middle East.[37]

The Iraqi Shiites are embittered by decades of Sunni tyranny in Iraq and centuries of Sunni dominance in the Middle East. Arab Shiites, until the United States overthrew Saddam Hussein, had not tasted power for centuries. Iraqi Shiites are determined to redeem their ostensible right to rule Iraq that was denied them in 1920, when the British successors to the Turks, inventing Iraq as a quasi-independent entity, rigged a plebiscite and phony parliament, installed a Hashemite puppet regime that the Shiites and Kurds never accepted, and paved the way to decades of Sunni tyranny.

The co-optation strategy has deeply enmeshed the United States in Iraqi tribal politics, lifting up certain tribes over others and corrupting them. Tribes are forming their own militias and creating new leaders adept at cutting deals and getting access to money that is supposed to pay for reconstruction. The predatory corruption of government officials and connected tribal leaders in Iraq is on a par with Afghanistan—pervasive, direct, and unrelenting. Iraq could very well explode again, as Shiite leaders demand greater power in the government and armed forces, and Shiite parties resist yielding it. Shiite and Kurdish leaders are stonewalling against integrating Sunnis into the Iraq army, and they have gathered the fingerprints, retinal scans, and home addresses of every Sunni "Awakening" fighter on the U.S. payroll.

Important political gains have been made in Iraq during Obama's watch. A national election was held in March 2010 in which a secular party led by former interim prime minister Ayad Allawi defeated the ruling government of Nuri Kamal al-Maliki. Allawi overcame his reputation as an American puppet to win a narrow victory, but he failed to assemble a ruling parliamentary coalition. Thus al-Maliki held onto power after accusing Allawi's party of fraud and vaguely warning that he remained the commander in chief. The key to al-Maliki is that he survived twenty-four years of brutally difficult exile in Iran and Syria as a functionary in a tiny, persecuted, anti-American, Islamist party, the Dawa Party. He developed close ties with Iran and Hezbollah, but he learned to trust only tiny cells of Dawa exiles. Al-Maliki owes his political prominence to his alliance with Moktada al-Sadr and the Mahdi Army, the very force that he subsequently put down to prove his mettle as a unifying national leader.

To make further progress that makes a real difference, Iraq needs an oil deal, a new constitution, a resolution over who owns the oil city of Kirkuk, and an election that brings more Sunnis into the government. Most difficult of all, Iraq needs to integrate large numbers of Sunni forces into the army and police force. Above all, it needs to get the U.S. Army out of Iraq, which is happening.

Obama has fulfilled his campaign promise to withdraw combat troops from Iraq and to gradually withdraw noncombat forces. Upon taking office he announced that 65 percent of America's force structure in Iraq would be removed by August 2010 and all combat troops, leaving up to 50,000 troops there in noncombat roles until December 2011. By April 2011 the United States was down to 47,000 troops, and Obama reiterated his determination to withdraw most of them by December. On Obama's watch the United States has relinquished one of its largest military bases in the Green Zone, the dramatically named Forward Operating Base Freedom. Shortly afterward, the administration announced its plan to keep indefinitely the entire Camp Victory complex (consisting of five large bases in Baghdad) and Camp Prosperity and Camp Union III (located near the new American embassy in the Green Zone). But Obama's official position is that the United States will relinquish all its military bases eventually.

As the United States winds down its formal role, the State Department is planning to double its presence in Iraq, to approximately 16,000 people, which will require a large contingent of private contractors that has to be housed somewhere. Moreover, the Army and State Department want to keep in place a regular U.S. military force that is large enough to counterbalance Iran, which has vast influence in Iraq. In the spring of 2011, Iraqis debated whether they should ask American troops to stay beyond December. Many Iraqis in the northern zones where Arabs, Kurds, and Turkmens compete for land want the United States to stay to prevent an ethnic civil war, while many others elsewhere want the occupiers to leave. Al-Maliki, who rarely consults

Parliament about anything, spent the spring and summer saying that this decision was up to Parliament, not him.[38] Then he took yes for an answer, accepting the December 2011 deadline.

Once an empire invades, especially a sentimental one like the United States, there are always reasons why it thinks it cannot leave. But sooner or later, conquered peoples have to be set free to breathe on their own and regain their dignity. As long as the U.S. Army was the ultimate power in Iraq, Iraq had no sovereignty. Shiites were viewed in the Sunni provinces as collaborators with the invader, and Sunnis viewed the Iraqi army as a creation of the invaders that put their enemies in charge.

The United States has, in effect, created a Sunni army in Iraq. The fate of this entity is a major, daunting variable. Sunni leaders protest constantly that the nation's interests against Iran are not being defended. If the Sunnis and Kurds can be integrated into what is euphemistically called the Iraq Army, Iraq has a chance of holding together as a semi-federalized state. There is no other option that averts another upsurge of death and destruction.

Advocates of breaking Iraq into three nations stress that parts of the country are already partitioned, all three of the major groups have their own military, and the Kurds have their own government and oil deal too. Ironically, the person now in charge of American policy in Iraq, Biden, was formerly a chief advocate of this view. But the majority of Iraqi cities and provinces still have Sunni and Shiite communities living side by side. Iraq cannot break apart without igniting a horrible civil war, one that Iran, Syria, Turkey, and Saudi Arabia would not sit out. The best hope is that Iraqis will decide for integration and sovereignty, as Obama contends. But it is up to Iraqis to decide whether they want a unitary state, a decentralized federation, three nations, or something else.

The situation in Iran, where the Bush legacy is disastrous, is equally perilous. Here there may be a chance of a breakthrough, although Obama has stopped saying so. In 2001 Iran had a few dozen centrifuges, and the government of President Mohammad Khatami helped the United States overthrow the Taliban regime in Afghanistan. Khatami negotiated with the United States in the wake of 9/11, closed Iran's border with Afghanistan, deported hundreds of al-Qaeda and Taliban operatives that had sought sanctuary in Iran, and helped establish the new Afghan government. The Bush administration could have spent the succeeding years negotiating with Iran, limiting its nuclear program, allowing it to buy a nuclear power reactor from France, and restraining it from flooding Iraq with foreign agents. Instead, Bush arbitrarily ended talks with Iran, consigning it to the Axis of Evil. Iran responded by electing an eccentric extremist, Mahmoud Ahmadinejad, to the presidency, developing more than 5,000 centrifuges, and threatening Israel.

We barely averted a catastrophe in 2006, when Bush and Cheney wanted to bomb Natanz with a nuclear weapon and the Joint Chiefs rebelled against Bush and Cheney.

Today there is a serious possibility that the Netanyahu government in Israel will carry out the bombing option. If it does, the entire region could explode into a ball of fire. That's the apocalyptic scenario. The hopeful one is a game-changer based on two or three years of sustained diplomacy. The United States could declare that it recognizes the legitimacy of the Islamic Republic of Iran. It could acknowledge Iran's right to security within its present borders and its right to be a geopolitical player in the region. It could accept Iran's right to operate a limited enrichment facility with a few hundred centrifuges for peaceful purposes. It could agree to the French nuclear power reactor and support Iran's entry into the World Trade Organization. And it could return seized Iranian assets. In return Iran could be required to cut off its assistance to Hezbollah and Hamas, help stabilize Iraq and Afghanistan, maintain a limited nuclear program for peaceful ends verified by the International Atomic Energy Agency, adopt a nonrecognition and noninterference approach to Israel, improve its human rights record, and stop its campaign of persecution against the political opposition it defrauded in the election of 2009.

Any deal of this sort would be a dramatic breakthrough in the Middle East. It would have a major impact on nearly every major point of conflict in the region. It would demonstrate that the United States understands that it cannot advance the cause of peace in the Middle East by isolating Iran. The election of 2009 embarrassed the clerical, political, and Revolutionary Guard reactionaries that rule Iran, leaving them in a weakened position politically, to which they responded by mounting a self-destructive culture war.

Obama responded by pulling back on his plan to explore negotiations with Iran. During the 2008 campaign he was willing to take sharp criticism from Hillary Clinton and John McCain on this issue. He wanted to press Iran's leaders to make concessions, or otherwise to strengthen the majority opposition in Iran that wants their nation to have constructive relations with the rest of the world. Obama could still be the ideal president to pull off a game-changing deal with Iran or at least to ratchet up the pressure on Iran's rulers to make gains for peace. On Obama's watch, Iran's clerical and political leaders have lost much of their day-to-day governing authority to the military, which tends to be more pragmatic than the clerics and Ahmadinejad. If Obama decides to deal with Iran, he will have to stand up to a firestorm of opposition in the United States and risk offending most of Israel's political establishment.

Other places exploded unexpectedly in his first term. Tunisia and Egypt overthrew their dictators within four weeks of each other in January and February 2011. In Tunisia, protesters overthrew President Zine al-Abidine

Ben Ali too quickly to require any help from the United States. The following month, Obama was very helpful to the Egyptian revolution, urging President Hosni Mubarak to resign from office and to "begin the transition now," although there were a few awkward days in mid-February when it wasn't clear what the latter phrase meant. Hillary Clinton and special envoy Frank G. Wisner, a former ambassador to Egypt, favored a gradual exit, partly in response to warnings from regional allies that pushing out Mubarak would destabilize the entire region. Three of Obama's advisers—deputy national security adviser Denis McDonough, speechwriter Ben Rhodes, and human rights specialist Samantha Power—urged Obama not to sell out the Egyptian protesters packed into Cairo's Tahrir Square. Tellingly, all three were holdovers from Obama's presidential campaign, true believers in "change you can believe in," although Power had been forced to resign from the campaign after she denounced Clinton as "a monster."[39]

Briefly there was a standoff between White House advisers who worried about what the rising generation of Arab democrats would think and State Department professionals who worried about what Israeli and Saudi leaders would think—until Obama instructed Robert Gibbs to explain that "now" meant "yesterday." When Mubarak resigned on February 11, Arab democrats beheld a realized impossibility—the opportunity to be ruled by leaders who did not condemn them to poverty and servitude.

Mubarak disastrously subjected Egyptians to thirty years of dictatorship and brutality. His regime helped to create Islamic terrorism by imprisoning, torturing, and exiling his opponents. He was a rock-solid ally of the United States and Saudi Arabia. He kept the peace with Israel, winning more aid from the United States than any nation except Israel. And he enriched his cronies by supplying Israel with natural gas cut from supplies to local Egyptian consumers. All of this fueled the rage of dispossessed Egyptians. For Islamic terrorist recruiters, Mubarak was a gift that kept giving. Ross Douthat aptly notes that Mubarak offered much of the Arab world a "constant vindication for the jihadi worldview." For many young Egyptians condemned to a bleak existence of stagnation and repression, it was a short step from hating Mubarak to hating the superpower that bankrolled him. One of them was Ayman al-Zawahiri, who found a home as Osama bin Laden's chief strategist; another was Mohamed Atta, who steered American Airlines Flight 11 into the World Trade Center.[40]

American presidents and diplomats backed Mubarak year after year because they could easily imagine something worse—a Khomeini-like anti-American Islamist, a Nasser-like anti-American secular pan-Arabist, or a Saddam-like anti-American fascist thug. American leaders realized that this calculation sold out the Egyptian people, but the day for dealing with that was always down the road. Obama made the same calculation until the so-called Arab street exploded in favor of Egyptian democracy. Whether Egyptian democrats actually get democracy will depend on their capacity to wrest power from an Egyptian army that has no intention of relinquishing its extraordinary privileges in Egyptian society. The middle-class professionals and students that overthrew Mubarak had no organizations to speak of, and the only opposition group with a strong organization, the Muslim Brotherhood, bided its time in the background.

The cause of Egyptian democracy has enormous challenges looming ahead, beginning with a crippled economy, an entitled army, and weak democratic organizations. "Arab democracy" itself is a concept fraught with dangers to religious and ethnic minorities, as majorities in numerous Arab nations contend that gays and lesbians should be stoned to death, and Muslim converts to other religions should be stoned too. Egypt has large majorities that favor both views, as well as repressive views about the rights of women; the prospect of an illiberal democracy is real there. In any nation lacking a tradition of democracy that makes a breakthrough to majority rule, it is difficult to establish the principle that obeying rules of fair play is more important than winning. Tunisia and Egypt have stronger traditions of national consciousness and thicker networks of civil society and middle-class professionalism than do most Arab nations; thus they were better candidates for democratic revolutions than their neighbors. The next hard case to come along, Libya, had none of these advantages, which required Obama to decide what he believes deep down.

On one level, Libya was an easy case. Libyan leader Colonel Muammar Qaddafi was an international pariah, a half-crazed megalomaniac and tyrant who brutalized Libyans for forty-two years and built nothing besides an oil industry and a resilient dictatorship. When Libyans joined the chain reaction of popular revolts sweeping the Arab world, Obama took a firm one-footed step in support of the rebellion, demanding on March 3, 2011, that Qaddafi immediately "step down from power and leave." Qaddafi had vengefully retaliated against the uprising, opening fire on protesters and vowing to fill the nation's streets with their blood. Obama declared that Qaddafi's "appalling violence against the Libyan people" destroyed his claim to legitimacy.[41]

This strong response, however, though emboldened by the Egyptian precedent, begged numerous questions. Where would Qaddafi go? What was he supposed to do if no country was willing to offer him sanctuary? How deeply should the United States intervene in Libya, besides freezing Libyan assets and airlifting refugees on military planes? Should the United States initiate or encourage collective action against Qaddafi through the U.N. Security Council? Was there any chance of getting a no-fly zone resolution through the Security

Council? Was this Libya's version of a national rebellion? Or was it closer to something that the United States usually tried to avoid, an African civil war? If it was a national rebellion, should the United States and its allies establish a no-fly zone to prevent Libyan planes from attacking protesters and armed opponents? If it was only the latest iteration of a civil war in a tribal society, did the United States and the international community have any business establishing a no-fly zone, and/or supplying the opposition, and/or fighting explicitly to overthrow Qaddafi?

Obama was reasonably clear about the main things. He wanted Qaddafi to resign and leave immediately. He feared that the Libyan revolt amounted to a civil war that could easily lead to a military stalemate. He wanted the Libyans to own their revolution. He was determined to restrict direct U.S. involvement to its relief efforts. He was opposed to putting American troops on Libyan soil. And, at first, he avoided taking sides between Hillary Clinton and Robert Gates on establishing a no-fly zone. Clinton said that she was open to destroying Libya's air defenses, although she did not press the point. Gates publicly opposed the no-fly option without absolutely ruling it out. Obama stated that it was an option on the table. In the early going John McCain and Connecticut senator Joseph Lieberman led the congressional fight to take military action in Libya.

For two weeks Obama stuck to his conflicted caution about intervening; he did not initiate or call for Security Council action to oppose Qaddafi. But on March 12 the Libyan opposition and the Arab League urged the Security Council to stop Qaddafi's forces from crushing the opposition. France, Britain, and Lebanon initiated a resolution, Obama signed on, and on March 17 the four nations formally sought authorization for a no-fly zone to protect civilians and civilian areas targeted by Qaddafi. This resolution passed by a vote of ten to zero, with five abstentions. For the first time ever, the U.N. took swift action to protect citizens from being killed by their government. In the Bosnian crisis it took more than a year before the U.N. got to the same point in 1999, intervening with air power. In the Libyan crisis it took a month. France and Britain issued strong statements on behalf of doing so; Russia, China, Germany, India, and Brazil abstained from voting; China, despite choosing not to use its veto, declared that it opposed any use of military force by the U.N. on principle.[42]

The resolution ruled out dispatching ground troops to Libya, and it passed barely in time to prevent a massacre of civilians in the opposition capital of Benghazi, a city of nearly 700,000. The White House assured Americans that U.S. forces would take the lead only in the early work of destroying Libya's air defenses, a puzzling assurance that evoked angry responses as the United States attacked Libyan forces. Eleven days passed before Obama addressed the nation on this subject. He seemed to be unsure what to say, while critics across the political spectrum protested that two wars were surely enough. Why was the United States intervening in Libya? How deeply did Obama plan to commit the United States to deposing Qaddafi? What did it mean to claim that the United States would play the leading role only briefly? Syria, Bahrain, and Yemen were flush with rebellions too; Syria was every bit as repressive as Libya; and the United States had recently looked the other way as Bahrainians were mowed down. What made Libya so different? Even if one assumed that Bahrain was beyond helping, because the Saudis would never permit a Shiite rebellion to succeed there, did Obama have plans for intervening in Syria and Yemen too?

Obama replied that America intervened to save Libyans from being massacred, which had to be a good thing. Not saving the people of Benghazi would have left a terrible moral stain on America's soul. By the time that Obama spoke he was already obscuring his very recent history of refusing to intervene in Libya, since he needed to sell Americans on his change of position. In Obama's telling, he pressed for an international mandate to save Libyan citizens because not doing so was not an ethical option for America.[43]

Obama walked Americans through the past month. Qaddafi had vowed to show no mercy to his people, going door to door, killing them like rats. Obama explained: "We knew that if we waited—if we waited one more day, Benghazi, a city nearly the size of Charlotte, could suffer a massacre that would have reverberated across the region and stained the conscience of the world." So American fighters struck Libyan forces on the outskirts of Benghazi, saving the city. They struck Qaddafi's forces in neighboring Ajdabiya, allowing the insurgents to drive them out. They hammered Libyan air defenses, setting up a no-fly zone, after which the United States handed over to NATO chief responsibility for enforcing the arms embargo and the no-fly zone and protecting Libyan citizens. From here forward, Obama announced, the United States would play a supporting role to NATO in the fight to protect Libyans: "While our military mission is narrowly focused on saving lives, we continue to pursue the broader goal of a Libya that belongs not to a dictator, but to its people."

America and its allies ended up in the right place, he implored—making a humanitarian intervention that stopped short of an explicit commitment to regime change. Obama did not mention that the Europeans had economic and strategic interests at stake in Libya, though that was implicit in the deal to make them lead the fight. He affirmed that America could not intervene every time that a government attacked its people, "but that cannot be an argument for never acting on behalf of what's right." The Libyan case was unusual, combining the undeniable prospect of "violence on a horrible scale" with the opportunity to prevent it through an international mandate. A month later, Obama tried to get the Security Council to condemn Syria's attacks on antigovernment protesters but was rebuffed, as Russia went back to warning that the U.N. was stirring up civil wars in the Middle East, and Lebanon was compromised by Syrian influence in Lebanon.[44]

Obama's case for intervening in Libya emphasized the necessity of fighting as liberally as possible. He was emphatic that being able to intervene with the blessing of the Arab League and the United Nations Security Council made all the difference in the Libyan case. His foreign policy was all about working cooperatively with other nations to build structures of collective security and shared responsibility. He had no truck with the contempt for multilateralism that marked the previous administration, or its sneers against "Old Europe."

But his trump argument for intervening in Libya was not the international mandate; that was merely the means to an end. Obama's trump was an ethical version of American exceptionalism. He put it bluntly:

> To brush aside America's responsibility as a leader and—more profoundly—our responsibilities to our fellow human beings under such circumstances would have been a betrayal of who we are. Some nations may be able to turn a blind eye to atrocities in other countries. The United States of America is different. And as President, I refused to wait for the images of slaughter and mass graves before taking action.[45]

In truth, the United States often looks away from massive violations of human rights in places where they occur episodically or frequently; it looked away from a nasty crackdown in Bahrain—where the Navy's Fifth Fleet resides—during this very period. The record of the United States in this area is not significantly better or worse than its NATO allies. But Obama made a deeply moral case for not making the perfect the enemy of the good. Regarding Libya he made a case for only one strategic interest, noting that America wanted the democratic revolutions in Tunisia and Egypt to succeed; if Qaddafi were allowed to slaughter his people, Tunisia and Egypt would be inundated with Libyan refugees. Obama did not add that Libya was an oil provider too, since that would not have helped with anything, and Gates had already contended publicly that the United States had no economic interests at stake there.

Not intervening in Libya was not conceivable if America was to be itself. It was imperative to strengthen liberal internationalist institutions and to develop new structures of collective security. And, Obama added on subsequent occasions, though not in his sell-the-war speech, it was terribly important not to get stuck in a military stalemate—his original misgiving about Libya.

So why not admit the obvious, that the goal of this intervention was to overthrow Qaddafi? Obama replied that the U.N. would never stand for outright regime change: "If we tried to overthrow Qaddafi by force, our coalition would splinter." Being explicit about it was a sure path to relying on the U.S. Army, a repeat of the Iraq war. Plus, Obama was determined to limit America's involvement in Libya to the point that, according to him, he was not required to win congressional authorization for the war—a claim that congressional leaders rightly disputed. According to Obama, the War Powers Resolution requiring presidents to halt unauthorized hostilities after sixty days did not apply to America's campaign in Libya because there were no U.S. troops on the ground and the military mission was constrained by the terms of a U.N. Security Council resolution. Thus, the "hostilities" threshold had not been breached, a remarkable position that left unanswered what one should call a campaign that showered Libya with drone attacks, dropped bombs on Qaddafi's compound, and spent $10 million per day on military efforts to expel Qaddafi from power.[46]

Obama tried something new in Libya, without announcing a doctrine for it—a half-in war effort in which the United States helped Europe, not the other way around. For the first time since NATO was created, the United States would not take the lead in a NATO war. Old-thinking critics derided it as "leading from behind." Obama had no slogan for it, but in effect, he told the Europeans: "We care, and we will help, but it's your neighborhood. Deal with it, especially the refugees and the overthrowing. And try to think about what happens after the dictator is gone."

All that Obama could do was ask for patience, trust, more patience, and an unwavering belief that America, to be itself, must do what it can, along with its allies, to make the Middle East come out right. If NATO and America kept the pressure on without overcommitting, Libya would get its chance to build a decent regime based on something besides fear and patronage. That was exactly what happened, refuting nearly everyone who had spoken up on this topic while the anti-Qaddafi rebellion played out. The fact that almost nobody liked how Obama did it had much to do with the lack of credit that he received for succeeding. But he did succeed, on liberal internationalist terms that set an important precedent.[47]

Obama wants Americans to take pride in the good works of American empire and to play better with others. In his thought, as in Niebuhr's, liberal internationalism and realism fold together, since working together is what ac-tually works to secure America's interests. Like Niebuhr, Obama combines a love affair with the American experiment with an ethical critique of American presumption. But Niebuhr had no real responsibilities for statecraft; he was free to write whatever he thought. Obama, responsible for the world's all-time superpower, and accountable to its electorate, has to work much harder at indulging its presumptions about itself.

Notes

1. Barack Obama, *The Audacity of Hope: Thoughts on Reclaiming the American Dream* (New York: Three Rivers Press, 2006), 279–280.

2. Obama, *The Audacity of Hope*, quotes 280, 285.

3. See Whitney J. Oates, ed., *Basic Writings of Saint Augustine*, 2 vols. (New York: Random House, 1948), II: *The City of God*, Book 19: 468–507; Reinhold Niebuhr, *Moral Man and Immoral Society: A Study in Ethics and Politics* (New York: Scribner, 1932); Niebuhr, *Christianity and Power Politics* (New York: Scribner, 1940); Niebuhr, *The Children of Light and the Children of Darkness* (1944; new edition, Chicago: University of Chicago Press, 2011).

4. See Reinhold Niebuhr, *Christian Realism and Political Problems* (New York: Scribner, 1953); Niebuhr, *The Irony of American History* (New York: Scribner, 1952). On Niebuhr's method, see Robin W. Lovin, *Reinhold Niebuhr and Christian Realism* (Cambridge: Cambridge University Press, 1995); Gary Dorrien, *Social Ethics in the Making: Interpreting an American Tradition* (Oxford: Wiley-Blackwell, 2009), 226–276.

5. Obama, *The Audacity of Hope*, 289.

6. Obama, *The Audacity of Hope*, 293.

7. Obama, *The Audacity of Hope*, 302–303.

8. Obama, *The Audacity of Hope*, 305.

9. Office of the Secretary of Defense, "National Defense Budget Estimates for the FY 2007 Budget (Green Book)," and "Financial Summary Tables Fiscal Year 2007," www.dod.mil/comptroller/defbudget/fy2007; Office of Management and Budget, "Department of Defense," www.whitehouse.govomb/budget/fy2007; Jim Garamone, "President Signs 2007 Defense Authorization Act," American Forces Information Service (October 17, 2006), www.defenselink.mil/News; Associated Press, "Senate Approves Pentagon Budget" (September 29, 2006), www.military.com/News; Renae Merle, "Pentagon Budget 'a Great Surprise,'" *Washington Post* (February 10, 2006), www.washingtonpost.com.

10. Obama, *The Audacity of Hope*, 307.

11. See Richard Wolffe, *Revival: The Struggle for Survival Inside the Obama White House* (New York: Crown Publishers, 2010), 244–245; Jonathan Alter, *The Promise: President Obama, Year One* (New York: Simon & Schuster, 2010), 232–233.

12. "Obama Signs Order to Close Guantanamo Bay Facility," CNN Politics, January 22, 2009, http://articles.cnn.com.

13. Bob Woodward, *Obama's Wars* (New York: Simon & Schuster, 2010), 70–71, 82–85; Peter Baker and Thom Shanker, "Obama Sets New Afghan Strategy," *New York Times* (March 26, 2009).

14. "Prepared Remarks of President Barack Obama: A New Strategy for Afghanistan and Pakistan," *New York Times* (March 27, 2009).

15. Woodward, *Obama's Wars*, 154–156; Peter Baker, "How Obama Came to Plan for 'Surge' in Afghanistan," *New York Times* (December 5, 2009); Wolffe, *Revival*, 238–242.

16. Bob Woodward, "McChrystal: More Forces or 'Mission Failure,'" *Washington Post* (September 21, 2009); Ben Smith, "A D.C. Whodunit: Who Leaked and Why?" *Politico* (September 22, 2009), www.politico.com/news; see Woodward, *Obama's Wars*, 175–177; Steve Luxenberg, "Bob Woodward Book Details Obama Battles with Advisers Over Exit Plan for Afghan War," *Washington Post* (September 22, 2010).

17. Woodward, *Obama's Wars*, 166–167.

18. Baker, "How Obama Came to Plan"; Woodward, *Obama's Wars*, 319–323.

19. Woodward, *Obama's Wars*, quotes 221, 239.

20. Michael Hastings, "The Runaway General," *Rolling Stone*, June 22, 2010, published in *Rolling Stone* issue of July 8–22, 2010; Baker, "How Obama Came to Plan"; Greg Jaffe and Ernesto Londono, "Obama Orders McChrystal Back to Washington After Remarks about U.S. Officials," *Washington Post* (June 23, 2010).

21. For a rebuttal that blasts the new "theology" of military social work and calls for a return to the military's "core competency" of killing and destroying, see Bing West, *The Wrong War: Grit, Strategy, and the Way Out of Afghanistan* (New York: Random House, 2011). For a conservative realist case against escalating in Afghanistan, see Andrew Bacevich, "Afghanistan: The Proxy War," *Boston Globe* (October 11, 2009); and Bacevich, *Washington Rules: America's Path to Permanent War* (New York: Metropolitan Books, 2010).

22. Barack Obama, "On a New Beginning," The White House: Office of the Press Secretary, June 4, 2009, www.whitehouse.gov/the-press; "President Obama Speaks to the Muslim World," June 4, 2009, youtube.com, uploaded by whitehouse.

23. Charles Hurt, "Obama Butters Them Up in Cairo," *New York Post* (June 4, 2009); Michelle Malkin, "Rainbows and Unicorns and a World Without the J-Word," June 4, 2009, www.michellemalkin.com/2009/06/04; Robert Spencer, "Platitudes and Naiveté: Obama's Cairo Speech," *Jihad Watch* (June 4, 2009), www.jihadwatch.org/2009.

24. Daniel Nasaw, "American Right Blasts Obama's Cairo Speech," *Guardian* (June 4, 2009), Hewitt quote, www.guardian.co.uk/world/2009; Frank J. Gaffney Jr., "America's First Muslim President?" *Washington Times* (June 9, 2009), www.washingtontimes.com/news/2009; Rick Moran, "Obama's Cairo Speech," *American Thinker* (June 4, 2009), www.americanthinker.com.

25. The Editors, "Obama in Cairo: Now What?" *National Review Online* (June 5, 2009), www.nationalreview.com/articles.

26. "Obama Seeks New Start with Muslims," Al Jazeera (June 5, 2009), Bishara and Abbas quotes, http://english.aljazeera.net/news; Barak Ravid Haaretz Service Agencies, "Israel: We Hope Obama Speech Heralds New Era in Mideast," Haaretz.com (June 4, 2009), www.haaretz.com/news.

27. Norwegian Nobel Committee, "The Nobel Peace Prize for 2009," October 9, 2009, http://nobelprize.org/nobel.

28. Wolffe, *Revival*, 37–38.

29. Barack Obama, "Remarks by the President at the Acceptance of the Nobel Peace Prize," December 10, 2009, www.whitehouse.gov/the-press-office.

30. See James Turner Johnson, *The Just War Tradition and the Restraint of War* (Princeton: Princeton University Press, 1981); Johnson, *Can Modern War Be Just?* (New Haven: Yale University Press, 1985); Frederick H. Russell, *The Just War in the Middle Ages* (Cambridge: Cambridge University Press, 1975); Michael Walzer, *Just and Unjust Wars: A Moral Argument with Historical Illustrations* (New York: Basic Books, 1977); John Howard Yoder, *When War Is Unjust: Being Honest in Just-War Thinking* (Maryknoll, NY: Orbis Books, 1996); Paul Ramsey, *The Just War: Force and Political Responsibility* (New York: Scribner, 1968); Gary Dorrien, *Social Ethics in the Making* (Oxford: Wiley-Blackwell, 2009), 471–472.

31. Obama, "Remarks by the President at the Acceptance."

32. Victor Davis Hanson, "Obama's Bad War," *National Review Online* (December 10, 2009), www.nationalreview.com/corner; Susan Davis, "Reactions to Obama's Nobel Peace Prize Lecture," *Wall Street Journal*, December 10, 2009, http://blogs.wsj.com/washwire.

33. Adam Serwer, "The Obama Doctrine and the Nobel Prize," *The American Prospect* (December 10, 2009), http://prospect.org/CSNC; John Nichols, "The Beat," December 10, 2009, www.thenation.com/blogs; Robert Siegel, interview with Katrina vanden Heuvel, National Public Radio, December 10, 2009, www.npr.org/templates.

34. Ruth Marcus, "Obama's Brilliant Nobel Speech," *Washington Post* (December 10, 2009), http://voices.washingtonpost.com; Joe Klein, "A Noble Lecture," *Time* (December 10, 2009), http://swampland.time.com/2009; Joe Klein, "A Noble Lecture," *Time* (December 10, 2009), http://swampland.time.com/2009; Rick Klein, "Humility of Hype: Neither Peace Nor Prize for Obama—Yet," ABC News, The Note (December 10, 2009), http://bogs.abcnews.com.

35. Walter Russell Mead, "Obama's Nobel Prize Speech," *Politico: The Arena*, December 10, 2009, www.politico.com/arena; see Mead, *Power, Terror, Peace, and War: America's Grand Strategy in a World at Risk* (New York: Knopf, 2004); Mead, *Special Providence: American Foreign Policy and How It Changed the World* (New York: Knopf, 2001).

36. On unipolarist ideology, see Gary Dorrien, *Imperial Designs: Neoconservatism and the New Pax Americana* (New York: Routledge, 2005); Charles Krauthammer, "The Unipolar Moment," *Foreign Affairs* 70 (1991), 23–33.

37. This discussion of Iraq and Iran briefly summarizes arguments I have made in Dorrien, *Economy, Difference, Empire: Social Ethics for Social Justice* (New York: Columbia University Press, 2010), 240–277.

38. Michael S. Schmidt and Tim Arango, "Iraq Must Decide Within Weeks if U.S. Troops Will Stay Past 2011, Top Official Says," *New York Times* (April 23, 2011); Tim Arango and Michael S. Schmidt, "Should U.S. Stay or Go? Views Define Iraqi Factions," *New York Times* (May 11, 2011), A6.

39. See Helene Cooper, Mark Landler, and David E. Sanger, "Policy Rift Muddles U.S. Message on Mubarak," *New York Times* (February 13, 2011); Peter Baker, "Cheer Leaders," *New York Times* (February 13, 2011); Laura Kind and Ned Parker, "Concessions Fail to Appease Foes of Government," *San Francisco Chronicle* (February 7, 2011).

40. Neil MacFarquhar, "Mubarak Faces More Questioning on Gas Deal with Israel," *New York Times* (April 23, 2011); Ross Douthat, "The Devil We Know," *New York Times* (January 31, 2011); see Lawrence Wright, *The Looming Tower: Al-Qaeda and the Road to 9/11* (New York: Knopf, 2006).

41. Mark Landler, "Obama Says Qaddafi Must Leave Libya Now," *New York Times* (March 4, 2011).

42. "UN Authorizes No-Fly Zone Over Libya," Al Jazeera (March 18, 2011), http://english.aljazeera.net/news; Edith M. Lederer, "Libya No-Fly Zone Approved by U.N. Security Council," *Huffpost World* (March 17, 2011), www.huffingtonpost.com/2011/03/17.

43. Barack Obama, "Remarks by the President in Address to the Nation on Libya," National Defense University, Washington, DC; The White House, Office of the Press Secretary, March 28, 2011, www.whitehouse.gov/the-press-office.

44. Obama, "Remarks by the President in Address," quotes; Neil MacFarquhar, "Push in U.N. for Criticism of Syria Is Rejected," *New York Times* (April 28, 2011).

45. Obama, "Remarks by the President in Address."

46. Obama, "Remarks by the President in Address"; Charlie Savage, "Two Top Lawyers Lose Argument on War Power," *New York Times* (June 18, 2011).

47. See Rod Nordland and Steven Lee Myers, "Chairman of Joint Chiefs Warns of Possibility of a Stalemate in Libya," *New York Times* (April 23, 2011).

7

Banks and Budgets

THERE IS NO INSTITUTION IN WHICH MORE IS AT STAKE for morality and social justice than a bank. And there is no document that is more charged with moral meaning, for better or worse, than a federal budget. Today the big banks are bigger and more dominating than ever, so soon after nearly destroying the economy and themselves. As usual, the people who are paying most for the destruction had little or no share in the excesses that caused it. The Republican Party has been overtaken by antigovernment extremists bent on savaging the social gains of the New Deal and Great Society. And the decision that Americans face between gutting Medicare and raising new tax revenue crystallizes the choice they must make about the kind of country they want to be.

A few months into Obama's presidency, the United States was still perched on the edge of an economic abyss when the Tea Party reaction galvanized Republicans, protesting about the national debt as though Obama had created it. Sometimes, when pressed on the point, Republican leaders acknowledged that George W. Bush exploded the debt. But nearly always they lionized Ronald Reagan as the model president—a classic case of cognitive dissonance, since Bush exploded the debt precisely by returning to Reagan's prescription of unpaid tax cuts combined with unpaid military increases.

Republican leaders, the new Republican base, and the Republican contenders for president all want to give yet another tax cut to corporations and the rich, never mind that that would worsen the debt. They propose to save money mostly on the backs of the poor and disabled—slashing food stamps and welfare, turning Medicare into a voucher program, reducing Medicaid to block grants, and abolishing the Affordable Care Act. They want to cut or abolish the capital gains tax and all taxes on interest, dividends, and inheritance. They want a balanced budget amendment to the constitution that caps federal spending at 18 percent of the total economy. They successfully forced Democrats to come to them in making huge budget cuts, only to walk away from historic deals in fits of extremism, which strengthened their leverage. They have no answer whatsoever to the question of how the financial industry should be prevented from frothing up another crash. And much of their party thrives on conspiracy theories about America's first black president.

The Tea Party is a throwback to the nativist Know Nothing movement of the 1840s and 1850s, which warned that German and Irish Catholic immigrants were destroying the country. The Know Nothings, when asked about their secret organizations, professed to know nothing. Antigovernment Republicans, when pressed to explain their insistence that Obama was born in Africa, somehow he espouses Islamic radicalism and radical Socialism simultaneously, and he is destroying America, profess that these convictions have nothing to do with feelings about his race. Racial justice, as an ideal, has seeped deeply enough into American society that no one admits to not believing in it. There is, however, a faction of the Tea Party that stormed into electoral politics primarily as a backlash against the Wall Street bailouts, not primarily from racial or ideological anxiety. Where were they to take their rage at the gross unfairness of the system? Why was no one taking a stand against the economic hazards of "too big to fail"? Who would put a stop to business as usual?

The Tea Party takes no interest in regulating Wall Street, and Wall Street is fighting not to be regulated. But there might have been no Tea Party had Wall Street not fallen in love with derivatives or gotten its way on everything for thirty years, and the Tea Party might have been a lesser affair had Obama cut the Wall Street oligarchy down to size. As it was, Obama and the Democratic Congress won a halfway decent financial reform after struggling with a financial industry that resisted any encroachment on its right to gamble away the economy.

Throughout 2009 it appeared likely that the big banks would suffer no infringements on business as usual. Two months into his presidency, at the March 27 meeting at which Obama told the thirteen biggest bankers that he was protecting them from the pitchforks, he asked them plaintively to help him help them. He and they were all in this together, he said, although they needed to show some respect for the public's rage about excessive compensation: "Excess is out of fashion." The big bankers nodded in fake agreement and told reporters at the White House that they were all in this together.[1]

The bankers realized what had just happened. They had gotten a reprieve they didn't deserve, though they thought they deserved it. This was the moment at which Obama could have won a political windfall by diminishing the power of the megabanks. Had Obama told the bankers that he planned to cut them down to an upper limit of 3 percent of GDP for a single bank and 2 percent for an investment holding company, the cheering would have resounded throughout the country. The bankers knew it; there were even a few likely Republican votes for ending "too big to fail." But the big bankers, having won a reprieve from a sympathetic president who wanted to work with them, took no interest in working with Obama. They geared up to defeat every financial reform that he and the Democrats proposed.

In June Obama unveiled a modest reform plan, which he called "a sweeping overhaul." He wanted enhanced regulation of financial institutions, stronger consumer protections, larger capital and liquidity requirements for large banks, and new regulations for over-the-counter derivatives and securitization. The key to his plan was to expand the reach of the Federal Reserve to regulate financial risk. Ineffective regulation, Obama noted, was a major factor in the financial meltdown, but so was the fact that the Fed had no supervisory authority over several companies that crashed, such as Bear Stearns, AIG, Lehman Brothers, and Countrywide Financial. To prevent the next meltdown the Fed had to have wider authority across the system, extending beyond its oversight of bank holding companies (firms owning more than one commercial bank) to regulate all financial companies large enough to pose a systemic risk in the event of failure. Obama, Summers, and Geithner advocated placing the authority in one place because vesting a committee of regulators with collective responsibility would be ineffective, lacking accountability. Obama called for a new consumer protection agency to oversee mortgages and credit cards; proposed to give the FDIC new powers to seize troubled banks; and required hedge funds, private equity funds, and venture capital funds to register with the SEC.[2]

All of this annoyed or alarmed the big bankers, even as Obama held back on what they cared about most—trading derivatives in the dark. His plan called for standard (plain vanilla) derivatives to be traded on an open exchange, but he took a pass on bespoke derivatives—the customized, one-of-a-kind type that blew up the system. Obama did not propose to curtail the use of bespoke derivatives; he merely asked for a clearinghouse to monitor prices and trades.

Three months later he gave a speech at Federal Hall, at the heart of Wall Street, declaring: "We will not go back to the days of reckless behavior and unchecked excess that was at the heart of this crisis, where too many were motivated only by the appetite for quick kills and bloated bonuses. The old ways that led to this crisis cannot stand." It was good theater and dead-on rhetoric, but the Obama plan merely proposed additional oversight for the existing system. By then Wall Street was regaining its swagger. In the first nine months of Obama's presidency the financial industry spent $344 million to oppose the expanded Fed, the consumer protection agency, the new rules for derivatives, and everything else smacking of reform, employing 1,537 registered industry lobbyists. This was twenty-five times the size of the pro-reform consumer and union lobbying group. The nine biggest banks, opting for togetherness of a sort, formed a joint lobbying powerhouse, the CDS Dealers Consortium. Citigroup alone hired forty-six lobbyists, notwithstanding that the federal government owns 34 percent of bailed-out Citigroup.[3]

All of that, plus a monolithic congressional Republican opposition, was arrayed against financial reform when the Obama administration took up the fight for a reform bill in the fall of 2009. In the early going the administration featured its proposal for a Consumer Product Safety Commission (CFPA) that regulated deceptive or abusive financial practices. Obama wanted the CFPA to require banks to offer plain vanilla versions of products, such as a thirty-year fixed-rate mortgage, in addition to whatever exotic products they offered. The aim was to allow consumers to buy something they understood and that had no risk of exploding. Industry lobbyists, however, drummed up Democratic opposition to the plain vanilla rule, causing Barney Frank and Christopher Dodd to drop it from the House and Senate bills they crafted, and both had to fight to keep the CFPA proposal alive.

Meanwhile Paul Volcker hit the lecture circuit to urge that banks should be prohibited from trading for their customers and themselves at the same time. In 1933 Carter Glass, a Senate Democrat from Virginia, and Henry Steagall, a House Democrat from Alabama, coauthored a landmark New Deal bill outlawing branch banking by national banks. Glass-Steagall created the Federal Deposit Insurance Corporation and erected a wall between commercial and investment banking, excluding commercial banks from the securities business. On Clinton's watch the wall came down, culminating twenty years of bank deregulation, as the Gramm-Leach-Bliley Act of 1999 allowed investment banks and commercial banks to merge. Clinton, Phil Gramm, and Larry Summers saw nothing wrong with fostering too-big-to-fail banks combining speculative investment and taxpayer-supported shelter, which opened the door to the megabank empires and mergers of the Bush years. Volcker, surveying the wreckage, implored that it was not too late to repeal Gramm-Leach-Bliley. In a world gone so awry, he implored, the seeming quaintness of this view was not a defect: "People say I'm old-fashioned and banks can no longer be separated from nonbank activity. That argument brought us to where we are today."[4]

By October 2009, Obama agreed with Volcker, but Geithner and Summers were opposed. Geithner contended that prohibiting banks from speculating for themselves would unnecessarily hamper America's wealth machine. Summers worried that the Volcker Rule would prompt many banks to opt wholly for speculative trading. If the big banks had to choose between gambling for themselves and taking care of customers, they would choose themselves. And if they got out of banking, the system would be plunged into another crisis. Summers warned Obama that Volcker's proposal was not as simple as it seemed. In fact, it was unrealistic and unworkable. What was Goldman Sachs, servicing virtually every player in the foreign exchange market, supposed to do with the Volcker Rule? Stop trading currencies? Geithner and Summers, though respecting Volcker's iconic status, admonished Obama that the financial world had left Volcker behind.

Summers usually won these battles in the early Obama administration. He bullied everyone, opposed proposals to change the system, and lectured repeatedly that "first, do no harm" is the touchstone of good policymaking. But the Volcker Rule made sense to Obama. In December the House passed a reform bill based on Geithner's strategy of requiring the banks to hold higher capital reserves. Obama wanted more than that, so Geithner relented, and Obama told Summers to get in line. On January 21, 2010, a year into Obama's presidency and two days after the Democrats lost Ted Kennedy's seat, Obama announced that he advocated Volcker's "simple and common-sense reform."[5]

Obama urged that America had made a serious mistake in allowing banks to stray from their mission of serving customers. The privileges of shelter, Obama stressed, should never have been yoked with speculation. The federal government, since the New Deal, has provided deposit insurance and other safeguards to ensure that America has a stable banking system. But these privileges were not created to give unfair advantages to banks operating hedge funds or private equity funds: "When banks benefit from the safety net that taxpayers provide—which includes lower-cost capital—it is not appropriate for them to turn around and use that cheap money to trade for profit." Worse yet, Gramm-Leach-Bliley allowed banks to make trades conflicting with the interests of their customers. The post-Clinton system allowed hedge funds and private equity firms inside banks to place risky bets, posing obvious risks of conflicted interest, which taxpayers subsidized. In Obama's view, the system was unacceptable on both counts, plus it fueled a riot of speculation. The best remedy for "too big to fail" was to draw a line between trading for customers and trading for yourself.[6]

Progressives shouted for joy at Obama's reversal, and Wall Street recoiled at his unexpectedly frontal challenge. This was not mere technocratic tinkering. This was using political power to change the system. In the spring the Dodd bill moved through the Senate in tandem with a Senate Agriculture Committee bill sponsored by Arkansas Democrat Blanche Lincoln. Unlike most reform bills, these two got stronger with each week of debate and amendment. Oregon Democrat Jeff Merkley and Michigan Democrat Carl Levin attached the Volcker Rule as an amendment to the Dodd bill, and in April the Securities and Exchange Commission set off another wave of public revulsion at Wall Street by filing a civil suit against Goldman Sachs for misleading investors in an opaque collateralized debt obligation (CDO) deal.

Goldman routinely shorted (betted against) CDOs that it created and marketed to investors—a showcase example of the unseemly but legal double-dealing that Volcker abhorred. According to the SEC, however, Goldman took a further step in its Abacus 2007 deal by creating a derivative that was designed to fail at the request of a client, John Paulson, who wanted to bet against it. Paulson is the head of a giant New York hedge fund that made billions betting against the housing market. The SEC said that Goldman misled investors by not disclosing that Paulson handpicked some of the bonds underlying the derivative, and Goldman said it had no obligation to do so.[7]

This case proved enlightening to a vaster public than the *Wall Street Journal*'s usual audience. The ostensible purpose of Wall Street is to raise money to finance making things in the real economy. But CDO deals are not investments. They do not create any actual bonds or mortgages or add anything of value to society. They are pure gambling on whether somebody else's bonds will succeed, inflating the housing bubble without financing a single house. They are like side bets at a casino, except the Federal Reserve, implicitly, protects these bets. Moreover, according to the SEC, Goldman looted its own customers. The star of the Abacus story was Goldman vice president Fabrice Tourre, who wrote in a January 2007 e-mail that crystallized the case: "The whole building is about to collapse anytime now. Only potential survivor, the fabulous Fab standing in the middle of all these complex, highly leveraged, exotic trades he created without necessarily understanding all of the implications of those monstruosities!!!"[8]

The Goldman case and a flock of media stories about Wall Street corruption incited public rage at a delicate moment, as Democratic senators competed to strengthen the financial reform bill. Lincoln's Agriculture Committee bill proposed to force banks to spin off their derivative trading to separate organizations, which Obama opposed. Minnesota Democrat Al Franken attached an amendment to the Dodd bill that prohibited banks from deciding who would rate their new securities, but this amendment was eliminated in the Dodd-Frank reconciliation bill.

More importantly, Ohio Democrat Sherrod Brown and Delaware Democrat Ted Kaufman proposed to limit the size of America's megabanks. Brown urged, "If we're going to prevent big banks from putting our entire economy at risk, we need to place sensible size limits on our nation's behemoth banks. The SAFE Banking Act prevents megabanks from controlling too much of our nation's wealth." No single bank should be allowed to risk more than 3 percent of the nation's gross domestic product, Brown and Kaufman contended. A cap on bank size would put an end to "too big to fail," and it would free up lending to small businesses that megabanks spurn. The Brown-Kaufman amendment imposed a 10 percent cap on any single bank or holding company's share of the U.S. total insured deposits. It limited the size of nondeposit liabilities to 2 percent of the nation's GDP for banks and 3 percent for nonbank institutions. And it established a 6 percent leverage limit for bank holding companies and select nonbank institutions.[9]

These caps were large enough to allow effective economies of scale. The Brown-Kaufman amendment, if passed, would have broken up the nation's six largest banks. Despite failing to win the support of Obama or the Senate Democratic leadership, it won thirty Democratic votes in the Senate and three Republican votes. It would have passed had Obama supported it. He did not support it because he believed the Volcker Rule was more effective.[10]

But the Volcker Rule proved easy to dismember, and it had a key Republican opponent, Alabama senator Richard Shelby, who supported a size limit. Procedural maneuvering by Shelby and Kansas Republican Sam Brownback blocked Merkley and Levin from attaining a Senate vote on the Volcker Rule. The Merkley-Levin amendment got a second life in an early version of the House-Senate conference bill, but in the end, the bill could not pass without the vote of Scott Brown, who gutted the Volcker provision, demanding exemptions for proprietary trading in Treasury bonds, bond issues by government-backed entities such as Fannie Mae and Freddie Mac, and municipal bonds. Banks were allowed to invest up to 3 percent of their tangible equity in hedge funds and private-equity funds, a huge loophole for the megabank holding companies, which led to more exemptions.[11]

Something similar happened to the rest of the reform bill. The Dodd-Frank Wall Street Reform and Consumer Protection Act required most derivatives to be traded on a public exchange and cleared through a third party to guarantee payment if one of the trading parties went out of business. It expanded the authority of the Federal Reserve, abolished the notoriously inept Office of Thrift Supervision, and established a new Financial Services Oversight Council chaired by the Treasury secretary. It established a new consumer agency and authorized regulators to impose higher capital reserves. It won greater authority for shareholders on how much corporate executives should be paid, and it called for new rules on the trading that financial companies do with their own accounts (proprietary trading).

These were significant victories over an overwhelmingly better-funded opposition. On signing the bill in July 2010, Obama justly boasted that it represented the strongest consumer financial protections in [American] history. But the lobbying and political opposition riddled the bill with poison pills and loopholes, especially carve-outs for select corporate users of derivatives, exemptions for foreign exchange swaps, and restricted scrutiny of corporate pension funds. The plan's heavy reliance on the Federal Reserve was a mixed blessing at best, as the Fed is very friendly to the big banks, and the new consumer protection agency is housed there. The bill did not require higher capital reserves or abolish gambling with CDOs. It took a pass on the biggest problem, that the ever-growing too-big-to-fail banks are too big to be regulated too. And Wall Street poured over $50 million per quarter into gutting the Dodd-Frank rules, winning victories on debit card fee caps, oversight of complex derivatives, and funding and leadership of the consumer protection agency. In the first quarter of 2011 alone, Wall Street spent $52 million to weaken the Dodd-Frank Act. Ten banks and trade groups, the usual players, led the parade of the powerful, accounting for 31 percent of the lobbying total: Financial Services Roundtable, American Bankers Association, Wells Fargo, JPMorgan Chase, Barclays, Securities Industry and Financial Markets Association, Goldman Sachs, Citigroup, Blackstone Group, and Investment Company Institute.[12]

Wisconsin Democratic senator Russell Feingold voted against the Dodd-Frank bill because it settled for half a loaf, which forced Obama to bargain for Scott Brown's vote. Two other Senate Republicans, Olympia Snowe and Susan Collins, helped carry the bill to the sixty-vote threshold in the Senate. Many Republicans echoed McConnell in warning that Dodd-Frank was a victory for Democrats and a defeat for the American people. As a party, the Republicans felt no responsibility for reforming a system that wiped out $13 trillion of wealth in eighteen months.

They opposed the consumer protection agency and thwarted the appointment of a strong director, Elizabeth Warren, despite the well-chronicled predatory lending and fraud that stoked the housing crash. They opposed transparency in derivative trading without explaining what Republican principle was at stake in preserving dark corners. Some Republicans regretted having voted for the bailouts, or at least claimed to do so after the Tea Party frightened them into repudiating their own emergency actions. But "we won't do it again" is no answer. Henry Paulson and the politicians who voted for TARP saved the country from replaying 1931. "Let them all crash next time" is not a realistic option, or an honest one.

But it was a winning sentiment in the dumbed-down midterm elections. The Republicans ran in 2010 as free-enterprise purists suddenly alarmed about the federal debt that their policies created. The same Republicans who routinely raised the debt ceiling under George W. Bush were suddenly opposed to doing so after a Democrat won the presidency. They were supposedly alarmed about America's mounting debt, but they opposed anything that yielded more revenue. They had no answer to why America began to have bank crises after dismantling the New Deal rules. They had nothing to say about how the federal government might prevent another meltdown. But they were brilliantly successful politically, gaining six Senate seats and retaking the House of Representatives with eighty-seven new Republican members, twenty-eight with Tea Party status, for a net gain of sixty-three seats, all of whom embraced the budget plan of Wisconsin representative Paul Ryan.

Savaging the Poor and the Vulnerable

The new congressional Republicans overread their election, as conservative Republicans are wont to do. In 1995, Newt Gingrich overread his midterm election mandate to impose his "Contract for America" on Americans, which proved disastrous for his party after he shut down the government. In 2005, George W. Bush told Americans that he had an electoral mandate to gamble their Social Security funds in the stock market, which got his second term off to a self-destructive start. The Ryan budget plan for 2012 is an overreach of this sort, to which Republicans subsequently added a screwball scheme that mucks with the Constitution.

Obama took the spiraling debt problem seriously, having appointed, in February 2010, a bipartisan commission to deal with it. In February 2011 he proposed a budget containing cuts in assistance to the working poor, home heating assistance, and other programs adding up to $1.1 trillion in savings over ten years. This was the customary Washington resort in this area, bashing poor people first. Obama seemed to believe he would win points from Republican and Democratic deficit hawks by slashing aid to people lacking lobbyists. The new Republican House, however, condemned the plan as a nonstarter. House budget chair Paul Ryan declared that gouging Medicaid and other programs for the poor was barely a beginning: "The President's budget spends too much, taxes too much, and borrows too much—stifling job growth today and leaving our children with a diminished future. In this critical test of leadership, the President has failed to tackle the urgent fiscal and economic threats before us." In Ryan's telling, Obama apparently believed that he could get away with ignoring the demands of the American people, as expressed in the midterm election. In this the president was amazingly mistaken: "We cannot tax, spend and borrow our way to prosperity. Where the President has fallen short, Republicans will work to chart a new course—advancing a path to prosperity by cutting spending, keeping taxes low, reforming government, and rising to meet the challenges of our time."[13]

This was Ryan's project for himself and his party. Two months later Ryan offered his plan to the House, where all but four Republicans committed themselves to it. In the election just passed, nearly all of them had claimed to be staunch defenders of Medicare, outraged by Obama's plan to cut Medicare spending. Then they voted to replace Medicare with a voucher program for all people currently under fifty-five years of age. Bait-and-switch politics was on.

According to the Ryan plan, the United States should abolish the federal government's guarantee to the elderly and the poor. Since 1965, the federal government has reimbursed doctors and hospitals for medical services to the elderly through the Medicare program, and the federal government has paid half to three-fourths of costs incurred by states for medical services to the poor and disabled through the Medicaid program. Medicaid is a matching program that insures as many people as meet the criteria for assistance. When states add Medicaid recipients, the federal government helps to meet the cost by matching a certain percentage.

The Ryan plan breaks both social contracts to the elderly and the poor. It privatizes and defunds Medicare, making the elderly find their own private health care with the help of a subsidy voucher up to a specified amount. It requires beneficiaries to pay $6,400 more to qualify for whatever the new Medicare program would be called. It makes deep cuts in Medicaid by turning it into a block grant with a fixed amount from the federal government to the states. It abolishes the Affordable Care Act, saving $725 billion by repealing the subsidies that the poor and disabled would have received to help buy health insurance. It achieves fully two-thirds of its $4.3 trillion in savings from low-income programs, cutting food stamps by 20 percent over ten years, removing more than 100,000 low-income children from Head Start, and cutting job-training programs. It does all this slashing and repudiating in the name of reducing the deficit, yet it blows a $4 trillion hole in the deficit with new tax cuts. The Ryan plan cuts the highest individual and corporate tax rates from 35 percent to 25 percent, which would be the lowest tax rate on high earners since 1931.[14]

A federal budget is, among other things, a statement about the kind of country that we want to be. In the House Republican vision, America would become the kind of country that sees no problem with leaving the elderly and dying to the mercies of insurance companies. Profit-based insurance companies do not provide decent coverage for the elderly and dying of modest means, and under the Ryan plan, states would drop Medicaid enrollees and cut services too. Medicaid is already inadequate, paying less than Medicare and private insurance, reflecting the weak political power of its beneficiaries. The Ryan plan, though dramatic, had no chance of passing in 2011; in the Senate it got forty votes. But it perfectly summarized what Republicans wanted to do, and still plan to do, establishing a dreadful benchmark for debt ceiling ultimatums and the elections of 2012.

In early April 2011, Obama averted a government shutdown by negotiating with House Republican leaders a spending reduction of $38.5 billion for 2011. This was a foretaste of baleful things to come. Obama cut Democrats out of the bargaining, negotiating directly with Majority Leader John Boehner, with whom he aimed chiefly at the politically weakest beneficiaries. Pelosi fumed at being shoved aside; more importantly, and rightly, Illinois representative Jesse L. Jackson Jr. blasted Obama for keeping government open on the backs of the poor and disenfranchised. Obama, incredibly, boasted that he negotiated "the largest annual spending cut in our history." Krugman replied that Obama had become a "bland, timid guy who doesn't seem to stand for anything in particular."[15]

That was not quite right, as Boehner pressed to eliminate federal funding for Planned Parenthood, and Obama cut him off, establishing what was not negotiable. On Friday, April 8, Obama and Boehner announced their last-minute budget deal. The next day Obama made his "largest cut" boast, and the outcry got his attention. Obama realized that he dangerously offended his liberal base by seeming to crow about cutting aid to people poor enough to need Medicaid. Four days later he stood up for progressive principles, countering a rush of Beltway chatter about breaking social contracts.

He began with some terribly elementary points: America is not about rugged individualism alone. Americans have always recognized their connections to each other. Some things can only be done together. Government is an instrument for doing some of these things. Without government there would be no military, public schools, or highways. Government programs such as Social Security, Medicare, and Medicaid exist because Americans believe that all citizens deserve a guarantee of basic security and dignity.[16]

It was sadly symptomatic that Obama found it necessary to go on like this, defending truisms from third-grade civics. We would not be a great country, he admonished, if we did not provide care for poor children, people with disabilities, and the elderly. Moreover, for the past century Americans have generally recognized that those who benefit most from America's way of life should give back a little more than others for the sake of the common good.

Pivoting to the debt crisis, Obama skipped over the deficits piled up by Reagan and George H. W. Bush, which, in his telling, were taken care of in the 1990s. Democrats and Republicans, despite their disagreements, came together in 1990, 1993, and 1997 to reduce the nation's deficit, and they did so in a way that mostly protected the middle class, America's social contract with the elderly, and its strategic national investments. Obama urged that this was what America needed to do again after losing its way for eight years. Two unfunded wars, an unfunded prescription drug benefit, and huge unfunded tax cuts sent the national debt soaring. Even with the unfunded wars, Obama noted, if the Bush administration and Congress had paid for the tax cuts and drug benefit, there would be no serious debt problem. As it was, when he took office the nation's projected annual deficit was over $1 trillion, and the economic meltdown necessitated emergency spending, which added to a serious debt problem.

Obama agreed with Ryan and the House Republicans that they had to start cutting something besides the discretionary 12 percent of the budget that deals with education, transportation, medical research, clean energy, national parks, food safety, air and water safety, and the like. Four things—Social Security, Medicare, Medicaid, and defense—take up two-thirds of the budget. But Obama was appalled that the House Republican budget proposed cuts of 70 percent in clean energy, 30 percent in transportation, and 25 percent in education. This was a strategy for losing the future, he warned. China is investing heavily in education and solar facilities. Brazil runs its cars on biofuels and is investing billions in new infrastructure. If Ryan-style pessimism and shortsightedness prevailed in American politics, America would lose the battle for a dynamic, healthy, prosperous future.

As for the Republican positions on Medicare and Medicaid, both were stunningly unworthy of America. Obama noted that Ryan and the Republicans wanted Medicare beneficiaries to pay $6,400 more to qualify for benefits, and they wanted to abolish guaranteed health care, forcing the elderly to shop for an insurance company with a voucher in hand. In addition, they wanted to reduce Medicaid to a block grant fraction of itself. Upwards of 50 million Americans would be told to fend for themselves, including grandparents who could not afford nursing home care without Medicaid, poor children, and children with autism or Down syndrome. Meanwhile, Republicans wanted to give another tax cut to the wealthy. Obama was incredulous: "That's who needs to pay less taxes? They want to give people like me a $200,000 tax cut that's paid for by asking 33 seniors each to pay $6,000 more in health costs. That's not right. And it is not going to happen as long as I'm President."

The House Republican plan was not about reducing the deficit, Obama contended. It was about changing the basic social compact in America. A chorus of pundits, led by *New York Times* columnist David Brooks, had praised Ryan for his courage and seriousness. Obama begged to differ on both counts, with Ryan sitting in front of him. There was nothing courageous or serious about giving millionaires and billionaires a trillion-dollar tax cut while asking the poor to take most of the hit for deficit reduction: "That's not a vision of the America I know. The America I know is generous and compassionate. It's a land of opportunity and optimism. Yes, we take responsibility for ourselves, but we also take responsibility for each other; for the country we want and the future that we share." It was simply false, Obama insisted, to claim that America must choose between investing in Americans and the country and getting control of the debt problem.

Obama was deadly earnest about controlling the debt problem; thus he had appointed the Bowles-Simpson fiscal commission in February 2010 and drawn upon some of its recommendations in devising his budget. The commission was cochaired by former Clinton White House chief of staff Erskine Bowles and former Wyoming Republican senator Alan Simpson. It issued its debt reduction plan in December 2010, providing the model for a similar group in the Senate calling itself "the Gang of Six" and a similar group bridging the House and Senate with which Biden worked closely.

The Bowles-Simpson group proposed to reduce the federal deficit by $4 trillion by 2020, principally by reducing spending and raising the retirement age. It called for discretionary spending cuts beginning at $50 billion and extending to 2020, capping government expenditures and revenue at 21 percent of GDP, simplifying the tax code and eliminating most tax breaks, cutting the top tax rate to somewhere between 23 and 29 percent, requiring equal percentage cuts in defense and nondefense areas, raising the retirement age for Social Security to 69 by 2075, raising the Social Security contribution ceiling from 86 percent of total potentially taxable wages to 90 percent, lowering Social Security benefits at the upper end, reforming the system of payments to physicians, cutting most agriculture subsidies, modernizing the military and civil service retirement systems, reducing congressional and White House budgets by 15 percent, increasing the gas tax up to 15 cents per gallon, and changing the budget process. Simpson and Bowles issued a cochairs' report that was more specific in some areas.[17]

The official commission report, though carefully vague in some areas, got nowhere, as the eighteen-member panel failed to muster a fourteen-vote supermajority for its plan. The group fell three votes short of the number needed to send the plan to Congress for a vote. But the Bowles-Simpson plan laid the foundation for the "balanced" plans that Democrats advocated and Boehner briefly considered, luring Democrats into budget negotiations in which they got hammered.

For Obama, it was just as well that the Bowles-Simpson plan never made it to Congress, which left him free to cherry-pick the parts that he liked. In February 2011 he proposed a $3.7 trillion budget that cut the deficit by $1.1 trillion over ten years, whereupon Ryan and the House Republicans erupted, ripping Obama's budget as a pathetic half measure. Budget-cutting hysteria commenced; Republicans turned a mere formality—raising the debt ceiling to $14.3 trillion—into a species of political hostage taking; and Obama revised his budget to prevent Republicans from shutting down the government. He centered his plan on a four-fold strategy to achieve $4 trillion of savings over twelve years.

The first plank was the spending cut of $1.1 trillion that he proposed in February and the deficit reduction of $38.5 billion that he had just negotiated with Boehner, which saved an additional $750 billion over twelve years.

The second plank was to cut current and future defense spending by $400 billion. Until now, Obama had relied on Gates to cancel unnecessary weapons programs and to make the Pentagon's procurement and management processes more efficient. Gates provided political cover for Obama by identifying business efficiencies and ordering, in January 2011, $78 billion in reduced military spending over five years. The Bowles-Simpson plan called for a military spending cut of $1 trillion over ten years. Now Obama asked Gates to find 40 percent of that figure during his last months on the job, before Gates retired in June 2011. Obama wanted the entire $400 billion to come from outside the special budget that his administration had devised to pay for the wars in Iraq and Afghanistan. Some of it came from the Pentagon; the rest had to be found in the defense programs of the State Department, Homeland Security, Veterans Affairs, intelligence, the Energy Department, and other national security agencies. Military spending, adjusted for inflation, grew by 7 percent per year every year from 2001 to 2011; with no adjustment the rate was 12 percent. Obama told the military that the years of growing at this scale every year had to stop; the Pentagon could save the entire $400 billion merely by limiting its spending increases to the expected rate of inflation. Besides eliminating waste and inefficiencies, he vowed, "We're going to have to conduct a fundamental review of America's missions, capabilities, and our role in a changing world." Progressives had waited over two years for that sentence.[18]

The third plank was to further reduce health care spending, but closer to the Bowles-Simpson plan than to the House Republican model. Obama declared: "Their plan essentially lowers the government's health care bills by asking seniors and poor families to pay them instead. Our approach lowers the government's health care bills by reducing the cost of health care itself." The reforms of the Affordable Care Act cut the deficit by $1 trillion; there were further wasteful subsidies to eliminate; there were savings on prescription drugs to be realized by using the full purchasing power of Medicare to attain greater efficiency and accelerate the availability of generic brands; and Medicaid was overdue to be strengthened and streamlined. Obama kept it short and vague on the main driver of rising health care costs—fee-for-service medicine. He had one sentence on this topic: "We will change the way we pay for health care not by the procedure or the number of days spent in a hospital, but with new incentives for doctors and hospitals to prevent injuries and improve results."

This is a major second-term issue; Obama merely put it into play. Fee-for-service medicine is an absurd incentive system that rewards as many procedures as possible, not good care. It treats physicians as independent contractors who get paid for running up the number of procedures. To be faced with upwards of twenty medical bills after a routine operation and brief hospital stay is no less absurd than if one had to separately pay off all the copilots, airline carriers, baggage contractors, and assorted others involved in a flight requiring a transfer. Obama did not say that health providers should be paid a salary, or even that physicians should be allowed bonuses based on good results. Although the American Medical Association is more liberal, female, hospital based, and public health–oriented than in the past, offending its other half was not in Obama's plan for his first term. When Obama visited and praised the Mayo Clinic and the Cleveland Clinic, he carefully refrained from mentioning that these gold standard hospitals keep their costs low by paying their physicians one-year contracts, with no bonuses, with contract renewals based on annual performance reviews. That is the other half of what health care reform needs to be about. Obama put a marker down and moved on, vowing to strengthen Medicare and Medicaid.[19]

He was committed to preserving Medicare and Medicaid "as a promise we make to each other in this society." Obama declared, "I will not allow Medicare to become a voucher program that leaves seniors at the mercy of the insurance industry, with a shrinking benefit to pay for rising costs. I will not tell families with children who have disabilities that they have to fend for themselves. We will reform these programs, but we will not abandon the fundamental commitment this country has kept for generations."

The fourth plank adopted the Bowles-Simpson emphasis on cleaning up the tax code without adopting its nonstarter about dramatically lowering marginal rates, although a few months later, bargaining with Boehner, Obama was willing to trade lower rates for new revenue. In April he started with the Bush tax cut for the rich, vowing not to roll over again. He got rolled in December 2010 because Senate Republicans gave him a choice between swallowing an extended tax cut for the rich and raising taxes on the middle class. Obama urged: "We cannot afford $1 trillion worth of tax cuts for every millionaire and billionaire in our society. We can't afford it. And I refuse to renew them again."

Beyond the politics of extending the Bush tax cuts, the problem of tax expenditures is a growing forest of itemized deductions. Obama supported deductions for homeownership and charitable giving, but he cautioned that they provide an average tax break of $75,000 for millionaires while doing nothing for middle-class families that don't itemize. He proposed limiting itemized deductions for the wealthiest 2 percent of Americans, saving $320 billion over ten years. Moreover, he wanted to reform the tax code to make it simple and fair, "so that the amount of taxes you pay isn't determined by what kind of accountant you can afford." Overall, he got to $4 trillion of savings very differently than the House Republicans, getting $2 trillion through spending cuts, $1 trillion through lower interest payments on the debt, and $1 trillion through cuts in tax expenditures, all of it armed with a trigger for deeper cuts if his plan failed to hit its targets.[20]

Reaction was swift and partisan. Ryan, whom Obama did not name specifically, said he was stunned by Obama's pathetically inadequate and partisan speech: "What we heard today was not fiscal leadership from our commander in chief. What we heard today is a political broadside from our campaigner in chief." Conservative columnist Russ Douthat, though allowing that Obama matched Ryan's $4 trillion of savings in the first decade, stressed that this was not the crucial thing in Ryan's plan. What really mattered was that Ryan achieved big savings after the Medicare cuts kicked in, ten years down the road. Obama had nothing that compared to breaking the government guarantee on health care: "Under the president's plan, we soak the rich in the short term, and then just keep going deeper into the red." Mychal Massie, chair of the black conservative Republican group Project 21, claimed that Obama took up the debt problem only because Republicans dragged him to the table: "So I guess it's no surprise that he's taken the low road and found enemies in corporate America and rushed to the liberal cure-all of taxing them and his defined wealthy among the population. Here again, the remedy to everything is cutting defense, raising taxes and class warfare." Charles Krauthammer was brutally disapproving: "I thought it was a disgrace. I've rarely heard a speech by a President so shallow, so hyper-partisan and so intellectually dishonest, outside of the last couple of weeks of a presidential election where you are allowed to call your opponent anything short of a traitor." Krauthammer noted that Obama's commission recommended bringing down the marginal tax rate to the mid-20s, but Obama said nothing about that while blasting Ryan and the House Republicans for recommending the same thing.[21]

Glenn Beck took offense at Obama's contention that Social Security and Medicare helped to make the United States a great country. Obama plainly disrespected the America that existed before the New Deal, Beck charged. Or at least, his handlers did; Beck is a chief purveyor of the Right-blogosphere convention that Obama is helpless without his speechwriters and teleprompter: "It shows his disdain for the country prior to FDR. It shows his disdain for the country. We were not a great country until the progressives took on creating medicare and social security. . . . This is an amazing statement. This is written for him. This is in a teleprompter. When he says there is no such thing as American exceptionalism, he means it." Fox news anchor Bill O'Reilly piled on, explaining that Obama's infatuation with government was very liberal and not very American: "The words 'tax reform' are interesting. I believe that is code for: tax the rich. You can see the intrusion of the nanny state, the feds doling out money to help citizens who cannot or will not help themselves."[22]

Krugman cheered that Obama finally said something that smacked of conviction and a willingness to fight. At his best, Krugman allowed, Obama was capable of making "a spirited defense of his party's values," which always shocked the Right when he did so, accustomed as it was to the accommodating Obama. Krugman appreciated that Obama capably defended the legacy of the New Deal and the Great Society. Obama did not propose to replace the Medicare system, which pays 70 percent of bills, with a voucher system paying 30 percent. He did not pretend that $3 trillion of tax cuts could be rendered revenue neutral. And he registered moral convictions about these things. But Krugman lamented that Obama was too civil and accommodating. He cared too much about seeming agreeable to independents and Republicans. He was too enamored of the word *bipartisan*, which, in Beltway usage, is nearly always code for a deal between wealthy conservative Democrats and wealthy very conservative Republicans. Above all, Obama conceded far too much to the Beltway obsession with debt reduction, overly indulging Beltway purveyors of the wrong crisis, which threatened to strangle the economic recovery.[23]

Krugman, Joseph Stiglitz, and other liberal mainstream economists rightly inveighed against the Beltway dogma that terrible things would happen if the government raised taxes and/or took on more debt. Terrible things were happening already, they noted, even as Wall Street soared through most of Obama's term in office. Bowles-Simpson types warned that bond traders were losing confidence in America, although at least Bowles-Simpson types acknowledged that getting more tax revenue was crucial to quelling the anxieties of bond traders. In Washington the debate centered on debt reduction and the best way to go about it. Krugman and Stiglitz pleaded that that was the wrong crisis to fix upon. The more important and urgent crisis was the stagnant economy that eviscerated the hopes and dreams of unemployed Americans.

Right up to the debt ceiling extortion of August 2011, and even after the fallout from it, the Treasury Department had no trouble selling debt, and it was able to borrow cheaply. The fearmongering in this area was about an eventual day of reckoning that mostly affected people at the upper end. Corporate profits climbed to record heights on Obama's watch, but companies were not hiring, even as they sat on $2 trillion of cash. Krugman and Stiglitz urged the political class to take on America's really-existing, highest-priority problem by investing in America's future. Official unemployment topped out at 9.2 percent in July 2011 and official black unemployment topped 16 percent. The real figures were twice as large, counting those who gave up reporting and those who never got into the system.

Where was the alarm about *this* crisis? Krugman rightly objected, and still does, that politicians are conditioned to look for trouble in the wrong places. The fearmongers fixate on "invisible monsters" instead of the employment crisis surrounding them. They elevate the hypothetical wrath of the bond market and the judgments of rating agencies that were wrong about everything for twenty years over the terribly real ravages of an underperforming economy.[24]

Stiglitz put it equally starkly in trying to dissuade Obama from giving highest priority to spending cuts. Bowles-Simpson was "a near-suicide pact," Stiglitz warned. If Bowles-Simpson or anything like it were carried out, it would surely lead to a recession, in this case a double-dip recession flowing out of the 2008 meltdown: "Growth would slow, tax revenues would diminish, the improvement in the deficit would be minimal." Stiglitz wanted Obama to push harder for job-creating investments in clean energy and infrastructure and to make deeper cuts in military spending. The key factor for economic sustainability, Stiglitz stressed, is the ratio of debt to gross domestic product. The Bowles-Simpson plan reminded Stiglitz of the austerity hawks he knew at the World Bank and International Monetary Fund who chained developing nations to structural adjustment programs. The IMF belatedly learned from its sorry experiences in East Asia, Argentina, and Latvia that monetary tightening and spending cuts do not lift nations out of economic malaise. But Bowles and Simpson had not learned it, nor had the imitators of Bowles-Simpson, let alone the Republicans that opposed any revenue enhancement.

The United States has underinvested in infrastructure, education, and technology for decades; thus it has many high-return opportunities. Stiglitz implores that this is what America's fiscal policy should focus upon. Tax revenues generated by fiscally driven economic growth more than repay low interest costs, which is a better deficit reduction plan than any lean-and-mean austerity scheme. Since America has low borrowing costs and the prospect of high returns, there is no reason not to make large-scale social investments. Stiglitz puts it bluntly: "We need to think about what kind of economy, and what kind of society, we want to create; and how tax and expenditure programs can help achieve those goals. Bowles-Simpson confuses means with ends, and would take us off in directions which would likely be counterproductive."[25]

America's biggest problem throughout Obama's presidency was its unemployment and underemployment crisis, but for two years, through the debt ceiling debacle of August 2011, Obama gave an occasional speech about making social investments and followed through with little or nothing. The Federal Reserve, under Bernanke, made an unprecedented effort to pump up the economy by buying federal debt. Between November 2010 and April 2011 the Fed bought $600 billion in Treasury securities, which boosted the stock market, lowered the cost of American exports, and allowed companies to borrow money at low rates. But all of that barely made a dent in the unemployment crisis. Even an aggressive monetary policy did not lift the nation out of its economic malaise. To "win the future," the United States has to risk aggressive investments in clean energy hardware, education, technological innovation, and a rebuilt infrastructure.[26]

Obama was slow to realize and to tell Americans that this is what his presidency needs to be about. In May 2011, 47 percent of Americans told pollsters it would be better for America to default on its debt rather than raise the debt ceiling and only 19 percent favored raising the debt ceiling. Never mind that raising the debt ceiling has always been a formality with no conditions. Americans suddenly believed that raising the debt ceiling was dangerous. They were ripe for fearmongering on this subject because most Americans seriously believe they are overtaxed, that taxes have never been higher, that the tax burden has never been higher relative to the size of the economy, and that most of the federal debt accrued since 2009 was generated by Obama's policies. However, all of these staples of Beltway chatter and political campaigns are false to the point of being howlers.[27]

According to the Bureau of Economic Analysis, in 2011 the total tax burden on Americans reached a fifty-three-year low, 23 percent of income. Throughout the 1970s, 1980s, and 1990s, Americans spent approximately 27 percent of their income on federal, state, and local taxes. In 1990, an American making $100,000 per year paid, on average, $27,300 in total taxes. In 2000 that figure was $28,700. The recessions and tax cuts of the succeeding decade lowered the tax average on $100,000 of income, by 2011, to $23,600. As a percentage of the nation's gross domestic product, American taxation is at its lowest level since 1950, 14.8 percent, which is far below the take in most wealthy nations. As for the debt myth, more than three-fourths of the federal debt that has mounted since 2009 is a product of George W. Bush's unpaid tax cuts, unpaid drug benefit, and unpaid wars, plus the financial meltdown.[28]

In essence, the United States is operating the world's only twenty-first-century superpower at the level of taxation that existed in the mid-1950s, when the Dow averaged 550 and Medicare did not exist. Obama pulled the average to a half-century low in December 2010 by extending the Bush tax cuts, signing off on a payroll tax cut, and accelerating depreciation for businesses. In a weak economy, when the government can borrow at cheap rates it *should* run high deficits, investing more in economic growth than the government takes from the private sector. Otherwise the United States is opting for a Japan-like lost decade. Once the recovery takes hold, it makes no sense to keep the United States on a 1950s tax basis. To get the tax revenue that the United States will need to get its fiscal house in order and to feed economic growth for a clean energy economy, the United States will need higher taxable income, or higher taxes, or both.[29]

Thirty years of tax-cutting political opportunism have produced an American majority that thinks it should never have to accept higher taxes for anything. It doesn't help that the people who are most alarmed about the federal debt insist that raising taxes on anything or anybody is anathema. The debt problem could be solved by political gridlock, but almost nobody wants that. Obama contends that he will not repeat the deal that he cut in December 2010, which sacrificed fair taxes on the wealthy to preserve the Bush tax cuts for income below $250,000. These extensions will expire on December 31, 2012. If Obama wins the 2012 election and Republicans control the House or Senate, the December 2010 scenario will recur. The Clinton tax rates could return via political gridlock, which would solve the debt problem.

That would not be a bad outcome, returning to the equilibrium that Bush dismantled. In the meantime the Republican Right took the nation hostage over the debt ceiling and extorted a terrible budget deal out of Obama. Until Obama took office, raising the debt ceiling was a routine and minor matter, in keeping with one of the few absolute proscriptions in the U.S. Constitution: "The validity of the public debt shall not be questioned" (14th Amendment, Section 4). Congress raised the debt ceiling seventeen times under Reagan, six times under Carter, and four times under Clinton. Under George W. Bush, Congress raised it seven times—three times with fifty or more Republican votes in the Senate. Then Obama took office, and suddenly, there were only two Republican Senators willing to support the nation's binding obligation to pay its debt; finding the votes for it was entirely on Obama and Democratic leaders. The next time there was only one Republican Senate vote in favor, and in 2010, zero Republican Senators supported raising the debt ceiling to $14.29 trillion, never mind that Reagan, Bush, Boehner, and even Ryan can be quoted that allowing the United States to default on its debt would be catastrophic for the nation.

With the coming of Obama and the Tea Party, Republicans ceased to be a normal party that took responsibility for governing. A powerful wave of Republican officials in the House and Senate claimed to believe that raising the debt ceiling was worse than defaulting on the federal debt and/or that defaulting would be no big deal. Michele Bachmann and Tim Pawlenty advocated no-deal obstructionism while campaigning for the presidential nomination;

Mitt Romney kept quiet when it mattered, then made a pitch for Tea Party obstructionist support; and all of the Republican contenders for president took a hard line against bringing new revenue into the equation. In Congress, antigovernment extremism prevailed in both Republican caucuses, especially the House of Representatives. Congressional Republican leaders, faced with a debt ceiling crisis of their making, worked with alarmed Democrats ostensibly to solve the crisis.

Two bipartisan congressional groups emerged in the wake of Bowles-Simpson to lay the groundwork of a budget debacle. One was the Senate-based Gang of Six. The other group bridged the House and Senate, working closely with Biden. Both groups devised debt reduction plans resembling Bowles-Simpson.

The Gang of Six consisted of Oklahoma Republican Tom Coburn, Georgia Republican Saxby Chambliss, Idaho Republican Michael Crapo, Virginia Democrat Mark Warner, North Dakota Democrat Kent Conrad, and Illinois Democrat Dick Durbin. This venture, a typical "bipartisan" enterprise, featured three hardcore conservative Republicans, two Blue Dog Democrats, and one liberal-leaning Democrat. The other group consisted of House majority leader Eric Cantor, a Virginia Republican; Arizona Republican senator Jon Kyl; Hawaii Democratic senator Daniel Inouye; Montana Democratic senator Max Baucus; South Carolina Democratic representative Jim Clyburn; and Maryland Democratic representative Chris Van Hollen.

Both groups crafted budgets aimed at achieving up to $3 trillion of savings in ten years. In both cases, Republicans forced the Democrats to come to them, obtaining agreements to bind budget cuts to the debt ceiling and not to raise taxes. Incredibly, Democrats agreed to a three-to-one rate of spending cuts to revenue increases, cutting $3 in government spending and revenue programs for every $1 raised in new revenue. In both cases, Republicans played their victory to the hilt by exacting maximum concessions before walking out. Coburn bailed from the Gang of Six just as its plan was about to be unveiled, contending that three-to-one was unacceptable and that he would not support any plan not linked to a balanced budget amendment to the Constitution. Cantor subsequently quit the Biden group, insisting that he would not accept any net increase in federal revenues and that he would only consider closing tax loopholes if any such change was coupled with offsetting tax cuts.[30]

That kicked the debt ceiling crisis upstairs to Obama, who tried to persuade Boehner to support a $4 trillion savings plan over ten years. Boehner briefly flirted with letting the Bush tax cuts for the wealthy expire in exchange for lowering the marginal tax rate and making deep cuts in Medicare and Medicaid. Obama was willing to gore sacred cows on his side, especially cutting

Medicare and raising the starting age for Medicare, in exchange for Republican concessions on increasing tax revenue. He reasoned that it might be easier to pass a colossal plan containing major concessions by both parties than to attain a smaller plan lacking reciprocal concessions. More precisely, he was willing to do bad things on a huge scale if it meant that Republicans would reciprocate by breaking their pledge not to raise taxes on anything or anybody. As it was, Democrats made major concessions and Republicans made none, but Boehner still backed out, because House Republicans refused to concede anything for any reason.

The fix was in before it played out on the verge of a default. Obama's concessions tallied over $2 trillion while Republicans conceded nothing. Republicans pressed for more, which they got, still at no cost. This was a winning pattern for Republicans, as they noticed. All they had to do was seem crazy enough to shoot the hostage. If Obama was willing to give up over $2 trillion, why should Republicans aim for more if the price was a pledge-breaking tax hike on billionaires or oil companies? Republicans claimed that they made a big concession merely by agreeing to find a way to raise the debt ceiling. Anything more than that was beyond the pale. If they, or at least a fraction of them, were to help raise the debt ceiling, they could only do it on terms that did not violate their Grover Norquist pledge to never raise taxes.[31]

Grover Norquist's Taxpayer Protection Pledge prohibits any measure that increases marginal rates for individuals and/or businesses and any measure that reduces deductions and credits, unless, in the latter case, reductions are matched dollar for dollar by reduced tax rates. Norquist, on his website, proudly displays Arianna Huffington's description of him: "The dark wizard of the Right's anti-tax cult." All but fourteen Republicans in the entire House and Senate have taken the Norquist pledge, and many in the Tea Party class are more stringent even than Norquist in judging what counts as a loophole or violation. Boehner gave up on a grand bargain with Obama after learning that even fantasy-size cuts on entitlements would not entice his group to close tax breaks for hedge funds, corporate jets, agribusiness, and oil and gas companies. Obama also wanted to limit deductions for high earners, which would have raised $300 billion, but all congressional Republicans and even most congressional Democrats were against that.[32]

The news got more ludicrous with each late-July day that America hurtled toward default. America cannot continue to pay the world's highest medical expenses and the world's largest military, with an aging population, while maintaining tax rates that are among the lowest in the world. The Congressional Budget Office projects that Medicare and Medicaid will increase to 9.3 percent of GDP over the next two decades from 5.6 percent in 2011 and that Medicare, on its present course, will run out of money in 2020. The status quo is unsustainable as the Baby Boomers retire, but in July 2011 American politics froze, perilously, at the choice between gutting Medicare and raising revenue. Perched on the edge of default, Congress needed to raise the debt ceiling but lacked a plan that could win 217 votes in the House of Representatives and 60 votes in the Senate. Was there a way for Republicans to keep their antitax pledge without cutting off 50 million Americans from their Social Security checks?

That question motivated McConnell to come up with a clever union of extremism and political cover, which didn't work either. McConnell proposed to dump the entire debt ceiling problem on Obama, empowering the president to do the necessary thing so Republicans could condemn him for doing it. The McConnell plan granted Obama extraordinary power to increase the government's borrowing authority, enabling Republicans to allow the debt ceiling to be raised without having to vote for it. Cosponsored by Harry Reid, this plan permitted three debt ceiling increments totaling $2.4 trillion, under the condition that Obama specified spending cuts of equal amounts. McConnell stipulated that Congress would have to vote on any debt limit increase proposed by the president, but the spending cuts would be chosen by Obama, not Congress. Thus the McConnell scheme reversed the normal legislative process by calling on Congress to disapprove a request by the administration in the expectation of a veto.[33]

This brazenly partisan scheme shifted all the blame for doing what was necessary to keep the government going onto Obama without getting any extra revenue. Republicans could vote against raising the debt ceiling, and condemn Obama for doing so, without being responsible for the consequences of a government shutdown. Democrats from purple and red states could vote against it too, since Obama only had to muster enough Democratic votes to sustain his veto. But that risked alienating Democratic voters in the most contested states. The McConnell scheme was a ploy to punish Obama for raising the debt ceiling three times before the November 2012 election, and it put the squeeze on vulnerable Democrats. For Republicans, it was too ingenious and, in some ways, politically attractive not to become part of the final deal. On the other hand, it was too cynical and accommodating for true-believing antitax ideologues, who protested that McConnell capitulated on the debt ceiling issue just as they were on the verge of a historic victory.

McConnell tried to look beyond the true believers, to November 2012. What mattered was to take down Obama. Every time that Obama raised the debt ceiling, that would be a bad thing meriting condemnation and reproach. If he lost the battle to raise it, that would be even worse. In either case, Republicans would not be responsible, which would help them take down Obama.

This odious proposal was vastly better than the Republican alternative. At least McConnell let go of threatening to sabotage the nation's credit rating. As

Obama acknowledged in a backhanded endorsement, McConnell's opportunism was a saving grace compared to Republican apocalypticism: "It is constructive to say that if Washington operates as usual and can't get anything done,
let's at least avoid Armageddon." Just for show, House Republicans countered
with a loony budget plan calling for a balanced budget amendment to the Constitution that capped federal spending at 18 percent of the total economy—the
Ryan plan by another name, this time by abusing the Constitution. The 18
percent benchmark would require draconian cuts into everything, including
Social Security; Obama aptly replied that savaging Medicare and Medicaid was
not in play for a decent American society, and "we don't need a constitutional
amendment to do our jobs."[34]

So-called "cut, cap, and balance" got through the House but was dead on
arrival in the Senate, wasting precious days as the default deadline approached.
House Republicans lined up to condemn the McConnell scheme as a sellout;
meanwhile Obama and Boehner quietly returned to wrangling over a monster
package, and the Gang of Six staged a showy comeback calculated to win hero-
rescuer honors. In both cases the plans that emerged were lopsidedly Republican—cutting the top income tax rate to between 23 and 29 percent; cutting
between $600 billion and $900 billion in discretionary spending over ten years by
imposing annual spending caps through 2015; cutting between $300 billion and
$600 billion from Medicare; eliminating the Class Act, a government program
of long-term health care insurance; changing the consumer price index formula
to save $100 billion in entitlement spending over ten years; and eliminating the
alternative minimum tax, which collects revenue from income sheltered in deductions and loopholes. All of this was designed to win Republican concessions
on eliminating $1 trillion of tax breaks and deductions and not cutting Medicaid,
but Boehner walked out again on a deal he had brokered, backing off from raising any new revenue, as his party demanded.[35]

A week before the debt ceiling deadline, Obama and Boehner gave dueling
speeches on national television. Obama pleaded that Congress had already
spent the money and that refusing to honor America's debt would wreck the
economy and stain the nation's honor. Americans had to find a way to move
forward together. Boehner, in reply, stood reality on its head. In his telling,
congressional Republicans had tried to find a compromise solution, but
Obama and the Democrats stonewalled for an extreme position. Boehner lamented that Democrats apparently couldn't say yes to anything. Up was down
and down was up. Boehner, a leading hostage taker, pretended that Obama
was the obstacle to a compromise, even as Boehner fronted for colleagues who
were willing to pull the trigger.[36]

Republican leaders had the upper hand throughout the ordeal because
nothing could happen without them, and their radical-right base was willing

to crash the economy. Obama had nothing to compete with that, except the threat of invoking the 14th Amendment, which he spurned. As it was, he kept imploring that sooner or later, reasonableness had to prevail, which turned out not to be true. In game theory, an unhinged player holds a huge competitive advantage; Republican leaders played it shrewdly. This was extortion on a staggering scale. Obama had already cut Medicaid, indefensibly, in April, which convinced Republican leaders that rolling him on Medicare would be easy. That was true to a point. Obama tried to give away $350 billion in Medicare cuts, but Republicans demanded $250 billion more out of Medicare by reducing payments for home health care and laboratory services. The grand bargain fizzled twice, as Boehner dropped out twice after failing to deliver on new revenue. Briefly, progressives rejoiced at Obama's failure to make history with Boehner, even as Obama offered to raise the entry age for Medicare—another terrible precedent. America needs to provide health care for all Americans at a price the nation can afford. Dropping Americans in their midsixties from Medicare would be a giant step in the wrong direction.

The point is not that Obama could have done something to produce a decent bill that would have passed Congress. That was impossible. House Republicans wanted the ridiculous "cut, cap, and balance" assault on Medicaid, Medicare, and Social Security, which passed the House by 234 to 190. The same people that contrived the debt ceiling crisis had the power to block everything short of a reactionary solution to it. In the end the stronger party won, despite controlling one-third of the government. Boehner and Reid pushed stopgap proposals in their respective chambers, both adhering to the Republican demand for no new revenue. Boehner's stopgap kicked the can down the road for six months, setting up another debt ceiling debacle for the election campaign. To get his plan through his party he added a balanced budget amendment to the Constitution; now House Republicans had to have a constitutional amendment merely to raise the *debt ceiling*. Reid's proposal cut $2.2 trillion over a ten-year period, including $900 billion in education, health care, nutrition, affordable housing, and child care, all to be determined later by committees, and it gave a pass to corporations and the wealthy from contributing anything to debt reduction. Republicans spurned this vengefully Republican plan because it spared entitlements.

The last congressional card had been played, two days shy of a federal default. Neither party had a tolerable proposal that it could get through the other party's chamber. Republicans complained that Obama led from behind, refusing to put a written plan on the table, which was true; Obama tried to limit the damage from the losing game in which he was trapped. In the end, on the threshold of default, he cut a deal with Boehner and McConnell that essentially adopted an even more Republican version of the Reid plan.

Throughout this tragi-farce Obama refused to threaten to invoke the 14th Amendment. He apparently believed that using his constitutional leverage would be unseemly and that Congress should not be given an out from doing its job. Some of us hoped, nonetheless, that he would use his authority if Congress failed to pass anything. If Obama had to defy and overcome Congress's inability to carry out its most important constitutional responsibility, so be it. Defending this position in court, if that proved to be necessary, had to be better than capitulating to political extortion.

Instead Obama allowed Boehner and McConnell to refashion the Reid plan to their liking, agreeing to spend the rest of his presidency wrangling over the specifics of an austerity regime: $1 trillion of discretionary spending cuts slashing education, Head Start, transportation, medical research, Meals on Wheels, worker training, clean energy, national parks, food safety, and air and water safety; $1.5 trillion of additional cuts to be determined by a congressional supercommittee stacked with Republicans who had not committed the unpardonable sin of advocating a revenue increase of any kind; and a default trigger option that slashed straight across everything, taking half its cuts from defense. The only evidence that a Democrat held the White House showed up in the Pentagon cut and in the deal's first-phase protection of Medicaid and Social Security. Medicare providers, however, were fair game from the beginning, and everything was on the table in the second phase.[37]

Obama damaged his presidency and the country by capitulating to extortion and bad policy. In December 2010 he inexplicably failed to demand a debt ceiling raise in exchange for caving on the Bush tax cuts; Obama explained that he expected Republicans to act responsibly when the debt ceiling came up. That didn't work out. Then he yielded to a party controlling one branch of government, repeatedly calling for reasonableness and moderation that never occurred, and acting as though Republicans, not he, held the ultimate weapon—the 14th Amendment. Boehner, urging House Republicans to approve the budget deal, stressed that it gave Republicans 98 percent of what they sought. The vote broke down that way, with House Republicans supporting it 174 to 66, and House Democrats, after months of pleading for a debt ceiling raise, splitting 95 to 95.

Dead-enders, Rush Limbaugh, and eight of the nine Republican presidential contenders railed against losing the other 2 percent. If one hustled for votes in Republican presidential primaries, one was not allowed to celebrate the Republican rout. Republican leaders in Congress, however, were thrilled with their victory, vowing to repeat it in perpetuity. McConnell, as usual, was frank, acknowledging that from the beginning he viewed the debt ceiling as "a hostage that's worth ransoming." If it were up to him, McConnell said, America would never increase taxes for anything, and the debt ceiling would be held up for ransom every time that a president of either party proposed to raise it.[38]

Others were less impressed with America's ransom deal. The Dow crashed by 1,500 points, and Standard & Poor's downgraded America's long-term credit rating to AA-plus. To be sure, S&P had no business rating anything after botching mortgage bonds for ten years, and its venture into political analysis ranged well beyond the sphere in which it supposedly possessed special expertise. S&P noted dolefully that America's debt was too high and that "new revenues have dropped down on the menu of policy options." Above all, it argued that American politics had become unstable: "The political brinkmanship of recent months highlights what we see as America's governance and policymaking becoming less stable, less effective, and less predictable than what we previously believed. The statutory debt ceiling and the threat of default have become political bargaining chips in the debate over fiscal policy."[39]

Many critics rightly noted that S&P greatly harmed the nation for ten years by not doing its job and then damaged it further with a strange downgrade that made no sense aside from the political commentary. Investors throughout the world, watching Greece, Spain, and Italy teeter on default, poured their money into U.S. Treasury bonds in utter disregard of the downgrade. The political commentary of S&P, however, was hard to fault. Fiscal policy, the firm stressed, is fundamentally a political enterprise, and "the debacle over the debt ceiling continued until almost the midnight hour." That was a warning to the politicians: Stop scaring the bean counters with hostage politics, uncontrolled debt, and intransigent demands. America probably would not have lost its S&P triple-A rating had it raised the debt ceiling with less drama or passed a budget with new revenue. As it was, Obama entered his fourth year in office coping with a historic downgrade, brutal cuts in spending that spare the wealthy and powerful, and a battered economy that yields high corporate profits but few jobs.[40]

To salvage a progressive presidency Obama has to assert his power, fight for social programs and economic rebuilding, and start using the 14th Amendment to end the politics of debt ceiling extortion. Liberal Democrats in Congress waited for Obama to plant a flag somewhere during the debt ceiling drama, which never happened. Obama offered up a swirl of concessions to get to a deal, accommodating an opposition that thrived on red lines. To the extent that Obama planted a flag for anything, it was for balance—but in the end he gave that away too, setting up months of rearguard fighting to restore balance in budget debates that put everything on the table and at risk.

The first three debt reduction groups came up short despite being made up of self-selected officials who wanted to get something done. Somehow the supercommittee was supposed to get something better, despite being made up of Republicans who were placed on the committee because they opposed the revenue proposals of the earlier groups. That was hopeless from the start, and the supercommittee failed. As for the debt ceiling, in truth there is no such thing. There is only the illusion of a debt limit that Congress passed during World War I to persuade taxpayers that it deferred to a legal brake on its borrowing authority. Congress controls the level of spending and taxation, and the debt ceiling fiction would not withstand a legal challenge to the 14th Amendment. Obama, and the country, cannot afford for him to dodge this issue.[41]

In the real world, many factors contribute to economic growth, and tax rates, though important, are not the most important factor. Creating a healthy and productive workforce is more important. Educating the workforce for twenty-first-century jobs and investing in research and technology are more important. Sustaining a middle class that buys goods and services is more important. Developing a strong infrastructure (the United States ranks twenty-third in the world) and saving for investment (most Americans have no savings) are at least as important as the usual fluctuations in tax rates. Above all, when a nation borrows money, nothing outranks the necessity of honoring its debt obligations. Tea Party Republicanism, however, fixates exclusively on one factor, defying what is known about the complexity of economic productivity. Coming out of the financial meltdown, the American economy has remained sluggish because of stagnant wage growth and weak consumer demand, not because the low taxes that Americans pay are somehow too high.

Obama realizes that the United States cannot move forward without making massive investments to build a clean energy economy with a revamped infrastructure. He has a pronounced tendency, however, when waxing on his spending cuts, to sound as though he only half-believes it. The economy lost one million public sector jobs during the second and third years of Obama's presidency, partly because the stimulus program ended too soon. When Obama speaks about the necessity of cutting the federal budget, he admonishes that governments must live within their means, just as families do, and that spending cuts are needed to put the economy on a sounder footing and to give businesses the confidence they need to grow and create jobs.[42]

But none of these things are true, however much they burnish Obama's image as a moderate-responsible type. Balancing the budget hurts economic growth. Even families go into debt to make investments in their future. As Krugman and Stiglitz contend, businesses in the postmeltdown period are not holding back because they lack confidence in the government's efficiency or competence. They are holding back because of weak consumer demand, lacking confidence because they lack customers. The Obama economy has been sluggish because of weak consumer demand caused by stagnant wages, job uncertainty, and the ongoing ravages of the mortgage disaster. In this situation, it was wrong to allow fear of the bond market to trump the jobs crisis. The interest rate on ten-year bonds, during Obama's first summer in office, was 3.7 percent. Republican leaders and the *Wall Street Journal* warned that any stimulus for job creation would send interest rates soaring. Two years later the interest rate on ten-year bonds was down to 3.03 percent, and fear of the bond market was still a religion in Washington, capturing all Republicans and many Democrats.[43]

In a democracy, a federal budget should be a reflection of the kind of country that citizens want to be. The impulse to avoid taking on excessive debt is healthy and correct in a strong economy. However, a nation with 14 million unemployed people and tremendous unused capacity in vital markets has no business slashing government spending in areas that serve human, social, and environmental needs. Moreover, even a recovering American economy cannot arrest its spiraling debt without significantly cutting defense and raising taxes. By the time that Obama found himself in a hostage situation facing default, he did the best that he could, short of invoking the 14th Amendment. The Congressional Progressive Caucus, relying on progressive tax policies that have no chance of being enacted, offers a better budget model—one that eliminates the federal government's budget deficit and stabilizes the national debt.

The Progressive Caucus is cochaired by Arizona Democratic representative Raúl M. Grijalva and Minnesota Democratic representative Keith Ellison. It proposes tax hikes on high incomes, superbrackets for extremely high incomes, limits on deductions, and raising the cap on payroll taxes. It eliminates the federal deficit by 2021 without slashing Social Security, Medicare, Medicaid, K-12 education, student loans, unemployment insurance, and scientific research—things that Americans overwhelmingly support.[44]

Specifically, on individual and corporate taxes, the progressive budget lets the Bush tax cuts expire, while maintaining marriage penalty relief, credits, and incentives for children, families, and education. It taxes all capital gains and qualified dividends as ordinary income and caps the benefit on itemized deductions at 28 percent. It repeals the upper-income tax cuts that Obama approved in the December 2010 tax deal. It replaces the estate tax deal of December 2010 with a progressive estate tax. It creates five additional income tax brackets, starting at 45 percent for married couples earning over $1 million per year and ranging up to 49 percent for earners making over $1 billion. (Currently the top tax rate is 35 percent for earners making more than $379,150.) The progressive budget taxes U.S. corporate foreign income as it is earned, as contrasted with the current policy of taxing it when earnings are repatriated to the United States. It eliminates subsidies for oil, gas, and coal companies and revives the Environmental Protection Agency's Superfund program that Congress gutted in 1995. It taxes credit default swaps, futures, option premiums, and foreign exchange spot transactions, and it charges a leverage tax (0.15 percent of covered liabilities) on the big banks.

On health care, the progressive budget includes a public option and tougher bargaining by Medicare. On Social Security, it increases benefits based on higher contributions on the employee side. On defense, it eliminates all emergency war funding (saving $674 billion over 2012 to 2016) and realigns conventional and strategic forces, scaling back all branches of the armed forces and eliminating unnecessary weapons systems. On jobs, it invests $1.45 trillion in job creation, education, clean energy and broadband infrastructure, housing, and research, and it creates a new infrastructure bank.

The contrast to the budget framework that Republicans extorted out of Obama is dramatic, yet nothing in the progressive plan makes heroic demands or calls for anything radical. Overall taxes as a share of GDP would remain significantly below European levels. The progressive budget rests on the principle that people should pay taxes on the basis of their ability to do so—a principle that polls very well even in red states. By rescinding the Bush tax cuts, this approach restores Clinton-era taxes on middle-class families, calling for shared sacrifice. The usual objection, supposedly devastating, is that the United States would become like France or Germany if it adopted progressive budget priorities. But in France and Germany, nobody goes hungry, health care is universally guaranteed, higher education is inexpensive, liberal internationalism prevails, and public transportation systems are highly advanced. The United States is in no danger of becoming like that. Moreover, the Germans have retained their manufacturing base while paying good wages—by working together and making good stuff. In the United States, this is said to be impossible.

The radical plan is the one that sailed through the House of Representatives with only four Republicans voting no; which got forty Republican votes in the Senate; and which Republicans topped off with a constitutional amendment pegged at 1966 levels of government spending. The Ryan plan savages Medicare down the road, which does nothing to reduce the deficit for ten years, so it savages aid to poor and vulnerable people to come up with immediate savings. It pretends that Americans are overtaxed, never mind that Americans are significantly undertaxed by any historical or comparative standard. It proposes another huge tax cut for corporations and the wealthy, never mind that this plan was supposed to be about reducing the national debt. It contends that America cannot afford Obama's health care reform, even though the health care bill is funded, and even though Ryan voted for Bush's tax cuts, wars, and drug bill, all unfunded.

Time columnist Joe Klein, puzzling that Republicans somehow believe that Ryan has given them a winning agenda, reaches for a psychological explanation. Republicans loathe Obama so much, Klein observes, that he drives them crazy, producing "wounded elephant screechings. . . . Indeed, the sheer hatred that Republicans have for Obama has led them to overreach, to latch onto Paul Ryan's outside-the-mainstream budget plan. They now face a presidential election where they are completely tied to the idea of destroying the most popular government program out there—Medicare."[45]

But Republicans did not have to hate Obama to reach for the Ryan plan. They latched onto Ryan because he fashioned the party's core ideology into a budget proposal, albeit with an extra dose of Reagan-throwback magical thinking about tax cuts paying for themselves. Shortly after the Ryan bill swept the House, the 235 House Republicans who voted for it got an earful at their town meetings. It turned out that some Republicans were incredulous at another huge tax cut. What did that have to do with reducing the national debt? Many others were enraged that House Republicans thought they could replace Medicare with a voucher. Two weeks later House leaders pulled back on replacing Medicare, insisting that they had the right position but were not inclined to press it at the moment. First their town meetings had to calm down. Then there would be another round of theater over the debt ceiling. Then they would refashion the Ryan plan as a balanced budget amendment to the Constitution. Then they would humiliate Obama and the Democrats in the debt reduction extortion and aftermath. Then, according to Ryan, the election would determine who was right about Medicare: "At the end of the day, I think 2012 is going to make the decision. The people are ahead of the political class."[46]

But the people support Medicare by 85 percent, and over two-thirds believe that the wealthy should pay more taxes.

Notes

1. Eric Dash, "Bankers Pledge Cooperation with Obama," *New York Times* (March 27, 2009).

2. "Obama's Financial Reform Plan: The Condensed Version," *Wall Street Journal* (June 17, 2009), http://blogs.wsj.com/washwire; Stephen Labaton, "Some Lawmakers Question Expanded Reach for the Fed," *New York Times* (June 17, 2009); Joe Nocera, "Only a Hint of Roosevelt in Financial Overhaul," *New York Times* (June 17, 2009).

3. Barack Obama, "Remarks by the President on 21st Century Financial Regulatory Reform," June 17, 2009, www.financialstability.gov/docs/regs, "a sweeping"; Barack Obama, "Remarks by the President on Financial Rescue and Reform," Federal Hall, New York, September 14, 2009, www.whitehouse.gov, "we will"; Simon Johnson and James Kwak, *13 Bankers: The Wall Street Takeover and the Next Financial Meltdown* (New York: Vintage Books, 2011), 191–192.

4. David Cho and Binyamin Appelbaum, "Obama's 'Volcker Rule' Shifts Power Away from Geithner," *Washington Post* (January 22, 2010); Louis Uchitelle, "Volcker Fails to Sell a Bank Strategy," *New York Times* (October 20, 2009), Volcker quote.

5. Barack Obama, "Remarks by the President on Financial Reform," The White House, January 21, 2010, www.whitehouse.gov, Obama quote; Richard Wolffe, *Revival: The Struggle for Survival Inside the White House* (New York: Crown Publishers, 2010), 171; Ron Suskind, *Confidence Men: Wall Street, Washington, and the Education of a President* (New York: HarperCollins, 2011), 363–389.

6. Obama, "Remarks by the President on Financial Reform."

7. See Binyamin Appelbaum, "A Difficult Path in Goldman Case," *New York Times* (April 20, 2010); Andrew Ross Sorkin, "When Deals on Wall Street Resemble a Casino Wager," *New York Times* (April 20, 2010).

8. Complaint, Securities and Exchange Commission v. Goldman Sachs & Co. and Fabrice Tourre, www.sec.gov/litigation, quote. Goldman subsequently paid $550 million to settle the case, without admitting or denying guilt, and Paulson was not indicted.

9. Senator Sherrod Brown, "Brown, Kaufman File Amendment on Too Big to Fail Legislation," Press Release (April 29, 2010), http://brown.senate.gov/newsroom.

10. David M. Herszenhorn, "Bid to Shrink Big Banks Falls Short," *New York Times* (May 7, 2010); Johnson and Kwak, *13 Bankers*, 228.

11. Yalman Onaran, "Volcker Said to Be Unhappy with New Version of His Rule," *Bloomberg Businessweek* (June 30, 2010), www.businessweek.com; John Cassidy, "The Volcker Rule," *New Yorker* (July 26, 2010).

12. Barack Obama, "Remarks by the President at Signing of Dodd-Frank Wall Street Reform and Consumer Protection Act," July 21, 2010, www.whitehouse.gov; see Reuters, "Senator Christopher Dodd's Financial Reform Bill to Give Huge Powers to Federal Reserve," *New York Daily News* (March 15, 2010); Paul E. Barrett, "The Wall Street Reform Fight We Really Need," *Bloomberg BusinessWeek* (April 7, 2010); Floyd Norris, "Fortunate Timing Seals a Deal," *New York Times* (April 23, 2010); David M. Herszenhorn, "House-Senate Talks Drop New Credit-Rating Rules," *New York Times* (June 15, 2010); John Heilemann, "Obama Is from Mars, Wall Street Is from Venus," *New York* (May 22, 2010); Brady Dennis, "Congress Passes Financial Reform Bill," *Washington Post* (July 16, 2010); Eric Lichtblau, "Ex-Regulators Get Set to Lobby on New Financial Rules," *New York Times* (July 27, 2010); Ben Protess, "Leading the Wall Street Lobby," *New York Times* (July 15, 2011).

13. Shawna Thomas, Luke Russert, and Kelly O Donnell, "Responses to Obama's Budget," First Read, NBC News, February 14, 2011, http://firstread.msnbc, quote; see "Partisan Reaction to Obama's Budget," *Business Journal Daily* (February 15, 2011), http://business-journal.com.

14. House Budget Committee, "Fiscal Year 2012 Budget Resolution—The Path to Prosperity: Restoring America's Promise," http://budget.house.gov/fy2012budget; see Carl Hulse, "House Approves Republican Plan to Cut Trillions," *New York Times* (April 16, 2011).

15. Jeff Zeleny, "President Adopts a Measured Course to Recapture the Middle," *New York Times* (April 10, 2011), Jackson quote; Paul Krugman, "The President Is Missing," *New York Times* (April 11, 2011); Carl Hulse, "Republicans and Democrats

Alike Claim Successes in Averting a Shutdown," *New York Times* (April 10, 2011); Jennifer Steinhauer, "2011 Budget Bill with Cuts Is Approved by Congress," *New York Times* (April 15, 2011).

16. Barack Obama, "Remarks by the President on Fiscal Policy," George Washington University, April 13, 2011, The White House, Office of the Press Secretary, www .whitehouse.gov.

17. "The Moment of Truth: Report of the National Commission on Fiscal Responsibility and Reform," December 2010, www.fiscalcommission.gov; see "Co-Chairs Proposal, National Commission on Fiscal Responsibility and Reform," November 10, 2010, Draft Document, www.fiscalcommission.gov.

18. Obama, "Remarks by the President on Fiscal Policy," quote; Thom Shanker and Christopher Drew, "Obama Puts Deficit Ball Back in Pentagon's Court," *New York Times* (April 15, 2011).

19. See Timothy Noah, "Hold the Mayo," Slate (July 23, 2009), www.slate.com; Steven Bush, "What's Wrong with Fee-for-Service," *Physician's News Digest* (May 1997), www.physiciansnews.com; Anthony L. Schlaff, "A Must for Health Care Reform: End Fee-for-Service Medicine," *Christian Science Monitor* (September 10, 2009), www.csmonitor.com.

20. Obama, "Remarks by the President on Fiscal Policy."

21. Carrie Dann and Shawna Thomas, "Ryan Strikes Back," First Read, NBC News, April 13, 2011, http://firstread.msnbc, Ryan quote; Russ Douthat, "The Middle-Class Tax Trap," *New York Times* (April 18, 2011); "Obama's Budget Deficit Plan: Bookerista Reaction," April 14, 2011, www.bookerrising.net, Massie quote; Jeff Poor, "Krauthammer's Take on Obama's Budget Address: I Thought It Was a Disgrace," *The Daily Caller* (April 14, 2011), http://dailycaller.com.

22. *The Glenn Beck Show*, Premiere Radio Networks, April 14, 2011; *The O'Reilly Factor*, Fox News Channel, April 13, 2011.

23. Paul Krugman, "Let's Not Be Civil," *New York Times* (April 18, 2001), "spirited defense"; Krugman, "Obama, Ryan and the Shape of the Planet," *New York Times* (April 13, 2011), krugman.blogs.nytimes.com; Krugman, "Let's Take a Hike," *New York Times* (April 25, 2011).

24. Paul Krugman, "Fears and Failure," *New York Times* (May 6, 2011), quotes; Krugman, "Springtime for Bankers," *New York Times* (May 2, 2011).

25. Joseph E. Stiglitz, "Why I Didn't Sign Deficit Letter," *Politico* (March 28, 2011), www.politico.com, quotes; see Joseph E. Stiglitz, *Globalization and Its Discontents* (New York: Norton, 2003); Stiglitz, *Making Globalization Work* (New York: Norton, 2006).

26. See Binyamin Appelbaum, "Stimulus by Fed Is Disappointing, Economists Say," *New York Times* (April 24, 2011).

27. See Lydia Saad, "U.S. Debt Ceiling Increase Remains Unpopular with Americans," Gallup, July 12, 2011, www.gallup.com/poll.

28. Dennis Cauchon, "Americans Pay Less Taxes," *USA Today* (May 6–8, 2011); Brian Montopoli, "Analysis Finds U.S. Tax Burden Lowest Since 1958," Political Hotsheet, CBS News, May 6, 2011, www.cbsnews.com; Derek Thompson, "Taxes at Lowest Level Since 1958," *The Atlantic* (May 6, 2011), www.theatlantic.com.

29. See Kevin G. Hall, "This Fact May Not Sit Well: Americans Are Under-Taxed," McClatchy Newspapers (May 5, 2011), www.mcclatchydc.com.

30. Associated Press, "Analysis: Oklahoma Senator's Departure Leaves Gang of 6 Without Critical Cog to Forge a Deal," *Washington Post* (May 19, 2011), Washington Post.com; Josh Boak, "New Urgency in Joe Biden's Budget Talks," *Politico* (June 8, 2011), www.politico.com; Andrew Taylor, "Crunch Time Looms as Biden-led Budget Talks Resume," Associated Press, June 21, 2011, www.msnbc.com.

31. See Mark Landler, "Obama Presses G.O.P. for Deal on Debt Ceiling," *New York Times* (July 11, 2011); Carl Hulse, "A Lofty Vision vs. Realpolitik," *New York Times* (July 11, 2011); Jackie Calmes, "Obama Grasping Centrist Banner in Debt Impasse," *New York Times* (July 12, 2011); Mark Handler and Carl Hulse, "Budget Talks Beginning to Take on a Testy Air," *New York Times* (July 12, 2011).

32. Americans for Tax Reform, "Who Is Grover Norquist?" www.atr.org.

33. Jackie Calmes, "Debt Talk Mired, Leader for G.O.P. Proposes Option," *New York Times* (July 13, 2011).

34. Jackie Calmes and Carle Hulse, "Fallback Moving to Fore as Talks on Budget Stall," *New York Times* (July 16, 2011), quotes.

35. Jackie Calmes and Jennifer Steinhauer, "Bipartisan Plan for Budget Deal Buoys President," *New York Times* (July 20, 2011); Editorial, "The Gang of Six Play," *Wall Street Journal* (July 21, 2011); Naftali Bendavid, Carol E. Lee, and Janet Hook, "Obama and Boehner Advance Toward Deal to Cut Deficit," *Wall Street Journal* (July 22, 2011).

36. "Text of House Speaker Boehner's Primetime Debt Speech," July 25, 2011, www.abc12.com.

37. Naftali Bendavid and Carol E. Lee, "Leaders Agree on Debt Deal," *Wall Street Journal* (August 1, 2011); Carl Hulse and Helene Cooper, "Leaders Declare Deal Framework to End Debt Crisis," *New York Times* (August 1, 2011); Carl Hulse, "House Passes Deal to Raise Debt Cap and Avert Crisis," *New York Times* (August 2, 2011); Naftali Bendavid and John McKinnon, "Uneasy House OK's Debt Deal," *Wall Street Journal* (August 2, 2011).

38. Editorial, "End the Debt Limit," *New York Times* (August 5, 2011), McConnell quote.

39. Eyder Peralta, "Standard & Poor's Downgrades U.S. Credit Rating," WNYC, August 5, 2011, www.wnyc.org/npr, quote; Binyamin Appelbaum and Eric Dash, "S. & P. Downgrades Debt Rating of U.S. for the First Time," *New York Times* (August 6, 2011).

40. Nelson D. Schwartz and Eric Dash, "Amid Criticism, S. & P. Standing by Debt Downgrade," *New York Times* (August 7, 2011), quote.

41. Lisa Mascaro, "GOP Announces Its Deficit 'Super Committee' Selections," *Chicago Tribune* (August 10, 2011).

42. Barack Obama, "Weekly Address: Cutting the Deficit and Creating Jobs," The White House, July 2, 2011, www.whitehouse.gov, quote.

43. See Paul Krugman, "What Obama Wants," *New York Times* (July 7, 2011); Krugman, "No, We Can't? Or Won't?" *New York Times* (July 11, 2011); Krugman, "The Wrong Worries," *New York Times* (August 5, 2011).

44. Congressional Progressive Caucus, "The People's Budget: Budget of the Congressional Progressive Caucus, Fiscal Year 2012," http://cpc.grijalva.house.gov.

45. Joe Klein, "Wounded Elephant Screechings," *Time* (April 14, 2011).

46. Jennifer Steinhauer and Carl Hulse, "Voters Attack Republicans on Medicare," *New York Times* (April 27, 2011); Carl Hulse and Jackie Calmes, "G.O.P. Rethinking Bid to Overhaul Medicare Rules," *New York Times* (May 6, 2011), Ryan quote.

8

What Kind of Country?

THE STORY OF OUR TIME IS THAT THE COMMON GOOD has been getting hammered for thirty years. Wages have been flat for thirty years, and inequality has worsened dramatically. One percent of the American population controls nearly 40 percent of America's wealth and a bigger chunk of its politics. The crash of 2008 wiped out $8 trillion of home value, crushing the nest eggs of wage earners. The banks that frothed up the crash are doing just fine. Much of the Republican Party is committed to delegitimizing Obama's presidency, and most of the Republican Party wants to bust public unions and break America's social contract with the poor and elderly.

All of this has created an opening for a democratic surge for social justice and equality. But so far, the common good is still getting hammered, and Obama has spent most of his presidency cleaning up an economic disaster and coping with a massive global credit contraction.

Throughout American history Americans have debated about the kind of country they want to be. Today America stands at the crossroads of a decision about the kind of country that America should be, which does not mean that a decision is necessarily imminent, since Americans are deeply polarized. According to the theory of "realignment" favored in political science textbooks, American politics decidedly "realigns" every thirty or forty years in the wake of a breakthrough election. In 1800 Thomas Jefferson's Democratic-Republicans overturned the rule of the Federalists. In 1828 the Democratic-Republicans split into Democrats and Whigs. In 1860 Abraham Lincoln's Republicans pulled off the last third-party triumph, finishing off the Whigs. In 1896 William McKinley consolidated the Republicans as America's majority party. In 1932 Franklin Roosevelt's election paved the way to the New Deal. In 1980 Ronald Reagan's election paved the way to the capitalist blowout of the past generation.[1]

There is still time for 2008 to be transformational in the sense of these historic elections, ending an era of American politics. But time and opportunity are running out as the Reagan era endures in bizarre forms. Economic inequality, always steep in the United States, got much steeper after Reagan's policies took hold. In 1981 the top 1 percent of the U.S. population held 32 percent of the nation's wealth and took in 11 percent of its annual income. Today these corresponding figures are 39 percent and 25 percent. The top 10 percent of the population hold more than 70 percent of the wealth. The bottom 50 percent hold 2 percent of the wealth. The share of America's income held by the top 1 percent has more than doubled since 1980, while the bottom 90 percent has, since 1975, coped with flat wages and mounting debt.[2]

For thirty years we have had perplexed debates about how to account for this trend line in an advanced democracy. How could a nation possessing a strong tradition of middle-class democracy allow the middle class to be eviscerated? Economic globalization, to be sure, unleashed the predatory logic of capitalism, setting off a race to the bottom that feeds on inequality and obliterates cultural values and communities that get in the way. But globalization alone does not account for the American willingness to turn American society into a pyramid.

From the late 1940s to 1975, productivity and wages soared together in the United States, creating a middle-class society. Meanwhile there were no bank crises, as New Deal reforms kept commercial banks out of the investment business. But wages flattened in the mid-1970s and have stayed that way ever since, while productivity kept soaring and commercial banks got deeply into the investment business. The rich got fantastically richer in the 1980s and 1990s while everyone else fell behind, taking on debt to keep from drowning and to keep up appearances, as urged by the advertising industry. During this period nearly every manufacturing-oriented society outperformed the United States in income growth *and* did so with more equitable distributions of income.[3]

Globalization heightened the necessity of using political power to defend the common good, but in the United States, the common good fell decidedly out of favor politically. The right to attain wealth was exalted over other values. The corporate race to low-tax and cheap-labor markets was rewarded with tax incentives. The religious, civic republican, and trade union communities of memory that historically kindled America's idea of a common good faded in American society, eclipsed by an ascending Christian Right holding very different social convictions. The American myths of Manifest Destiny and American exceptionalism were refurbished for political usage. Political campaigns became coded with racist images of black criminals and welfare queens. Liberals were redefined as guilty types that coddled criminals, imposed affirmative discrimination, and taxed working people to pay for welfare programs. Xenophobic slurs against immigrants were recycled from the least attractive chapters of American history. America passed three-strike laws and binged on prison expansion, filling its prisons with racial minorities. And social issues were shrewdly used to get working-class and middle-class voters to vote against their economic interests.

In the economic sphere the consequences were devastating, fueling a surge for inequality. As late as 1963, the top-bracket tax rate for individuals was 88 percent. From 1964 to 1981 it was 70 percent. Reagan cut it to 50 percent on his first pass and astoundingly got it down to 28 percent in 1988; he also slashed the top rate on capital gains from 49 percent to 20 percent and made it easier for the superwealthy to pay most of their taxes at the capital gains rate. Policies favoring the financial industry and real estate over manufacturing and local communities were enacted, and corporations whittled their tax bills to nothing by exploiting loopholes and exemptions designed for them. The United States hollowed out its industrial base that paid decent wages, providing incentives to firms that made things to make them elsewhere. By the end of the 1980s, the top fifth of the population earned more than half the nation's income and held more than three-quarters of its wealth, while the bottom fifth received barely 4 percent of its income.

George H. W. Bush, after further exploding Reagan's debt, and Bill Clinton, succeeding Bush, restored some balance to the tax picture, which produced Clinton's budget surpluses of the late 1990s. But Wall Street fell in love with derivatives on Clinton's watch, with his help, and the financial sector began to gamble trillions of dollars on credit-default contracts. George W. Bush, succeeding Clinton, took no interest in regulating Wall Street's mania for extra yield, and his administration blew up the Clinton gains with tax cuts, two wars, and a drug benefit.

By the end of the Bush administration, the inequality blowout of the 1980s looked modest, as did the Reagan recession. The chair of the Federal Reserve, on a Friday late in Bush's term, warned Congress that America might not have an economy by the succeeding Monday. That weekend many Americans began to focus on whether they wanted to entrust John McCain with America's financial and economic meltdown.

Contrary to the views of apologists for unleashed global capitalism and some of its radical critics, politics matters. Thomas Friedman, in his best-selling books on "turbo-capitalism," enthused that economic globalization—the integration of the national economy into the global economy through trade, direct foreign investment, short-term capital flows, and flows of labor and technology—has "flattened" the world. Global capitalism reduces national politics to minor tweaks, he contended. There is no third way in political economy anymore; there isn't even a second way. Any nation that wants a growing economy has to wear a one-size-fits-all "golden straightjacket" that unleashes the private sector, deregulates capital markets, minimizes government bureaucracy, eliminates tariffs on imported goods, privatizes state-owned industries and utilities, and allows direct foreign ownership and investment. Once a nation takes this path, Friedman claimed, there are no important political issues to debate. All that remain are "Pepsi or Coke" choices involving slight nuances of taste, policy, and local traditions. The "core golden rules" of the global economy have replaced most of what national politics used to be about.[4]

But the apologists for turbo-capitalism, which academics call "neoliberalism," exaggerated the demise of national politics and the futility of attempts to channel economic forces. Neoliberals were credulous about the self-correcting capacities of the market. They ignored that unionism and the NGO movement have globalizing capacities too and that governments were far from passé in this area before the global economy crashed. After the crash, governments stepped up dramatically, spending trillions of dollars to save capitalism from itself. Germany put up more than $700 billion, and Britain spent one-fifth of its national GDP to save its banking systems. By March 2009 the governments of Europe, North America, and the leading Asian capitalist powers had spent or guaranteed over $11 trillion to save the system.

The neoliberal boosters overlooked that governments played huge roles in setting up this system, defending and perpetuating it, deciding whether to regulate it, and dealing with its implications for equality, trade agreements, racial and gender justice, human rights and the rights of workers, immigration, and the environment. They played down the roles of the International Monetary Fund (IMF) and World Bank in enforcing neoliberal doctrine. They thought it didn't matter that economic oligarchies in emerging and advanced economies entrenched themselves in national governments, rigging the game whenever possible.

Then came the crash of 2007, which played out dramatically a year later. The crisis that Obama inherited was thirty years in the making. Government was denigrated, and private wealth was prized over the public good. Speculators gamed the system, and regulators looked the other way. Mortgage brokers, bond bundlers, rating agencies, and corporate executives made fortunes selling bad mortgages, packaging them into securities, handing out inflated bond ratings, and putting the bonds on balance sheets. The chief rating agencies, Moody's and Standard & Poor's, instead of exposing financial risk, handed out triple-A ratings that stoked the lunacy, being paid by the very issuers of the bonds they rated.

So many plugged-in bankers, investors, brokers, and traders rode this financial lunacy for all it was worth, caught in the terribly real pressure of the market to produce constant short-term gains. Banks got leveraged up to fifty-to-one (Bear Stearns's ratio at the end) and kept piling on debt. In some cases subprime mortgage bonds were actually created to allow investors, using credit-default swaps, to bet against them. There was so much money to be made that firms could not bear to leave it aside for competitors to grab.

Obama inherited a global deflationary spiral exacting portfolio contractions of 30 to 40 percent and a free-falling economy that had nearly doubled its unemployment rate in one year. Deflation, once started, has a terrible tendency to feed on itself. Income falls in a recession, which makes debt harder to bear, which discourages investment, which depresses the economy further, which leads to more deflation. Obama helped to break the spiral by coddling Wall Street and by pumping a trillion dollars of life support into the system. It worked well enough that eight months into his presidency, the fear of a depression had been forgotten and Wall Street was soaring. A year later, the nonpartisan Congressional Budget Office estimated that in the past quarter alone the stimulus package had created or saved 3.3 million jobs and lowered the unemployment rate by 1.8 percentage points. By then it was clear that Democrats would pay a fearsome midterm electoral price for Obama's aggressiveness in saving the economy. Or at least, that was the reason that Republicans featured in explaining why the Obama administration had been such a disaster.[5]

Many Americans are ideologically opposed to any politics that tries to rectify severe discrepancies in wealth, and the race to the bottom unleashed by economic globalization has convinced many people that nothing can be done about it. But both versions of this verdict are nonstarters for any moral perspective that maintains a connection to biblical teaching about wealth, poverty, and the good society. Moreover, the view that nothing can be done is untrue. If we think that we cannot do anything about economic disparities, we will soon be stampeded into believing that Social Security is unsustainable, Medicare and Medicaid should be gutted, and we might as well abolish what remains of the progressive tax system. Tellingly, American politics has reverted to debates about these very things, all rolled up with the politics of fear and loathing.

Imagining the Hateful Obama

Obama is a lightning rod for the politics of fear and loathing. Millions of Americans did not dream up, by themselves, their convictions that Obama was born in Kenya, his teenaged mother forged an American birth certificate so he could run for president, he imbibed radical Socialism from a father he never knew, or his real father was an American Communist poet, he wrote *Dreams from My Father* to hoodwink prospective voters, or he got a 1960s revolutionary to write *Dreams from My Father* for him, he forged a political career by exploiting his friendships with Communists and anti-American activists, he sympathizes with radical jihad, and his presidency is a conspiracy to inflict anticolonial rage on America. There is a paranoid literature on these themes and a seemingly insatiable market for it. It is anchored in best-selling books, spewed in countless right-wing websites, and legitimized with appearances and commentary on Fox television.

Jerome R. Corsi, a conspiracy theorist with a doctorate in political science from Harvard, is the king of this genre. Brad O'Leary, another early entrant, warned in *The Audacity of Deceit: Barack Obama's War on American Values* that Obama aims to destroy America's economy, bar Christianity from public life, legalize late-term abortion on demand, ban the use of firearms, and turn the U.S. Treasury into an ATM for the United Nations. Orly Taitz, the "queen of the birther movement," holds out against Obama's birth certificate and plugs for a conspiracy about Obama getting into Harvard as a foreign exchange student. Aaron Klein, a Fox News regular and columnist for the *Jewish Press*, updates Corsi's "radical connections" trope and adds birther material in *The Manchurian President: Barack Obama's Ties to Communists, Socialists, and Other Anti-American Extremists*. Jack Cashill, in *Deconstructing Obama*, contends that *Dreams from My Father* is a cunningly subversive stew authored by Bill Ayers that Obama is not smart enough to have written. Other titles in this burgeoning field include *Culture of Corruption: Obama and His Team of Tax Cheats, Crooks, and Cronies*, by Michelle Malkin; *The Post-American Presidency: The Obama Administration's War on America*, by Pamela Geller (with Robert Spencer); and *Obama: The Postmodern Coup*, a warmed-over Trilateral Commission conspiracy tale by Webster Griffin Tarpley.[6]

In the weeks leading up to the Democratic and Republican conventions of 2008, the nation's number one best-seller was Corsi's *The Obama Nation: Leftist Politics and the Cult of Personality*, which established the template for a gusher of anti-Obama alarmism. For Corsi, *The Obama Nation* was a campaign second coming, having made his early fame in 2004 by smearing John Kerry's military record as a Swift Boat commander in Vietnam. In Corsi's telling, Kerry was a fraud whose Silver Star and three Purple Hearts only appeared to top George W. Bush's military record. Corsi was an avid blogger for FreeRepublic.com, out of which his anti-Kerry book *Unfit for Command* was spawned with coauthor John O'Neill. The book rocketed to a number one best-seller, but on its way up, O'Neill claimed that he hadn't known that his longtime friend Corsi had showered the Right blogosphere with scurrilous opinions about Hillary Clinton, Islam, Muslims, Pope John Paul II, Kerry, and other targets of his bigotry. "HELLary," according to Corsi, was a "FAT HOG" who couldn't keep her husband satisfied because she was probably a "lesbo." Islam was "a worthless, dangerous Satanic religion." Muslims were "RAGHEADS" and "Boy-Bumpers." Muslims, Corsi wrote, were much like the pope in the latter regard: "Boy buggering in both Islam and Catholicism is okay with the Pope as long as it isn't reported by the liberal press." And "Commie Kerry" was "anti-Christian and anti-American," with suspicious connections to Jews.[7]

None of this disqualified Corsi from respectful treatment on Fox television or from attracting a prestige publisher for *The Obama Nation*. Corsi actually boosted his stature in 2007 by charging that President Bush secretly plotted to merge the United States with Canada and Mexico. In the fevered atmosphere of the Far Right, some dramatic explanation was needed for Bush's inexplicable "sympathy" for Mexicans. Corsi's book, *The Late Great USA*, offered an accusatory explanation lacking any evidence. The following year he wrote *The Obama Nation* for a conservative imprint of Simon & Schuster directed by Mary Matalin, a confidante of the Bush family and former aide to Dick Cheney. In Corsi's telling, an Obama presidency "would be an *abomination*" because Obama is a lying, corrupt, anti-American Socialist and elitist who covered up his commitments to radical causes, plotting to subvert America with every waking breath.[8]

The Obama Nation pilloried Obama for employing a literary imagination and for taking literary license in telling his story. The Obama candidacy, Corsi argued, was nothing without Obama's story and the campaign's cult of personality, but Obama lied about his story, which made him untrustworthy. Obama's speech at Selma in 2007 laid Corsi's foundation. Speaking to a commemorative gathering at Brown Chapel a month after he launched his presidential candidacy, Obama set up a climactic rhetorical run by mistakenly asserting that President Kennedy financed the airlift that brought Obama's father to Hawaii: "This young man named Barack Obama got one of those tickets and came over to this country. And he met this woman whose great-great-great-great-grandfather had owned slaves, but she had a different idea, there's some good craziness going on, because they looked at each other and they decided that we know that in the world as it has been it might not be possible for us to get together and have a child. But something's stirring across the country because of what happened in Selma, Alabama, because some folks are willing to march across a bridge. So they got together and Barack Obama, Jr., was born. So don't tell me I don't have a claim on Selma, Alabama. Don't tell me I'm not coming home when I come home to Selma, Alabama. I'm here because somebody marched. I'm here because y'all sacrificed for me. I stand on the shoulders of giants."[9]

Corsi, not exactly prizing the feeling of the occasion, belabored the obvious literal impossibilities: Obama's father came to Hawaii in 1959; Kennedy took office in 1961; the Selma march occurred in March 1965, four years after Obama's birth; the Kennedy family had nothing to do with the first airlift of young Kenyans to America. Corsi saw nothing but lying, lying, lying in Obama's peroration, plus presumption at linking himself to Kennedy: "So Obama is again lying about history to claim JFK had anything to do with bringing his father to the United States to study." By the time that Corsi wrote his book, there was an ample literature in the Right blogosphere on this subject; often critics added that Obama had never lived in Selma, either, so he was lying again. But Obama's spiel was a romanticized riff on heroic continuity and "some good craziness going on." To his audience of civil rights movement veterans, it was a variation on a stock biblical trope, "so great a cloud of witnesses" (Hebrews 12:1), where chronology was not the point. As for his bit about the Kennedy family, Obama confused the first airlift with the second one, which the Kennedys did finance.[10]

Obama's rhetorical shape-shifting at Selma established his debased moral character for Corsi, who piled on for 300 pages. Repeatedly he complained that Obama's memoir refigured characters as composites and dispensed with chronology when it served his literary purpose, exactly as Obama explained in the introduction. He blasted Obama for withholding key information until late in the book, never mind that the whole point was to tell the story of how Obama learned it. The artistry meant nothing to Corsi, who saw only holes, deceit, and distraction. He demanded a memoir that enumerated the faults of Obama's father and mother from the outset, so that readers could feel superior to them and know where this story was going.

Corsi seized on Obama's remembrance, during his preadolescence in Indonesia, of being stunned by a *Life* magazine picture of a black man "who tried to peel off his skin." In Obama's telling, this experience "was violent for me, an ambush attack," one that conveyed to him that his race was a problem. Reporters found no such issue of *Life*, or any other magazine picture of the time, and Obama suggested that perhaps it was an advertisement for skin bleaching agents that had wounded him. That was plausible, as skin bleaches have been marketed to African Americans since the 1850s. The incident occurred when Obama was eight or nine years old; he was in his early thirties when he wrote about it; and he was forty-seven when reporters queried him about it. Obama acknowledged that the magazine part of the story was less vivid for him than the hurt it produced. Corsi knew better, declaring that Obama had lied again; it was only a question of determining the type of lie. Either Obama was a hypothetical liar who imagined an invented memory so forcefully that it became real for him, or he made up the story as a vehicle for delivering a guilt-mongering point straight out of Frantz Fanon's chapter on "The Fact of Blackness" in *Black Skin, White Masks.* The second option seems worse to Corsi's fans in the Right blogosphere, so they usually opt for it.[11]

Corsi could see no reason why Obama might have felt any racial angst while growing up in Hawaii; thus, nearly everything that Obama said on this topic fell into the category of "liar" or doubtful, except for the Frank Marshall Davis factor. Corsi judged that Davis probably did encourage Obama to think of himself as a victim of racial injustice. That would explain how Obama came to admire Malcolm X, came to believe his own childish fantasy about a black man ripping off his skin, and dwelt on Fanon's fantasy about a serum that turned black skin white. In any case, Corsi stressed, Davis was the first of many anti-American radicals that Obama befriended over the years.[12]

Corsi had long chapters of guilt by association on the latter theme, establishing the baseline for wilder speculation. Saul Alinsky, Jerry Kellman, Bill Ayers, Bernadine Dohrn, Jeremiah Wright, and Rashid Khalidi were the key players. In Corsi's account, Obama perfected Alinsky-style radicalism by working for Kellman. Ayers and Dohrn, the Weather Underground revolutionaries of the 1960s who got respectable later on, were neighbors and acquaintances of Obama's in Chicago. Obama absorbed black liberation theology from Wright; and Obama was influenced by Columbia University professor Khalidi's pro-Palestinianism.

In much of this discussion, Corsi explicated his material more objectively than was often the case with his successors, stopping short of wild theories about Obama's foreign birth or Davis being his real father. On the other hand, Corsi enabled some of the worst anti-Obama material by roughing up Michelle Obama, describing her as "the Angry Obama" who scared ordinary Americans. Michelle Obama did not come as naturally to elitism as her husband, Corsi allowed. However, she spouted snotty howlers about not being proud of her country until her husband ran for president, and during her years at Princeton, "she indulged in the luxury of experiencing alienation, instead of being grateful for the opportunity." Corsi shuddered at picturing the arrogant, radical, and ungrateful Obamas in the White House, although he admonished readers not to say that Obama's Christianity was a fraud or that he was secretly a Muslim. Charges on these topics already filled the Right blogosphere when Corsi wrote *The Obama Nation.* Having come a bit late to the birther movement, Corsi did not troll in this area in his first Obama book; later he compensated with a best-seller titled *Where's the Birth Certificate?: The Case that Barack Obama Is Not Eligible to be President.* This book's moment of glory was brief, zooming to number one on Amazon's best-seller list before it was released in April 2011, the same week that Obama unveiled his birth certificate.[13]

Though the wild stuff about outward conspiracies sells at high volume, its reliance on outward claims makes it subject to refutation. Donald Trump, after losing the birther issue, tried to switch to a race-baiting campaign centered on Obama's admission to Columbia and Harvard, but Trump's polls plummeted, and he spared Americans of a spectacle presidential campaign. The best conspiracy argument, it turned out, operates differently. It has all the usual right-wing charges about Obama's ostensible radicalism and otherness, but it works from the inside out as a claim about his alienated psyche. Dinesh D'Souza, a popular conservative writer and former Reagan staffer, ventured into this area with typical boldness. A Dartmouth graduate and native of Mumbai, India, D'Souza grew up as part of India's first postcolonial generation, and in his telling, he has a keener ear for Obama's postcolonial animus than do other conservatives.

Corsi caught some of it, arguing that "Obama's black rage" is closer to Fanon's postcolonial experience than to the urban African American experience of racial discrimination, housing segregation, and economic inequality. Obama seethes with racial resentment, Corsi assured, but not because he has ever experienced deprivation or oppression. Obama's racial crisis during his youth was a Fanon-like crisis of racial identity; it was primarily about wearing a white mask in a world owned by whites. But Corsi did not develop this insight, partly because he believed that Obama fabricated most of his racial angst anyway. To the extent that Obama had a racial crisis, it was a struggle for a self-determined racial identity, but *Dreams from My Father* was filled with lies, so Corsi put it aside, focusing on Obama's attraction to white radicals and Jeremiah Wright. *The Obama Nation* offered up a familiar stew of categories and accusations.[14]

D'Souza goes whole hog for the postcolonial thesis. In September 2010 he got the cover of *Forbes* magazine for a stunning piece of race-baiting titled "How Obama Thinks." The usual right-wing interpretations of Obama, D'Souza urged, are inadequate, not wrong. To fit Obama into some strand or tradition of American history is to misunderstand him, for Obama does not relate to American history. Obama's vision has nothing to do with the dream of the American founders for a new order of the ages; it has no real affinity with the civil rights movement; and it is not even best understood as a species of Euro-American Socialism. The key to Obama is African anticolonial rage. D'Souza explained that Obama is a seething anticolonialist dedicated to avenging the defeat of his father: "Incredibly, the U.S. is being ruled according to the dreams of a Luo tribesman of the 1950s. This philandering, inebriated African socialist, who raged against the world for denying him the realization of his anti-colonial ambitions, is now setting the nation's agenda through the reincarnation of his dreams in his son."[15]

This article electrified the sector of the Right that longed for a better account of Obama's obvious illegitimacy as an American leader. Rush Limbaugh, Glenn Beck, and Newt Gingrich heaped praise on D'Souza's brilliant insight and courageous truth telling, which helped the book version skyrocket to number four on the best-seller list in its first week. *The Roots of Obama's Rage* repeatedly admonishes that Obama's father was a raging, radical, drunken, philandering Black Man from Africa. It claims that Obama's positions are too radical and bizarre to make sense as any kind of American progressivism. And it disclaims any personal animosity. D'Souza explains that he is darker skinned than Obama, but not black, unlike Obama, and that he liked Obama's 2004 Democratic convention speech. There are two Obamas, D'Souza says. "Obama I" is a sunny healer and unifier who wowed the 2004 convention with a speech resounding with conservative themes. "Obama II," however, is arrogant, controlling, and vengeful:

> This is the Obama who lambasts the banks and investment houses and forces them to succumb to federal control; the Obama who gives it to the pharmaceutical and the health insurance companies, bending them to his will; the Obama who demonizes his predecessor and his opponents, portraying them as the source of all the problems that only he can solve.[16]

With so much arrogance at play, D'Souza explains, plus will-to-power and vengefulness, it makes sense that Obama supports environmental regulations, wants the rich to pay higher taxes, and plans to withdraw American troops from Iraq and Afghanistan. But D'Souza cautions that the usual Right complaint that Obama is an anti-American Socialist is slightly off. Obama has a twisted affection for his country, even as he harms America at every turn, and Socialism isn't really the point for him, even though most of his policies are Socialist. For D'Souza, the anticolonial theory explains everything that Obama does as president, including the moments when he pretends to be a healer to keep the façade going. Obama is "dedicated to a campaign of revenge" on behalf of his defeated father: "Obama is on a systematic campaign against the colonial system that destroyed his father's dreams. With a kind of suppressed fury, he is committed to keep going until he has brought that system down. And according to his father's anti-colonial ideology, which Obama has internalized for himself, that system is the military and economic power of the United States of America."[17]

In D'Souza's telling, *Dreams from My Father* is a revelation of Obama's commitment to destroy everything smacking of Western colonialism. Thus Obama gave it an unusual title, stressing *from*. Obama's mother, D'Souza says, taught Obama to idolize his father, and she had anti-American prejudices to match. As a youth Obama imbibed the anticolonial folklore of

Hawaii and Indonesia. The defining moment of Obama's youth was the day that his father explained anticolonialism to Obama's fifth-grade class. As a student, Obama consumed a diet of "oppression studies," D'Souza's moniker for American liberal arts education. Upon making his pilgrimage to Kenya, Obama dedicated himself to fulfilling his father's dream, which filled him with hatred, "but it was a calm hatred, an ideological hatred" of the system and social hierarchies that Western colonialism created. This hateful dream consumes Obama and his presidency, D'Souza contends: "It is a dream that, as president, he is imposing with a vengeance on America and the world."[18]

As a domestic policy, D'Souza explains, postcolonialism is always about humbling the overclass by subordinating it to the power of government. Obama is obsessed with sticking it to the rich, although, admittedly, Obama is not as stridently anticapitalist as his father was. D'Souza notes that Obama's father was a postcolonial African Socialist—not a Communist—who wanted to use the power of the state to take over the economy and to abolish everything that remained of British rule in Kenya. The elder Obama clashed with Jomo Kenyatta over socialism versus capitalism, demanding a Kenyan state that nationalized the means of production. In D'Souza's telling, Obama, like his father, wants to use the power of the state to bring down the overclass. But for Obama, Socialist ideology is not indispensable for this purpose. Obama is comfortable with corporate capitalists, he persuaded the insurance companies to support health reform, and he provided millions of new customers to them. D'Souza reasons that Obama is happy to deal with the capitalist class as long as it is willing "to succumb to a government leash and to being told what to do by Big Daddy Obama."[19]

In foreign affairs, in this telling, Obama-style anticolonialism is equally straightforward, though operating in reverse, seeking to diminish American power. D'Souza claims that Obama does not want to win the war in Afghanistan; in fact, Obama wants the United States to lose in Afghanistan, to strike a blow for anticolonialism: "His only concern is how fast he can get America out." The only reason that Obama escalated in Afghanistan was to provide political cover for his anti-imperial animus to get the United States out of the Muslim world. Similarly, D'Souza contends, Obama does not care if Iran and North Korea attain nuclear weapons; his only concern in this area is to lessen the nuclear capability of the United States and its allies.[20]

That would seem to convict Obama of anti-Americanism too, but D'Souza wants to be fair. Obama has an affection of some kind for the country that lifted him to power, D'Souza allows. To be sure, Obama does hate Republicans—"They are not just wrong; they are evil." Obama's nice-talk about civility and working together is just for show; Obama regards Republicans as the enemy, the neocolonial party. Working with them would be pointless. But D'Souza acknowledges that Obama does not hate his country. At least, Obama does not hate his fantasy of what America should become—a humbled, mediocre, postcolonial nation that does not think of itself as an exception to history. D'Souza explains that Obama regards himself as a defender of America's interests, because he thinks that America and the world would be better off if the United States lost its great power. This vision of the United States is apparently therapeutic for Obama's twisted psyche, D'Souza observes, "but it is a ridiculous one for America in the twenty-first century."[21]

The anticolonial thesis ostensibly explains Obama's determination to expand government power at home and to diminish American power abroad. According to D'Souza, it also explains why Obama seems "so distant, detached, and even bored." It is draining enough to have to act white for the public, but Obama has an extremely eccentric and advanced case of the "acting white" problem. Obama is caught in a time machine, D'Souza contends. He has no real connection to American history. Even his relationship to the civil rights movement is totally contrived for a political purpose, not something that he feels. At the level of feeling and imagination, Obama reads himself into a different story, the Mau Mau rebellion in Kenya, which the British crushed with vicious brutality. For Obama, D'Souza argues, the story that matters is the battle of African guerilla movements against Europe's marauding colonial armies. Obama yearns for the heroic grandeur and moral clarity of the black Africans who stood up against their white oppressors. George Washington pales by comparison, as does the "dull and thin" world of global summits to which Obama drags himself as president of the United States.[22]

Take a breath. Obama's life and presidency are consumed with rage and revenge? He does not think like an American or identify with the United States? He is bored by the presidency? The civil rights movement means nothing to him? He does not believe in American liberal democracy? He escalated in Afghanistan and Pakistan in order to strangle American power? He laments, daydreaming in the West Wing, that he didn't get to fight the British in Kenya in 1952? What is beyond ludicrous?

D'Souza says that Obama is crafty in spreading his anticolonial poison, such as after the Gulf of Mexico oil spill: "Time and again he condemned 'British Petroleum'—an interesting term since the company long ago changed its name to BP." Fascinating, except that Obama never said "British Petroleum" in the event that D'Souza describes, let alone time and again. Straining to tag Obama, of all people, as an advocate of racial revenge, D'Souza descends to a level of race-baiting that would have embarrassed Lee Atwater or George Wallace. He misrepresents *Dreams from My Father* to the point of standing the book on its head. Somehow, in D'Souza's telling, Obama absorbed anticolonial vengeance from a father that he idolized, never mind that

Obama met his father only once; he knew very little about him throughout his youth; in his memoir he described the pain that he felt upon learning about his father's life; and D'Souza has no theory about how Obama internalized his father's ostensible ideology.[23]

Above all, it is perverse to stigmatize Obama as an obsessed anticolonialist on the evidence that his writings contain critical remarks about imperialism. The United States was founded as an anticolonial rebellion, and Obama says nothing about empire or colonialism that is not standard fare for liberal Democrats. Obama's most radical position is something that he shares with Harry Truman and Richard Nixon—that the poor and vulnerable should be provided with health coverage. Since Obama has the same ideology as John Kerry and Hillary Clinton, what is the point of making him out as a vengeful anticolonialist who wants to put whitey down and take whitey's money?

But that question answers itself, and Gingrich embraced the answer as a platform for a presidential candidacy. D'Souza's account was, to Gingrich, profound, brilliant, and utterly convincing. Gingrich told *National Review Online* that to understand Obama, one has to understand "Kenyan, anticolonial behavior"; otherwise, Obama is "outside our comprehension," exactly as he likes it: "This is a person who is fundamentally out of touch with how the world works, who happened to have played a wonderful con, as a result of which he is now president." Gingrich charged that Obama is "authentically dishonest," a trick that he mastered as an Alinsky-style community organizer: "He was being the person he needed to be in order to achieve the position he needed to achieve." For absurdity, it would be hard to top this particular politician presuming moral superiority over this president.[24]

For months it appeared that Gingrich's naked race-baiting of Obama, piled on top of his distinctly repugnant career in politics, would disqualify him from breaking into the top tier of Republican presidential contenders. But that was sadly not to be, and much of the Republican base wants to believe ludicrous things about Obama.

The Good Society

In 1985, a few years into the Reagan era, a group of academics led by sociologist Robert Bellah tried to account for what was happening to America morally, socially, and politically. Bellah's coauthors were Richard Madsen, William M. Sullivan, Ann Swidler, and Steven M. Tipton; the book they wrote was *Habits of the Heart: Individualism and Commitment in American Life*. In the wake of Reagan's massive electoral victory over Walter Mondale, a symbol of New Deal liberalism, the Bellah group disputed Reagan's campaign slogan that it was "morning in America."[25]

The Bellah group countered that America was wracked with terrible prob-lems of economic injustice and moral cynicism. In the past, they argued, the antisocial ravages of American individualism were mitigated by the influence of Biblical religion and civic republicanism in American life. These moral languages taught an ethic of community stewardship and provided a litmus test for assessing a society's moral health. The test was how society deals with the cluster of problems pertaining to wealth and poverty. Scripture condemns inequality and oppression, taking the side of the poor against the principali-ties and powers that exploit them. Republican theory from Aristotle to the American founders assumed that a free society could survive only if there is an approximate equality of opportunity and condition among citizens.

The Bellah group acknowledged that these moral convictions had always been contested in the United States. But now they were being erased from America's cultural memory. American youth no longer knew or cared about the biblical sources of the American experiment or the social gospel dream of a cooperative commonwealth. A new and largely unchurched American generation voted for Reagan and cheered his broadsides against liberalism, the welfare state, the feminist and peace movements, the mainline churches, and the unions. The dominant trend in American life, according to the Bellah group, was toward an atomized society that reduced all moral and social issues to the languages of possessive or expressive individualism. In national politics, the triumph of Reaganism symbolized this trend, just as Reagan himself mythologized it.

Habits of the Heart struck a cultural nerve. The book's portrait of an in-creasingly rootless and narcissistic American middle class was heralded as a telling critique of the loss of community in American life. In the academy the book fueled an upsurge of communitarian social theory, which began with Michael Sandel's landmark critique of the liberal ideology of the "unen-cumbered self," *Liberalism and the Limits of Justice* (1982). Communitarians criticized the egocentrism of America's dominant culture, contending that American conservatism and liberalism were overly preoccupied with indi-vidual rights and individual success. Both of America's dominant political traditions eroded the connections between individuals and their families, communities, and nations. Both traditions rationalized the assaults of global capitalism on communities, mediating institutions, and the environment. Communitarians resurrected John Dewey's understanding of democracy as a "great community" of shared values and his conception of politics as the project of continually re-creating the public. The more progressive versions of communitarian theory followed the Bellah group in stressing the wealth and poverty test of a society's moral health.[26]

To be sure, *Habits of the Heart* had many flaws and limitations. It was decidedly focused on the moral condition of professionally oriented, middle-class, mostly white Americans. The book lauded Martin Luther King Jr. as an exemplar of the United States' best moral traditions, but it offered no account of the African American culture that produced him. It took a liberal feminist perspective for granted without discussing feminism or the implications of its argument for feminism. It could be read as a nostalgic lament for a lost Christian America, even as the Bellah group disavowed that reading. The book seemed strangely removed from important debates of the time over racial, cultural, and sexual politics. These drawbacks made the book ripe for hijacking by conservatives who waved off its animating concern with social justice.[27]

With all its limitations in method and perspective, however, *Habits of the Heart* portrayed the eclipse of moral community in the United States in ways that reflected far beyond its focus on upwardly mobile white professionals. The Bellah group stressed that many Americans no longer took ethical instruction from character-shaping communities of any kind. Asked to explain their moral values, Americans increasingly fell back on their society's ethos of the sovereign consumer. The religious and republican moral languages of America's past were being displaced by an individualistic pursuit of success or emotional satisfaction that placed highly tenuous selves at the center of a meaningless world.

Moreover, the Bellah group cautioned that this sorry picture affected not only those who belonged to no community. Even for most Americans who identified with some religious, cultural, or political community, the ethic of individual rights and success provided the primary operative frame of moral reference. For the Christian Right, American capitalism folded seamlessly into the Christian gospel. Mainline churches, on the other hand, struggling to stay in business, took the therapeutic option, providing undemanding communities of care for religious consumers and preaching an innocuous gospel that threatened nobody.

Habits of the Heart called for a renewal of morally generative communities of memory that cared about social justice. It warned that the erosion of America's religious and democratic traditions had seriously weakened the force of the biblical/republican ethic in American life. Many Americans claimed to believe that poverty could be alleviated by private charity. This belief was closely tied to the dominant American dream of becoming a star, a dream assiduously promoted by commercial culture. The Bellah group contrasted two American dreams, both deeply rooted in U.S. history. In the dominant dream, one attained enough success to stand apart from others, not have to worry about them, and perhaps look down on them. The second dream was that of living in a good society, "a society that would really be worth living in."[28]

A good society would subordinate private interest to the common good, the Bellah group argued. It would reduce the punishments of failure and the rewards of success. It would resist the relentless capitalist drive to turn labor

and nature into commodities. It would expand opportunities for socially use-
ful work and promote economic democracy by expanding the cooperative
and community development sectors. It would recognize that commercial
society is at war with the world's natural ecology and its social ecology. *Habits
of the Heart* called for a new social ecology that strengthened the social ties
that bind human beings to each other.

That came right to the edge of saying, twenty-six years ago, what must
be said today—that American democracy and the world's ecology are being
routed by the unsustainable demands of corporate capitalism. The earth's
ecosystem cannot sustain a U.S.-level lifestyle for more than one-fifth of the
world's population. The economy is physical. There are limits to economic
growth. Global warming is melting the Arctic ice cap at a shocking pace, as
well as large areas of permafrost in Alaska, Canada, and Siberia, and destroying wetlands and forests around the world. Everything on the planet that is
frozen is melting. We have to find alternatives to a system that constantly
demands more freedom for itself to pile up more wealth for the few while
treating the destructive aspects of its activity as somebody else's problem.

The Bellah group did not foresee twenty years of unleashed greed in the
financial sector. It did not foresee the abolition of the Glass-Steagall wall sepa-
rating commercial banks and investment firms, or Wall Street's soaring traffic
in derivatives. Yet it saw the problem clearly enough to write a sequel, *The
Good Society* (1991), that stressed the necessity of creating structural alternatives to corporate capitalism. *The Good Society* made a programmatic argument for expanding the cooperative sector, reducing the anxiety and cynicism
of economic life, building a movement for economic democracy, and helping
people to be secure enough to make commitments to each other and pursue
activities that are good in themselves.[29]

Shrewdly, the Bellah group insisted that its social vision passed Reinhold
Niebuhr's tests for realism. They appealed to Niebuhr's passion for justice,
his commitment to democracy, his emphasis on the limits of politics, and
his commitment to re-creating the public. They portrayed Niebuhr's work
as an important corrective to Dewey's idealistic liberalism, suggesting
that Niebuhr was right about the inevitability of violence and collective
egotism. The Bellah group accepted Niebuhr's thesis that politics is about
the struggle of competing interests for self-promoting power. Movements
based on ethical concern for the common good or religiously inspired good
do not change structures of power. In the social arena, power can be challenged only by power.

The Bellah group absorbed these lessons deeply enough to understand that
they could not simply return to a pre-Niebuhrian progressivism. The social
gospel movement mistakenly thought that a cooperative commonwealth was

literally achievable, partly because it refused to accept that group egotism is inevitable. Any worthwhile social ethic had to absorb Niebuhr's point that every social gain creates the possibility of new forms of social evil.

To the Bellah group, however, relinquishing the idea of a good society on these grounds was a nonstarter, no matter what Niebuhr said against it. The common good emerges from discussion and struggle. It is never settled definitively. But some idea of it is necessary to provide a vision of what is worth struggling for and to test the boundaries of possibility. The Bellah group observed that in the dominant version of the American dream, there is no such thing as a good society or the common good. There is only the sum of individual goods. The sum of individual goods, however, when organized only by capitalism, eventually produces a common bad that destroys personal goods along with society.

We have accumulated a staggering common bad since the Bellah group wrote its books on the common good. Celebrants of neoliberal globalization exaggerated the futility of political attempts to channel economic forces. They were far too credulous about the self-correcting capacities of the market, which supposedly made it unnecessary to regulate banks and investment firms. They waved off the huge imbalances between economies relying on debt-financed consumption and those promoting oversaving and production-oriented exports. Above all, they wrongly supposed that America's widening chasm between productivity and wages could be bridged with more and more borrowing. In 1955, corporate taxes yielded 27 percent of federal revenue; by the end of the Bush administration, that figure was down to 9 percent, and giant corporations like Boeing, General Electric, Verizon, and Citigroup paid no taxes at all—erasing even the memory that it wasn't always so.

Community and Meaning

The progressive communitarian perspective I have just explicated is, to be sure, well to the left of Obama's. Some forms of communitarian theory place a high value on authority, and some are politically moderate forms of "third way" politics in which communitarianism becomes a vague rationale for "responsibility," usually defined as the political middle ground, wherever it happens to be. Obama is skilled at bending communitarian thought to the latter purpose, aiming at the middle ground where every national election is decided. But Obama *is* a communitarian, mostly of a progressive-leaning type. His thought was shaped in the 1980s and early 1990s when debates over communitarian criticism reenergized the field of political theory.

Obama is devoted to a deliberative politics of the common good that builds up new and old communities of memory to achieve a good society. The civic republican language of identity, pragmatic engagement, civil society, and communities of faith is second nature to him. It was the basis of his work as a community organizer, which led him to join a Christian community. It is the basis of everything that he says about the optimum relationship between politics and religion. It is the basis of his insistence that freedom, equality, and community go together in a healthy society. It is the basis of his untiring insistence that common solutions have to be found that mediate rival ideological positions. Harvard intellectual historian James Kloppenberg aptly observes, "Obama understands that the power of our principles of liberty and equality depends not on the fervor with which they are proclaimed but on the deliberative process from which they are developed. That process requires us to debate, test, and revise the meaning of our ideals in practice rather than genuflecting reverentially before them."[30]

Democracy is the work of practically and continually renewing society. Obama had an astute and reflective grasp of it as an organizer, as he showed in an article for *Illinois Issues* in 1988. This article, "Why Organize? Problems and Promise in the Inner City," had some clunky sentences lacking noun-verb agreement that later evoked sneers from anti-Obama bloggers. But those who claim that Obama was incapable of writing his two books overlook that he never had a speechwriter before he became famous, he wrote every sentence of the 2004 convention barnburner that launched his fame, and his early article on organizing bore the marks of his later thought and style. For Obama, communitarian theory helped to make sense of long-running debates among African Americans over integration versus nationalism, accommodation versus militancy, and Booker T. Washington versus W. E. B. Du Bois. By the 1980s, Obama observed, these historic debates usually played out as an argument between advocates of economic self-development and electoral politics. In Chicago, the black community was pretty much stalemated over this binary choice until Harold Washington swept to the mayor's office in 1983, after which the party politics group had four years of glory and pride. Then Washington died and the old stalemate returned.[31]

Obama held out for the community organizing alternative to a bad choice between self-help and going political. There had to be a way to hold together the strengths of the two predominant approaches, he urged. The community organizing strategy proposed that there are solutions to the grinding problems of inner-city communities, that these communities only lack the power that is necessary to solve their problems, and that the only way to build up power that makes a difference is to organize people and money around a common vision. Doing this requires building up broad-based organizations that unite religious congregations, block groups, parent associations, and similar groups. Obama implored that every obstacle to building such organizations is a reason why they are needed. To build one is to gain voice and power for the needs of communities, breaking the "crippling isolation" that makes poor and vulnerable people believe that there is no solution. Community organizing, Obama concluded with a rhetorical flourish, brings out the beauty and strength of ordinary human beings: "Through the songs of the church and the talk on the stoops, through the hundreds of individual stories of coming up from the South and finding any job that would pay, of raising families on threadbare budgets, of losing some children to drugs and watching others earn degrees and land jobs their parents could never aspire to—it is through these stories and songs of dashed hopes and powers of endurance, of ugliness and strife, subtlety and laughter, that organizers can shape a sense of community not only for others, but for themselves."[32]

Eighteen years later, now as a U.S. senator, Obama addressed a conference on "Building a Covenant for a New America," sponsored by Jim Wallis's Call to Renewal organization and *Sojourners* magazine. Most of his keynote speech was straight out of *The Audacity of Hope*, which was about to be published. In both places he expounded on the difference between being religiously faithful in an open-ended way and claiming religious certainty in a publicly problematic way. Obama stressed that he was "anchored" in his faith but not rigid or dogmatic about it. Here, as elsewhere, he walked a tightrope between saying more than one should say as a public official and not saying anything to avoid controversy. Too many Democrats took the path of saying as little as possible, even when they had a religious faith to cover up. Obama admitted that he took that tack in his 2004 Senate race, which nagged at him. Faced with a far-out opponent who made dramatic statements about how Jesus Christ would vote, Obama stayed off the religious issue and waited for election day.[33]

But that ceded the religious issue to conservatives like Alan Keyes and Pat Robertson. Obama realized that he needed to do better than that. At the conference, though not in the book, he put it directly—in a passage that echoed *Habits of the Heart* and Harvard sociologist Robert Putnam's research on the dwindling social capital of Americans. Putnam reported that Americans were increasingly isolated, lacking vital ties to social or community networks of any kind; in his arresting image, "bowling alone" had become commonplace. Obama replied that human beings need meaning and connection even when they behave otherwise. Something terribly important is missing in the busyness and materialism of modern American life, he argued. Busy materialism violates the spiritual nature of human beings. Obama contended that most people want a sense of purpose, "a narrative arc to their lives," even if they keep to themselves, numb themselves to the world, and bowl alone:

They're looking to relieve a chronic loneliness, a feeling supported by a recent study that shows Americans have fewer close friends and confidants than ever before. And so they need an assurance that somebody out there cares about them, is listening to them—that they are not just destined to travel down a long highway towards nothingness.[34]

He acknowledged that he spoke from experience. He grew up with no religious faith or community, and when he worked as an organizer with Christians in Chicago, he sang their songs and shared their values: "But they sensed a part of me that remained removed, detached, an observer in their midst. In time, I too came to realize that something was missing—that without a vessel for my beliefs, without a commitment to a particular community of faith, at some level I would always remain apart and alone."[35]

By then, heading into a presidential campaign, Obama had become adept at talking about his spiritual sensibility. On the campaign trail, he readily found his preacher voice. Later, running the country, it was harder to find, or at least, it was harder to find occasions to use it. There were notable exceptions. Obama's audience at the Nobel Prize speech was intently quiet through most of the speech, but near the end he jolted the secular Norwegians into an emotional standing ovation with his peroration about reaching for the world that ought to be, "that spark of the divine that still stirs within each of our souls." On January 12, 2011, speaking to a grieving and polarized community and nation, Obama the pastor reemerged.

Four days earlier, Arizona representative Gabrielle Giffords had convened one of her regular outdoor gatherings, which she called "Congress on Your Corner," outside a supermarket in Tucson. A gunman, Jared Lee Loughner, drew a pistol, shot Giffords in the head, and opened fire on the crowd of approximately twenty-five people. Six people were killed and thirteen were wounded; Giffords was critically wounded. A bitter national controversy erupted over gun control and the toxic political atmosphere surrounding immigration and health reform. Loughner had used a nine millimeter Glock 19 semi-automatic pistol with a thirty-three-round magazine that he purchased legally, despite a documented history of mental problems, and Giffords had received threats for taking liberal positions on immigration and health reform. A few months earlier, Giffords had noted on MSNBC that Sarah Palin's published target list for the 2010 election depicted the crosshairs of a gun sight over Giffords's district. Giffords protested, "When people do that, they have got to realize there are consequences to that action." In the aftermath of the shooting, Pima County sheriff Clarence Dupnik declared at a press conference: "When you look at unbalanced people, how they respond to the vitriol that comes out of certain mouths about tearing down the government—the anger, the hatred, the bigotry that goes on in this country is getting to be outrageous. And unfortunately, Arizona, I think, has become the capital. We have become the mecca for prejudice and bigotry."[36]

Loughner's ability to buy a semi-automatic and fire over twenty shots in a few seconds was one issue. The prevailing atmosphere of hatefulness and bigotry was another. Dupnik's suggestion that this massacre had some connection to Tea Party activism was something else, and not helpful or true. Obama walked into a cauldron of grief and anger in Tucson, acknowledging immediately that nothing he could say would "fill the sudden hole torn in your hearts." He applied Psalm 46 to Tucson: "God is within her, she will not fail." He moved, in a pastoral fashion, through the roll of the slain, making personal remarks about each victim, ending with a nine-year-old girl, Christina Taylor Green. He reported that Giffords had opened her eyes that day; in the manner of black church repetition, he said it four times.[37]

And he spoke against the accusatory mode. "Scripture tells us that there is evil in the world, and that terrible things happen for reasons that defy human understanding." It was imperative not to rush to simple explanations and accusations, he implored: "For the truth is none of us can know exactly what triggered this vicious attack. None of us can know with any certainty what might have stopped these shots from being fired, or what thoughts lurked in the inner recesses of a violent man's mind. Yes, we have to examine all the facts behind this tragedy. We cannot and will not be passive in the face of such violence. We should be willing to challenge old assumptions in order to lessen the prospects of such violence in the future. But what we cannot do is use this tragedy as one more occasion to turn on each other. That we cannot do. That we cannot do."

When we suffer tragedies, Obama observed, we are awakened to our mortality. We remember that we have only a little while on this earth, and that in this fleeting time "what matters is not wealth, or status, or power, or fame—but rather, how well we have loved and what small part we have played in making the lives of other people better." He had a black church "close," a take-home message about Christina jumping in rain puddles in heaven, but before Obama got there, he had a quintessentially Obama pre-close: "We may not be able to stop all evil in the world, but I know that how we treat one another, that's entirely up to us. And I believe that for all our imperfections, we are full of decency and goodness, and that the forces that divide us are not as strong as those that unite us."

What Kind of Country?

What kind of country should the United States want to be? For two centuries, Americans have given two fundamentally different answers to this question.

The first is the vision of a society that provides unrestricted liberty to acquire wealth. The second is the vision of a realized democracy in which democratic rights over society's major institutions are established. In the first vision, the right to property is lifted above the right to self-government, and the just society minimizes the equalizing role of government. In the second view, the right to self-government is considered superior to the right to property, and the just society places democratic checks on social, political, and economic power.[38]

Both of these visions are ideal types, deeply rooted in U.S. history, that reflect inherent tensions between classic liberalism and democracy. Both have limited and conditioned each other in the American experience. But in every generation one of them gains predominance over the other, shaping the terms of political possibility. From 1980 to 2008, the unleashed capitalist vision prevailed in American politics. Now we are in a national conversation about whether capitalism or democracy should have the upper hand.

To the founders that wrote the U.S. Constitution, *liberal* was a good word, referring to the liberties of white male property owners, while *democracy* was a scare word, referring to the vengeance and stupidity of the mob. From the beginning, democratic movements countered that liberty must be fused with democracy. The building blocks of American liberal democracy emerged from the early struggles between the parties of liberty and democracy: an open society, checks and balances, enumerated powers, consent of the governed, due process, the republican safeguards of *Federalist* Number Ten, separation of church and state, and disagreements over who deserved to be enfranchised, whether liberty could tolerate much democracy, and whether the American idea included republican democracy or a strong federal state.

In the nineteenth century the Jeffersonian/Jacksonian party of democracy prevailed about republican democracy; the Federalist/Whig Party of the state prevailed about a federal state; both parties compounded the United States' original sins against Native Americans and African Americans; the Republican Party emerged to challenge chattel slavery; and the Progressive movement embraced the idea of a centralized government. The latter development turned the party of democracy into the party of the state, changing the meaning of "liberal" in American politics. Before the Progressive Era the Federalist/Whig/Republican tradition stood for the consolidation of the national union, while Jacksonian and populist democrats stood for decentralized power, small-town values, and farming interests. The Progressive movement changed this picture by democratizing liberal ideology. Progressives converted to national governance, laying the groundwork for the New Deal, while Republicans became the party of antigovernment individualism and big business.[39]

The party of democracy, despite its racist and sexist history, made gains for social justice by demanding that society recognize the rights and humanity of groups lacking privileged status. The logic of democracy put the question to privileged groups: Why should only you have access to education, property, wealth, health care, and other social goods?

Democracy and the common good go together. Obama did not exaggerate when he spoke at Tom Harkin's steak fry in 2006: The unleashed capitalist vision of the Republican Party is about dismantling democratic governance. It is about breaking up government piece by piece, privatizing Social Security and Medicare, abolishing programs for the poor and vulnerable, cutting taxes for corporations and the wealthy, abolishing public schools, replacing police with private security guards, letting Wall Street do whatever it wants, and turning public parks into privately owned playgrounds. Obama rightly stressed that this vision of a society favoring the interests of corporations and the rich lies behind almost everything that Republicans do in Congress. It is the view that America is at its best when Americans deny that they owe obligations to each other.

Obama stopped putting it this starkly after he won the presidency because he had no chance of winning Republican cooperation on anything if he did not tell Republicans that he expected better than that. In his 2010 State of the Union address he told Republican leaders that if they were going to insist that no business could get done in the Senate without sixty votes, they had to take responsibility for governing: "Just saying no to everything may be good short-term politics, but it's not leadership. We were sent here to serve our citizens, not our ambitions. So let's show the American people that we can do it together."[40]

He knows that cooperation across party lines to solve the nation's problems will not happen, yet he keeps calling for it. Obama wants to be the Ronald Reagan of his party, a forward-looking optimist who changes the course of history. He wants to do it by winning independents and a significant minority of Republicans to his idea of good government, just as Reagan won over independents and the Blue Dog Democrats. But nobody doubted where Reagan stood ideologically, and Obama has no chance of winning anything more than token Republican cooperation. Reagan was the most ideologically defined president of the past half century and the only ideological movement leader to be elected president. Obama doubts that his worldview serves him as well. To succeed, he believes, he must keep proving that he cares more about civility and cooperation than about fighting for a principle.

Obama rightly hopes that he will inherit a less obstructionist opposition if he wins a second term. He will be a lame duck, the Tea Party will fade, and more Republicans will accept him as a legitimate president. Perhaps something closer to normal politics will resume. But the big issues that loom ahead will have to be fought over because America cannot build a clean energy economy, rebuild the nation's infrastructure, make massive investments in education, lift the cap on Social Security, break the financial oligarchy, and scale back the military empire on Republican terms. The big things that must be done contradict Republican ideology. Even defending the financial and health care reforms that Obama has achieved will require more fighting than he put up to attain them. Obama wants to "win the future" by inspiring Americans to believe that they can still do big things. Surely, he implores, America can build new airports like the Chinese and build fast trains like the Europeans and Chinese.[41]

But to win the future, the party of the common good must struggle with conviction for a just society, telling a galvanizing story about the struggle for it. The saddest irony of Obama's presidency is that he has fallen short on conveying what he believes in and is willing to fight for. Campaigning in 2008, Obama was eloquent and inspiring, using his story to paint a vision of America's vibrant, cosmopolitan, communitarian future. Governing afterward, he mostly coped and adapted, leaving his supporters perplexed about where he wanted to take the nation.

As this book goes to press, in the aftermath of the debt ceiling fiasco, Obama has belatedly returned to the cause of making socially beneficial investments that create jobs and scale up. Washington has embarked on a miserable season of self-defeating federal budget cuts. And a social movement that protests against economic injustice and raises hell against America's economic oligarchy has belatedly arisen.

The United States is caught in a deflationary cycle fueled by a global credit contraction. Income is falling, making debt hard to bear, which discourages investment, which further depresses the economy, which yields more deflation. To slash government spending in this situation is to further weaken demand, which leads to lost output and lost tax revenue. If the Democrats do not discover their nerve, or if the Republicans take over, we will follow Britain into a self-inflicted vicious cycle of low growth, high unemployment, and budget-cutting austerity. In Britain, the Conservative government of David Cameron has kept its pledge to slash over 100,000 public sector jobs. A year later, Britain's economy is flatlining at 0.1 percent growth, and other European nations are vainly trying to renew their economies by slashing their public sectors.

The United States has underinvested in infrastructure for decades, and it cannot move forward without making massive investments to build a clean energy economy. Labor costs, equipment costs, and the cost of capital will never be lower than they are today. A national infrastructure bank, once started, would get serious money plowed into infrastructure rebuilding.

If we can spend trillions of taxpayer dollars bailing out banks and setting up bad bank "Aggregator" contraptions to eat their toxic debt, we ought to be able to create good public banks at the state and federal levels to do good things. Public banks could finance start-ups in green technology that are currently languishing and provide financing for cooperatives that traditional banks spurn. They can be established at the state level, following the leads of North Dakota and Washington, to create state credit machines not dependent on Wall Street. They can be established at the federal level by congressional mandate or by claiming the good assets of banks seized by the government, or both.

Today, America's superwealthy minimize their income taxes by treating themselves mostly to the capital gains rate—all perfectly legally, owing to the favors that Washington showers on the superwealthy. Investment managers earning billions of dollars per year are allowed to classify their income as carried interest, which is taxed at the same rate as capital gains. Constantly we are told that the investor class would lose its zeal for making money if it had to pay taxes on its actual income or if the capital gains rate were raised. But this assurance lacks any evidence whatsoever. No investor spurns a promising investment because of the tax rate on a potential gain. A decent tax system would have additional brackets for the highest incomes, as the United States once did. It would have a bracket for $1 million earners and a bracket for $10 million dollar earners and a bracket for $100 million earners and so on. It would lift the cap on the Social Security tax, taxing salaries above $102,000 per year, or at least, as Obama proposed in 2008, creating a "doughnut hole" that adds a Social Security tax for individuals earning more than $250,000.

There is still time for an Obama administration that pushes hard for decent tax policies and that facilitates creative planning for economic democracy.

Heading into the fourth year of Obama's presidency, there is suddenly the prospect of an actual political Left that counterbalances the power of Wall Street and the Tea Party. American politics has had no Left for decades—no coalition of trade unions, Socialists, community organizers, progressives, and radical social movements. When professional class liberals are the leaders of the Left opposition, there is no Left opposition. Liberal-leaning politicians and professional class liberals are establishment functionaries who are supposed to hold the system together from the middle. They can be allies of a Left movement, playing a crucial role in shaping and enacting policies. But they cannot take the place of social movements and organizations that struggle for social justice.

Obama and every elected liberal Democrat have been hampered by the lack of a significant political Left. Until September 2011, there was nothing resembling a social movement to break the grip of America's economic oligarchy. For three years, and for thirty years of stagnant wages and accelerating inequality, there was an opening for a populist explosion demanding a full-employment economy and a curtailment of Wall Street's speculation and gouging. Finally, a smattering of mostly youthful protesters set one off. They would not have succeeded had they operated like conventional trade unions and social justice groups. And the long-term success of Occupy Wall Street depends on its ability to build constructive coalitions with these very groups.

Obama still has an essentially progressive vision of the presidency that he wants to have. He is still the most compelling human being to reach the White House in decades. And he is still a figure of singular promise in American politics. To fulfill that promise he has to overcome his own cautious, accommodating temperament, and progressives have to believe it is still possible.

Notes

1. See V. O Key. "A Theory of Critical Elections," *Journal of Politics* 17 (1955), 3–18; Walter Dean Burnham, *Critical Elections and the Mainsprings of American Politics* (New York: Norton, 1970); Burnham, "Periodization Schemes and 'Party Systems': The 'System of 1896' as a Case in Point," *Social Science History* 10 (August 1986), 263–314; Paul Kleppner (Westport, CT: Greenwood, 1981); Jerome M. Clubb, William H. Flanigan, and Nancy H. Zingale, *Partisan Realignment: Voters, Parties, and Government in American History* (Beverly Hills, CA: Sage Publications, 1980). Parts of this chapter adapt material from Gary Dorrien, "The Common Good," *Christian Century* (April 19, 2011), and Dorrien, *Economy, Difference, Empire: Social Ethics for Social Justice* (New York: Columbia University Press, 2010), 145–152.

2. See Edward N. Wolff, *Top Heavy* (New York: New Press, 1996); Wolff, "Recent Trends in Household Wealth in the United States: Rising Debt and the Middle-Class Squeeze—An Update to 2007," *Working Paper No. 589* (Annandale-on-Hudson, NY: Levy Economics Institute of Bard College, 2010); Kevin Phillips, *The Politics of Rich and Poor* (New York: Random House, 1990); Joseph E. Stiglitz, "Of the 1%, by the 1%, for the 1%," *Vanity Fair* (May 2011); G. William Domhoff, *The Power Elite and the State: How Policy Is Made in America* (Hawthorne, NY: Aldine de Gruyter, 1990).

3. See Eamonn Fingleton, *Unsustainable: How Economic Dogma Is Destroying American Prosperity* (New York: Nation Books, 2003); Doug Henwood, *After the New Economy* (New York: New Press, 2005); Barry Bluestone and Bennett Harrison, *The Deindustrialization of America: Plant Closings, Community Abandonment, and the Dismantling of Basic Industry* (New York: Basic Books, 1982); Michael J. Piore and Charles E. Sabel, *The Second Industrial Divide: Possibilities for Prosperity* (New York: Basic Books, 1984).

4. Thomas L. Friedman, *The Lexus and the Olive Tree: Understanding Globalization* (New York: Anchor Books, 2000); Friedman, *The World Is Flat: A Brief History of the Twenty-First Century* (New York: Farrar, Straus and Giroux, 2005); Jagdish Bhagwati, *In Defense of Globalization* (New York: Oxford University Press, 2004).

5. Congressional Budget Office, "CBO Report: Estimated Impact of the American Recovery and Reinvestment Act on Employment and Economic Output from April 2010 through June 2010," August 2010, Washington, DC.

6. Brad O'Leary, *The Audacity of Deceit: Barack Obama's War on American Values* (Los Angeles: WND Books, 2008); Aaron Klein, *The Manchurian President: Barack Obama's Ties to Communists, Socialists, and Other Anti-American Extremists* (Washington, DC: WND Books, 2010); Michelle Malkin, *Culture of Corruption: Obama and His Team of Tax Cheats, Crooks, and Cronies* (Washington, DC: Regnery, 2009); Pamela Geller with Robert Spencer, *The Post-American Presidency: The Obama Administration's War on America* (New York: Threshold Editions, 2010); Webster Griffin Tarpley, *Obama: The Postmodern Coup* (Joshua Tree, CA: Progressive Press, 2008); Jack Cashill, *Deconstructing Obama* (New York: Threshold Editions, Simon & Schuster, 2011); see Max Blumenthal, "Queen of the Birthers," *The Daily Beast* (July 30, 2009), www.thedailybeast.com; Cashill, "Is Khalid al-Mansour the Man Behind Obama Myth?" *WorldNetDaily* (August 28, 2008), www.wnd.com.

7. Jerome R. Corsi, *The Obama Nation: Leftist Politics and the Cult of Personality* (New York: Threshold Editions, 2008); John E. O'Neill and Jerome R. Corsi, *Unfit for Command: Swift Boat Veterans Speak Out Against John Kerry* (Washington, DC: Regnery, 2004); "MMFA Investigates: Who Is Jerome Corsi, Co-Author of Swift Boat Vets Attack Book?" Media Matters, August 6, 2008, http://mediamatters.org/research/200408060010, quotes; Kenneth P. Vogel, "Wild Theories of 'Obama Nation' Author," *Politico* (August 13, 2008), www.politico.com.

8. Jerome R. Corsi, *The Late Great USA: The Coming Merger with Mexico and Canada* (Los Angeles: WND Books, 2007); Corsi, *The Obama Nation*, quote x.

9. Barack Obama, "I'm Here Because Somebody Marched," Brown Chapel A.M.E. Church, Selma, Alabama, March 4, 2007, www.youtube.com.

10. Corsi, *The Obama Nation*, quote 33.

11. Barack Obama, *Dreams from My Father: A Story of Race and Inheritance* (1995; New York: Three Rivers Press, 2004), 51; Corsi, *The Obama Nation*, 65–66, 82–83; Richard Cohen, "Obama's Back Story," *Washington Post* (March 27, 2007); Kristen Scharnberg and Kim Barker, "The Not-So-Simple Story of Barack Obama's Youth," *Chicago Tribune* (March 25, 2007); Frantz Fanon, *Black Skin, White Masks* (New York: Grove, 1967).

12. Corsi, *The Obama Nation*, 70–91.

13. Corsi, *The Obama Nation*, quotes 230, 233; Jerome R. Corsi, *Where's the Birth Certificate?: The Case That Barack Obama Is Not Eligible to Be President* (Washington, DC: WND Books, 2011).

14. Corsi, *The Obama Nation*, 80–84.

15. Dinesh D'Souza, "How Obama Thinks," *Forbes* (September 27, 2010).

16. Dinesh D'Souza, *The Roots of Obama's Rage* (Washington, DC: Regnery Publishing, 2010), quote 19.

17. D'Souza, *The Roots of Obama's Rage*, quote 199.

18. D'Souza, *The Roots of Obama's Rage*, quotes 127, 35.

19. D'Souza, *The Roots of Obama's Rage*, quote 172.

20. D'Souza, *The Roots of Obama's Rage*, quotes 52, 55.

21. D'Souza, *The Roots of Obama's Rage*, quotes 170, 218.

22. D'Souza, *The Roots of Obama's Rage*, quotes 198, 199.

23. D'Souza, *The Roots of Obama's Rage*, quote 47.

24. Robert Costa, "Gingrich: Obama's 'Kenyan, Anti-Colonial Worldview,'" *National Review Online* (September 11, 2010), www.nationalreview.com.

25. Robert Bellah, Richard Madsen, William M. Sullivan, Ann Swidler, and Steven M. Tipton, *Habits of the Heart: Individualism and Commitment in American Life* (Berkeley: University of California Press, 1985; third edition, 2008).

26. Michael Sandel, *Liberalism and the Limits of Justice* (Cambridge: Cambridge University Press, 1982); see William Sullivan, *Reconstructing Public Philosophy* (Berkeley: University of California Press, 1982); Michael Walzer, *Spheres of Justice: A Defense of Pluralism and Equality* (New York: Basic Books, 1985); Alasdair MacIntyre, *After Virtue: A Study in Moral Theory* (Notre Dame: University of Notre Dame, 1984); Amitai Etzioni, *The Spirit of Community: Rights, Responsibilities, and the Communitarian Agenda* (New York: Crown Publishers, 1993).

27. See Vincent Harding, "Toward a Darkly Radiant Vision of America's Truth: A Letter of Concern, An Invitation to Re-Creation," in *Community in America: The Challenge of Habits of the Heart* (Berkeley: University of California Press, 1988), 67–83.

28. Bellah et al., *Habits of the Heart*, quote 285.

29. Robert Bellah, Richard Madsen, William M. Sullivan, Ann Swidler, and Steven M. Tipton, *The Good Society* (New York: Knopf, 1991).

30. James T. Kloppenberg, *Reading Obama: Dreams, Hopes, and the American Political Tradition* (Princeton: Princeton University Press, 2011), quote 265.

31. Barack Obama, "Why Organize? Problems and Promise in the Inner City," *Illinois Issues* (1988), republished 2008, http://illinoisissues.uis.edu.

32. Obama, "Why Organize?"

33. Barack Obama, "'Barack Obama Speaks Out on Faith and Politics: 'Call to Renewal' Keynote Address," June 28, 2006, www.sojo.net; Barack Obama, *The Audacity of Hope: Thoughts on Reclaiming the American Dream* (New York: Three Rivers Press, 2006), 195–226; see Kloppenberg, *Reading Obama*, 141–144.

34. Obama, "'Barack Obama Speaks Out'"; Robert Putnam, "Bowling Alone: America's Declining Social Capital," *Journal of Democracy* 6 (January 1995), 65–78.

35. Obama, "'Barack Obama Speaks Out.'"

36. Michael Falcone, Amy Walter, and Z. Byron Wolf, "Arizona Shooting Touches Off Fierce Debate Over Political Rhetoric," ABC News, The Note, January 9, 2011, http://blogs.abcnews.com, quotes; Peter Grier, "Jared Lee Loughner: What Is Known About Tucson, Arizona Shooting Suspect," *Christian Science Monitor* (January 10, 2011).

37. The White House, Office of the Press Secretary, "Remarks by the President at a Memorial Service for the Victims of the Shooting in Tucson, Arizona," January 12, 2011, www.whitehouse.gov.

38. This section adapts material from Gary Dorrien, "Beyond State and Market: Christianity and the Future of Economic Democracy," *Cross Currents* (Summer 1995), 184–204.

39. See Michael J. Sandel, *Democracy's Discontent: America in Search of a Public Philosophy* (Cambridge: Harvard University Press, 1996), 3–24; Arthur M. Schlesinger Jr., *The Cycles of American History* (Boston: Houghton Mifflin, 1986), 23–49; Robert Dahl, *A Preface to Economic Democracy* (Berkeley: University of California Press,

1985); Howard Zinn, *A People's History of the United States, 1492–Present* (New York: HarperCollins, 1995); Gary Dorrien, *Economy, Difference, Empire: Social Ethics for Social Justice* (New York: Columbia University Press, 2009), 143–144.

40. Barack Obama, "Remarks by the President in Sate of the Union Address," The White House, Office of the Press Secretary, January 27, 2010, www.whitehouse.gov.

41. Barack Obama, "State of the Union Address, 2011," January 25, 2011, www.npr.org/2011/01/26.

Index

About the Author

Gary Dorrien is the Reinhold Niebuhr Professor of Social Ethics at Union Theological Seminary and professor of religion at Columbia University. His fifteen previous books in social theory and ethics, philosophy, politics, and theology include the award-winning *Social Ethics in the Making* (2009) and *Kantian Reason and Hegelian Spirit* (2012).